PEACE WITH NATURE

50 Inspiring Essays on Nature and the Environment

PEACE WITH NATURE

50 Inspiring Essays on Nature and the Environment

Foreword by **President Halimah Yacob**

Editors

Tommy Koh
Ambassador-at-Large

Lye Lin Heng
National University of Singapore

Shawn Lum
Nature Society (Singapore)

NATURE SOCIETY SINGAPORE EST. 1954

World Scientific

Published by

World Scientific Publishing Co. Pte. Ltd.
5 Toh Tuck Link, Singapore 596224
USA office: 27 Warren Street, Suite 401-402, Hackensack, NJ 07601
UK office: 57 Shelton Street, Covent Garden, London WC2H 9HE

National Library Board, Singapore Cataloguing in Publication Data
Name(s): Halimah Yacob, author of foreword. | Koh, Tommy T. B. (Tommy Thong Bee), 1937– editor. | Lye, Lin Heng, editor. | Lum, Shawn K. Y., editor.
Title: Peace with nature : 50 inspiring essays on nature and the environment / foreword by President Halimah Yacob ; editors, Tommy Koh, Lye Lin Heng, Shawn Lum.
Description: Singapore : World Scientific Publishing Co. Pte. Ltd., [2023]
Identifier(s): ISBN 978-981-12-8201-0 (hardcover) | 978-981-12-8272-0 (paperback) | 978-981-12-8202-7 (ebook for institutions) | 978-981-12-8203-4 (ebook for individuals)
Subject(s): LCSH: Environmental protection--Singapore. | Environmentalism--Singapore.
Classification: DDC 333.72--dc23

British Library Cataloguing-in-Publication Data
A catalogue record for this book is available from the British Library.

For any available supplementary material, please visit
https://www.worldscientific.com/worldscibooks/10.1142/13561#t=suppl

Desk Editor: Jiang Yulin

Typeset by Stallion Press
Email: enquiries@stallionpress.com

Printed in Singapore

The editors (from left to right) Shawn Lum, Lye Lin Heng and Tommy Koh, meeting in a rainforest.

President's Foreword

In 1967, a plan to transform Singapore into a Garden City was unveiled. The Garden City vision was introduced by founding Prime Minister Lee Kuan Yew — a well-coordinated effort across government agencies, the nature community and our citizens to make Singapore greener and more liveable. After six decades of greening efforts, we now enjoy a beautiful network of green spaces on our urban island. We have transitioned from Garden City to a City in A Garden, and now aim to be a City in Nature. A City in Nature is more than having many species of native plants and wildlife in our small city-state — it should also be a place where Singaporeans feel joy to be around nature and have a shared sense of stewardship over it.

This book, *Peace with Nature*, features the stories of 50 Singaporeans who have served — and saved — Singapore's natural heritage in different ways. Some of the stories recount milestones in Singapore's greening or nature conservation efforts. Others tell the tale of how a love for nature become lifelong hobbies, careers, or volunteering efforts. Yet other stories chart the growth of Singapore's relationship with nature.

One of the Awards given out by my Office is the President's Award for the Environment (PAE). This award recognises individuals, organisations, and educational institutions that have made outstanding contributions to Singapore's environment and to its sustainability efforts.

I am heartened that a number of contributors to this book are past recipients of the PAE. They include two of the inaugural recipients, Professor Tommy Koh and Dr Geh Min, along with Professor Leo Tan, Dr Tan Wee Kiat, Mr Eugene Heng, Mrs Kirtida Mekani, Dr Shawn Lum, and Dr Joseph Koh. Many other contributors to this book are internationally recognised experts in the study or protection of nature.

It is heartening to know that there are so many Singaporeans from all walks of life, who love nature and the environment. We all have the power and responsibility to co-exist in Peace with Nature, and I hope the readers of this book will find it enlightening and inspiring.

Halimah Yacob
President of the Republic of Singapore

Contents

Introduction

Why do residents of a small country, whose share of humanity's ecological footprint is not likely to nudge the earth system as much as its larger neighbours, make the effort to do something for nature and the environment? What compels some Singaporeans to become environmental champions? What contributions have Singapore made to environmental protection? How might Singapore's work in this field go beyond sustainability in the city-state to impact environmental management regionally and even globally?

This volume captures the voices of 59 who have made substantive contributions to the local and global environmental movement or to the study and protection of Singapore's rich natural heritage. Our hope is that the stories in this volume will serve as a useful resource for interested readers, that it provides a good overview of environmental management and the conservation of nature in Singapore, and that it lays down a marker for future environmental efforts. The voices captured in this volume tell a relatively little known but significant part of Singapore's first 70 years as an independent country. Equally important to us, however, is that these are simply compelling and fascinating stories told by a remarkable group of people.

This is the first attempt to showcase in one volume the words of Singapore's leaders in the environment community. Many might be surprised that this had not been done earlier. Given that the three of us have worked in different facets of the environment for years, and that our respective networks offer good coverage of the many people who have worked in this space for decades, a volume such as this was crying out to be done (or at least we thought so). This volume, however, took an interesting path on the way to becoming the collection of stories that you hold in your hand.

All three of us have dedicated a large part of our careers to environmental issues. Our respective professions require us to speak in public, but for a senior diplomat, speeches, policy statements, and managing dialogue and negotiations define much of the job. In a diplomatic career spanning over 50 years, Professor Tommy Koh has given countless speeches, written articles, and crafted opinion pieces on a wide range of topics. A recurring one has been the environment.

The editors came up with a list of 50 writers, which grew as co-authors were brought onboard. We suggested a topic for each contributor, and while the completed essays did cover the range of ideas requested, some stories evolved beyond initial promptings. The final product, we feel, is better off for it, as each piece is a personal and passionate expression from an expert in their sphere.

The writers are people we have admired and with whom we have worked. Some we have known for decades; others are more recent acquaintances who will lead Singapore's efforts in their fields for decades to come. They are people who have distinguished themselves in areas such as international policy, biodiversity research, environmental law, education, nature conservation, and communications. All are recognised authorities in their fields, but just as importantly, they have consistently and generously given their time, experience and expertise to Singapore, beyond the confines of their jobs.

The editors have engaged with nature from the time they were children. Professor Koh was a scout, Prof Lye lived close to nature in the East Coast, and Shawn Lum spent his free time either at the beach or looking after pets. They have also held positions with the Nature Society (Singapore). One (Koh) has been its Patron for over 30 years, another (Lye) served as its Legal Advisor as well as Vice-President, and the third (Lum) was its president for 15 years. It is not surprising, therefore, that nature and wildlife essays feature heavily — about two-thirds of the essays are about biodiversity or nature more generally. Of these, birds are the subject of five essays. Insects are the focus of four, mammals three, and another three essays cover various habitats. There are personal accounts and musings as well.

The professions of the editors are also reflected in the essay topics. Environmental policy is the subject of four essays. Environmental law and international negotiations are featured. Many essays are written by professors in the biodiversity field. Prominent environment writers, nature advocates, and those working in sustainability fields are represented, along with a good number from leaders in the private sector.

Authors include nature and policy professionals, active members of civil society, and those who have gained prominence in natural history research through parallel amateur careers; three contributors have gained prominence as experts in their nature-related hobbies in addition to their high-profile day jobs in business and medicine. Eighteen authors write in their specialist academic capacity, another 14 as members of non-governmental organisations, with NParks (five), other government agencies (five), and the private sector (four) accounting for the other writers.

Our collective experience in the environment field, while acceptable (we think), includes gaps that are reflected by omissions in this volume. Achieving sustainability and harmony with the living world will require a broad basket of solutions as well as changes in lifestyles and values. Technology will be critical, whether in renewable energy, green transport, carbon capture, efficient yet nature-friendly agriculture, advanced environmental and biodiversity monitoring, and many other fields.

Food security, sustainable tourism, environment-linked social enterprise, and humanitarian efforts that have nature-positive outcomes do not feature in this book. Neither do we highlight the growing movement within faith communities to protect nature and the environment. These fields deserve consideration and attention in Singapore, and their absence from this volume do not mean that we do not think they are important to achieving a sustainable and thriving living world. Perhaps this gives the editors incentive to undertake a second volume as they expand their environmental horizons?

Throughout the three years and the beguiling journey that spanned conception to completion of this book, there has been one constant: the title. Peace with Nature was a vision of Professor Koh's that strongly resonated with each of us. The editors have witnessed the loss of vast swathes of wilderness and the expansion of built areas around the world. But we have also seen remarkable transformations in sanitation, public health, and the regeneration of nature when it is given a chance. We have seen the environment go from being a cause of activists to a way of life and a rich source of career opportunities. We have seen enough positive change to believe that our children truly have a chance to live in a world at peace with nature. And we hope that this vision resonates enough with you that we will work together to make it reality.

About the Contributors

Chapter 1 — The Built Environment in Harmony with Nature

Esther An has been instrumental in establishing CDL's leadership in sustainability for nearly three decades. CDL is ranked top real estate company on the Global 100 Most Sustainable Corporations in the World since 2020. Named by Reuters as one of 25 trailblazing women leaders in climate 2023, Esther's pioneering ESG initiatives include publishing the first sustainability report in Singapore in 2008 and issuing the first green bond by a Singaporean company in 2017. She sits on the Global Reporting Initiative (GRI) Supervisory Board, GRESB Foundation Board and UN PRI Real Estate Advisory Committee; and chairs the World Green Building Council Corporate Advisory Board and the Asia Pacific Real Estate Association's ESG Committee.

Chapter 2 — Primates of Singapore

Andie Ang pursued her M.Sc. at the National University of Singapore (NUS), studying the ecology of critically endangered Raffles' banded langurs, before completing her Ph.D. at the University of Colorado, Boulder, USA, working on the conservation of leaf monkeys in Vietnam. She is currently the Head of Primate

Conservation and Singapore Programmes at Mandai Nature. She is also a Deputy Chair in the IUCN Species Survival Commission (SSC) Primate Specialist Group. Since 2018, Andie has served as the President of the Jane Goodall Institute (Singapore), a charity organisation aimed at promoting greater awareness and protection of nature and wildlife.

Sabrina Jabbar leads the Monkey Guards programme at the Jane Goodall Institute (Singapore). Since 2013, she has been actively involved in collaborating with agencies and nature groups for an integrated approach to foster harmonious co-existence between people and macaques. Together with ACRES, the Monkey Guards project was first piloted in 2014. Monkey Guarding has since been adopted by the Macaque Working Group as one of the modern approaches to resolve human-macaque conflicts. Today she is also actively engaged in cross-border collaborations to share and exchange knowledge on smart and effective approaches to help people and macaques.

Chapter 3 — Cities and Biodiversity

Lena Chan is Senior Director of the International Biodiversity Conservation Division, National Parks Board, Singapore. Her duties include being the National Focal Point for the Convention on Biological Diversity and a Governing Board member of the ASEAN Centre for Biodiversity. She has published papers on ecology, parasitology, and book chapters on urban conservation biology. She co-authored the *Handbook on the Singapore Index on Cities' Biodiversity* and co-edited a journal supplement on a comprehensive biodiversity survey of the Bukit Timah Nature Reserve.

Chapter 4 — Business and Our Natural World

Jessica Cheam is the Founder and Managing Director of Eco-Business, Asia-Pacific's leading independent media and business intelligence organisation dedicated to sustainable development. She is recognised as a sustainability pioneer with two decades of experience in media, sustainable development and ESG issues globally. She serves as an independent, non-executive director for two Singapore-listed companies Wilmar International and ComfortDelGro. She is a regular columnist for national newspapers and is an ESG committee member of the Singapore Institute of Directors. She is accredited with INSEAD's Certificate of Corporate Governance, the CFA Institute Certificate in ESG Investing, and specialises in advising boards on sustainability strategy.

Chapter 5 — From Plant-blind to Botanist

Dr Chong Kwek Yan is a Senior Researcher at the Singapore Botanic Gardens, National Parks Board (NParks), where he coordinates a Tropical Forest Ecology Research Programme. This programme is anchored by a Long-Term Forest Ecological Monitoring project that maintains a network of permanent research plots in Singapore's nature reserves and parks. His main research interests are in vegetation ecology, urban ecology, and invasion ecology.

Chapter 6 — Coral Reefs in the Urban Seascape

Chou Loke Ming is Emeritus Professor at the National University of Singapore (Department of Biological Sciences). He devoted much of his research career to the study of marine biodiversity, specifically coral reefs. He is a Fellow of the Singapore National Academy of

Science and an Honorary Fellow of the Singapore Institute of Biology. In recognition of his contributions, he was given the "Green Leaf Award" from the Ministry of Environment in 1994, the "SeaKeeper of Singapore Award" from the International SeaKeepers Society in 2016, and the "ASEAN Biodiversity Hero Award" from the ASEAN Center for Biodiversity in 2022.

Chapter 7 — Working with the IPCC: A Singapore Boy's View of Climate Change

Dr Winston Chow is a Lee Kong Chian Research Fellow and an Associate Professor of Urban Climate in Singapore Management University's (SMU) College of Integrative Studies. He is a Co-Lead Principal Investigator in the ongoing Cooling Singapore Initiative, leading research into how a digital urban twin enables climate-resilient urban design, and assessing how Singapore's urban heat risks can be minimised under a warming climate. In SMU, Dr Chow teaches interdisciplinary courses on climate change and urban sustainability. Lastly, Winston was a Lead Author for the Intergovernmental Panel on Climate Change's 6th *Assessment Report on Impacts, Adaptation and Vulnerability* on urban climate issues.

Chapter 8 — My Personal Journey with Nature

Dr Chua Ee Kiam is a Senior Consultant with the National Dental Centre, Clinical Associate Professor with Duke-NUS and Honorary staff member of the Lee Kong Chian Museum. He still finds time to excel in his favourite past-time — nature photography, focussing on the tropical rainforests and intertidal areas. He has written award-winning books on nature, including *Nature in Singapore – Ours To*

Protect; *Pulau Ubin – Ours To Treasure*; *Chek Jawa – Discovering Singapore's Biodiversity*; *Borneo's Tropical Eden – Sabah*; *Singapore's Splendour – Life on the Edge*; *Wetlands in a City*; *Rainforest in a City*; *Footprints on an Island – Rediscovering Pulau Ubin*; *Moments of Wonder*.

Chapter 9 — Singapore and the Protection of the Marine Environment

Dr Tara Davenport is currently an Assistant Professor at the Faculty of Law, National University of Singapore (NUS) where she teaches Principles of Property Law, Law of the Sea, and International Regulation of Shipping. She is also co-head of the Oceans Law and Policy Team at the Centre for International Law (CIL) at NUS, Deputy Director of the Asia-Pacific Centre for Environmental Law (APCEL), member of the Executive Council of the Asian Society of International Law, and member of the Editorial Board of the *Asian Journal of International Law and Ocean Development*, and *International Law Journal*.

Chapter 10 — The Importance of Birds to Humanity

Vinayagan Dharmarajah (Vina) is the Regional Director (Asia) of BirdLife International. He oversees the delivery of BirdLife's Strategy in Asia which includes the conservation of threatened avian species including hornbills, migratory shorebirds, bustards, vultures and cranes, and promoting the important roles they play. He also serves on the board of SAVE (Saving Asia's Vultures from Extinction), a consortium addressing the threats faced by Asia's vultures. Vina has a degree in law (LLB) from the University of Bristol and an LLM in International Business Law from the Sorbonne-Assas

International Law School. He serves concurrently as BirdLife's Head of Governance.

Chapter 11 — Greening Singapore: From Garden City to City in Nature

Kenneth Er is the Deputy Secretary (Planning) at the Ministry of National Development. Formerly the Chief Executive Officer of National Parks Board (NParks) from 2014 to end May 2023, he played a key role in the conceptualisation of the City in Nature vision, one of the five pillars under the Singapore Green Plan 2030, and led NParks to realise the vision by conserving and extending Singapore's natural capital island-wide. As the lead agency overseeing greenery and biodiversity conservation of our City in Nature in Singapore, NParks manages more than 400 gardens and parks, four nature reserves, island-wide Park Connector Network and streetscape greenery. NParks also oversees veterinary services. His research interests are in conservation biology, forest ecology, and avian ecology.

Dr Leong Chee Chiew joined the Singapore Botanic Gardens in 1983 as a research officer. In 1990, he was appointed Deputy Executive Director of the National Parks Board (NParks). When the Parks and Recreation Department merged with NParks in 1996, he became the Deputy Chief Executive Officer (Specialist Services Department). He is currently the Commissioner of Parks and Recreation; Director-General, Plant Health; Director-General, Wildlife Trade Control; and also Executive Director (National Parks, Gardens & Nature Reserves Cluster).

Chapter 12 — Speaking up for Nature

Dr Geh Min is an Ophthalmologist with a strong interest in environmental issues. She served as President of Nature Society (Singapore) from 2000 to 2008 and as a Nominated Member of Parliament (2005 to 2006). She was a recipient of the inaugural President's Award for the Environment (2006), the Stellar Awards — Celebrating Women (UNIFEM) (2006), the Honorary Watermark Award (2007), the SMA Merit Award (2007) and the Patrons of the Arts Award (Friends of the Arts Award) (2017 and 2018). She currently serves on several boards and advisory councils including Nature Society (Singapore), World Wide Fund for Nature (Singapore) Limited and BirdLife International (Asia).

Chapter 13 — The Role of Financial Institutions and the Environment

Piyush Gupta has been the Chief Executive Officer and Director of DBS Group since 2009. He was previously Citigroup's CEO for Southeast Asia, Australia and New Zealand. Piyush is Chairman of the Board of Trustees, Singapore Management University; Vice-Chairman of the Institute of International Finance; and Vice-Chairman of the Executive Committee, World Business Council for Sustainable Development. He has a keen interest in nature, and serves as Co-Chair of BirdLife International's Advisory Group, a global conservation NGO.

Helge Muenkel is the Chief Sustainability Officer at DBS. He is responsible for developing DBS' overarching sustainability framework and driving sustainability initiatives across the bank.

He acts as Secretary to the bank's Board Sustainability Committee (BSC), and chairs its Group Sustainability Council. Helge also represents DBS in several global and regional working groups, is alternate director in Climate Impact X Pte Ltd, and sits on the Impact Advisory Panel of the Asia Impact First Fund. Helge holds a Master's Degree in Economics from Munich University (major in Development Economics) as well as a postgraduate degree in sustainability from Cambridge University. He is also a Chartered Financial Analyst (CFA).

Chapter 14 — Sungei Buloh

R. E. Hale's career with HSBC was spent mainly in Hong Kong, Japan, Malaysia, and in Singapore where he was the first recipient of the Singapore Green Leaf Award in 1991. Retiring from commercial banking in 1995, he was elected director of various public companies. Apart from birdwatching and a general love of nature, he is a dedicated philatelist. He also researches Singapore's 19th century commercial history and the people who made it happen. His 2016 book *The Balestiers* was followed by *Fraser's Hill and Lewis J. Fraser of Singapore* in 2018 and *The Pioneer Merchants of Singapore* in 2022.

Chapter 15 — From Engineering to Diplomacy

Hazri Hassan joined the Ministry of the Environment in 1990 as an engineer focusing on solid waste management and public health engineering. At present, as Divisional Director of International Policy at the Ministry of Sustainability and the Environment, his job entails formulating strategies and approaches for bilateral, regional and international issues to advance Singapore's efforts in the environmental and sustainability space. Hazri was appointed as Singapore's first non-resident Permanent Representative to the United Nations Environment Programme (UNEP) in 2016, where he takes part in international decision-making on the best means to resolve pressing global environmental issues.

Chapter 16 — Our Water, Our Life, Our Future

Eugene Heng, JP, BBM, is the founder and CEO of Waterways Watch Society. He started his environmental journey in the 1980s, first as an environment coordinator at the foreign bank he worked for. Eugene was later appointed to the Government Parliamentary Committee (Environment) from 1995–2000. He went on to serve in several advisory committees relating to environmental issues in Singapore, including the Water Focus Group, the Policy Study Workgroup on Physical and Environment Sustainability and the Singapore Green Plan 2012 Coordinating Committee. He also served as a PUB board member from 2001–2005 and was a pioneer member of the Public Hygiene Council.

Chapter 17 — The Battle to Conserve Nature in Singapore

Ho Hua Chew (M.Sc. – Landscape Ecology, Design & Management (Imperial College); M.Sc. – Applied Ecology & Conservation (East Anglia); Ph.D. – Philosophy (University of Washington)) is past Chairman of the Nature Society (Singapore)'s Conservation Committee and helped formulate its conservation proposals for various nature areas as well as its *Master Plan for the Conservation* *of Nature in Singapore* (1990). He continues to help in coordinating NSS' conservation activities and projects, including feedbacks to the government on land-use and development plans, biodiversity surveys, etc. He was awarded the Outstanding Advocate of Our Time (2016) by The Singapore Advocacy Awards.

Chapter 18 — Insects of Singapore: The Uncountable that Counts

Hwang Wei Song is Curator of Entomology and Senior Lecturer at the Lee Kong Chian Natural History Museum, National University of Singapore (NUS). His research work includes improving insect biodiversity knowledge through species discovery and creating better access to species information, especially for Singapore and Southeast Asia. He specialises in True Bugs (Hemiptera), particularly the predominantly predatory assassin bugs (Reduviidae). As an educator, Wei Song teaches for the NUS College and mentors students and interns from all walks of life, and anyone who is interested in insect biodiversity, museum curation and science communication.

Chapter 19 — History of Sustainable Energy in Singapore and Its Future Role

Er Edwin T.F. Khew, PBM, is a former Nominated Member of Parliament (NMP), Singapore, and currently the Chairman of the Sustainable Energy Association of Singapore (SEAS), President of the Plastics Recycling Association, Singapore (PRAS), Emeritus President of the Institution of Engineers, Singapore (IES), and a Supervisory Board Member of Solar Energy Research Institute of

Singapore (SERIS). He has an Executive MBA from the National University of Singapore, a Bachelor's in Chemical Engineering from the University of Queensland, Australia, and is Honorary Fellow and a Chartered Engineer of the Institution of Engineers, Singapore.

Chapter 20 — Butterflies of Singapore

Khew Sin Khoon is the Group Chief Executive Officer of CPG Corporation, a multinational built-environment consultancy firm. His passion for butterflies started more than five decades ago, when he collected butterflies in his home garden in Malaysia. He holds Honorary Research appointments with NParks' National Biodiversity Centre and the Lee Kong Chian Natural History Museum. An architect by training, he believes that nature and development can co-exist in harmony. In 2004, he founded "ButterflyCircle", an online community of butterfly enthusiasts and photographers. He is the author of *A Field Guide to the Butterflies of Singapore, 2010 & 2015.*

Chapter 21 — A Social Compact in Co-creating a City in Nature

Joseph K H Koh is a retired ambassador, an amateur spider scientist, and a passionate conservationist. He was President of the Asian Society of Arachnology (2015–2017), and Chairman of WWF Singapore (2017–2020). He has been Chairman of the Friends of Bukit Timah Forest (FOBTF) since 2016. Joseph received the prestigious President's Award for the Environment in 2021. Joseph was intimately involved in the dialogue between nature groups and the Land Transport Authority (LTA) over the Cross Island Line

(2013–2019). The views expressed in this essay do not necessarily represent those of the FOBTF and WWF Singapore.

Chapter 22 — The Importance of Environmental Law

Dr Koh Kheng Lian, Emeritus Prof. Faculty of Law, NUS, was formerly Director of APCEL, and IUCN-CEL Regional Vice-Chair for South and East Asia. Other appointments include — Consultant, ADB/IUCN-CEL/NUS *Capacity Building in Environmental Legal Education*; and Director, Ministry of Foreign Affairs *Capacity Building on Urban Environment*. She served as a legal officer in the Secretariat of UNCITRAL, 1980–1986, Vienna. An awardee of the Elizabeth Haub Prize in Environmental Law 2013, the Singapore Women's Hall of Fame 2014, and the Environmental Lawyer of the Year (ASEAN) 2020, her publications including conference papers numbering over 200. She currently serves on the Board of Governors of ICEL.

Chapter 23 — Nature-based Solutions to Climate Change

Professor Koh Lian Pin is the Vice Dean of Research at the Faculty of Science and the Kwan Im Thong Hood Cho Temple Chair Professor of Conservation at the National University of Singapore (NUS). He is also the Director of the Centre for Nature-based Climate Solutions, and the Tropical Marine Science Institute (TMSI) at the University. Professor Koh has 20 years of international research experience in the field of sustainability and environmental science, having worked in institutions across Europe, Australia, the United States and Singapore.

Chapter 24 — My Green Journey

Tommy Koh is an Ambassador-At-Large, at the Ministry of Foreign Affairs and an Emeritus Professor of Law of the National University of Singapore. He is the Patron of the Nature Society (Singapore) and was made a Champion of the Earth by the UN Environment Programme (UNEP) for his leadership role at the 1992 Earth Summit. He was the President of the Third UN Conference on the Law of the Sea. For this and other achievements in negotiations, he was given the Great Negotiator Award by Harvard University.

Chapter 25 — The Herpetological Society and Youth Outreach

Law Ing Sind is a conservationist, co-founder of the Herpetological Society of Singapore (HSS) and a zoology graduate from the University of Reading. His keen eyes often find him interesting animals and behaviours to document in Singapore. His interest in the natural world was piqued when he was young, having his very own sighting of a snake feeding on a toad at the tender age of 10. His interests in writing and photography are intertwined and he often finds one aiding the other.

Law Ingg Thong is one of the six co-founders of HSS. A zoology graduate from the University of Reading, he has had an interest in herpetofauna since 2011 and has spent the past few years helping as an independent researcher in comprehensive biodiversity surveys and other research projects around Singapore. He also has an interest and passion for the fields of bioacoustics and ecology.

Sankar Ananthanarayanan is a co-founder of HSS and a current PhD student pursuing his doctorate in tropical ecology at the National University of Singapore. Sankar has always been passionate about herpetology, conservation biology, and communication science. As the first president of HSS, he often found himself using the skills from all three fields in tandem to efficiently run the society and further the goals of the society.

Serin Subaraj is one of the six co-founders of HSS. He has worked as a Wildlife Consultant and field biologist in environmental consultancy since 2008. He has conducted a vast array of surveys and fieldwork around many countries in Southeast Asia. He has led multiple research and consultancy teams studying terrestrial fauna. He is currently enrolled with Curtin University as a research masters student studying tiger snake populations and behaviour in Perth.

Chapter 26 — From Railway Land to Rail Corridor

Leong Kwok Peng currently chairs the Conservation Committee of Nature Society (Singapore) (NSS), serving as a "front man" for engagement with many of the government agencies. He was former Vice-President and Chair of the Marine Conservation Group. He helped publish *Singapore Waters – Unveiling Our Seas*, and also coordinated the Coral Reef Rescue from Pulau Ayer Chawan in the mid-1990s. He joined NSS in the 1980s. He is a chemical engineer, and has spent many years in the petrochemical and water treatment industry before venturing into outdoor education to run school camps and inspire children to love nature.

Chapter 27 — Colugos in Singapore

Dr Norman Lim is a lecturer at the National Institute of Education, Nanyang Technological University (NTU). Norman teaches a variety of undergraduate and postgraduate courses, ranging from animal diversity, biostatistics, to ecology and conservation. Having an interest in understudied vertebrates, he focuses on the ecology and conservation of terrestrial vertebrates, and recent research projects include investigating the ecological impacts of free-roaming dogs, habitat connectivity of colugos, and habitat selection of small mammals. He has been a member of the IUCN Pangolin Specialist Group since 2012, and serves as an Associate Editor for *The Raffles Bulletin of Zoology* since 2013.

Chapter 28 — Cities and Climate Change

Jolene Lin is Associate Professor of Law at the National University of Singapore (NUS). She is also Director of the Asia-Pacific Centre of Environmental Law (APCEL). Jolene's research focusses on climate change law and transnational environmental law. Her recent publications include *Governing Climate Change: Global Cities and Transnational Lawmaking* (Cambridge University Press, 2018) and *Climate Change Litigation in the Asia Pacific* (Cambridge University Press, 2020). She is currently co-writing a book on climate change litigation in the Global South (Oxford University Press, 2024). Jolene enjoys travelling, hiking and exploring Singapore's amazing public playgrounds with her two children.

Chapter 29 — Nature Society (Singapore)

Shawn Lum is a botanist and forest ecologist. He taught at the National Institute of Education for over 20 years before moving to the Nanyang Technological University Asian School of the Environment in 2015. His work has largely focused on the dynamics and capacity for regeneration of isolated pockets of tropical rainforest. Shawn is a member of the Nature Society (Singapore) and served as its President from 2015 to 2023. He was born on a large island (Honshu), raised on a much smaller one (Oahu), and has made his life on an even smaller one (Singapore).

Chapter 30 — The Legal Protection of Nature in Singapore

Lye Lin Heng, PBM, is Hon. Fellow, Law Faculty, National University of Singapore, where she taught Environmental Law and Property Law for many years. She is Hon. Advisor and former Director, Asia-Pacific Centre for Environmental Law (APCEL). She was Vice-Dean (Graduate Programs), and initiated the NUS multi-disciplinary M.Sc. (Environmental Management) [MEM] programme, chairing the programme from its inception in 2001 till her retirement in 2019. Her publications include journal articles and books on Singapore's Environmental Laws. She is Hon. Advisor to the Nature Society (Singapore) and WWF Singapore. She was a member of the Board of Governors, IUCN Academy of Environmental Law and its co-Chair, Teaching and Capacity-Building Committee.

Chapter 31 — When We Nurture Nature, Nature Nurtures Us

Kirtida Mekani is a multi-faceted individual who dedicates her efforts to the four key pillars in her life — the environment, education, arts, and business. As a business leader, Kirtida has proven expertise in fundraising, institutional advancement, and capacity building. In education, she has spearheaded forward-thinking initiatives in schools across the nation. In 2015, Kirtida was bestowed the prestigious President's Award for the Environment. She was also nominated for the Singapore Women Award in 2014, and recognised as a 2012 Community in Bloom (CIB) ambassador. Kirtida is also an accomplished artist and author of her book, *Compassion for Life Through Nature: The Essence of Jeevdaya*.

Chapter 32 — Here be Dragonflies: An Ode to Singapore's Flying Dragons

Marcus Ng is an independent writer and researcher. His interests include the natural histories of Singapore and Malaysia; insects of Southeast Asia (in particular dragonflies and moths); and the natural and human histories of Singapore's coasts and islands. He was the curator of *Balik Pulau*, a special exhibition on Singapore's islands at the National Museum of Singapore, and two thematic galleries featuring the William Farquhar Collection of Natural History Drawings: *Danger and Desire* and *Magic and Menace*.

Robin Ngiam is a biodiversity consultant who has worked on dragonflies since 2005, spanning taxonomy, ecological surveys, conservation policies, environmental impact assessments (EIAs), training courses, outreach and guided tours. He has extensive publications on dragonflies from Singapore and Borneo (Sarawak). Sharing a passion for dragonflies, Robin and Marcus wrote *A Photographic Guide to the Dragonflies and Damselflies of Singapore*, which was published in 2022.

Chapter 33 — Hard Truths from a Flawed Naturalist

Peter K. L. Ng is in the Department of Biological Sciences and an associate in the Lee Kong Chian Natural History Museum at the National University of Singapore (NUS). He has been teaching in the university since 1990, has helped establish a multitude of teaching modules, and also been involved in various administrative tasks for the university and government agencies. He has worked on a wide variety of animals and issues in Singapore and the region, focussing on aquatic animals including fish and crabs.

Chapter 34 — The Re-introduction of the Oriental Pied Hornbill to Singapore

Ng Soon-Chye is a gynaecologist by profession, with sub-speciality in infertility. He was responsible for the first in-vitro fertilisation ("test-tube") baby in Asia, delivered in 1983 in Singapore. He pioneered the technique of SUZI which is the precursor of the current micro-injection (ICSI) technique, with the world's first delivery in 1989. He still practises at Novena Specialist Centre. He has a passion for nature, especially bird-watching, and since his younger days, has been involved with the Malayan Nature Society (Singapore branch) and now, the Nature Society (Singapore) (NSS). He did bird-ringing in the 1970s with David Wells, when the forests of Malaya were still pristine.

Marc Cremades is the Vice President and Team Lead for Attractions Development at the Mandai Wildlife Group. He is the founding member of the team, and is leading the conceptualisation and implementation of a new generation of wildlife parks in Singapore: Bird Paradise and Rainforest Park. He has over 30 years of experience in the study and management of conservation and breeding programmes for animals in Singapore, and across five continents. Many of these have been recognised with awards, and published in books, films and TV documentaries. Other notable projects include the creation of a Protected Natural Park in Madagascar and an Oscar nominee movie.

Chapter 35 — How Much for the Environment?

Euston Quah is Albert Winsemius Chair Professor of Economics at the Nanyang Technological University, with research interests in Cost-Benefit Analysis and Environmental Economics. He has published over 100 papers in journals, and lead opinion articles in media. Widely cited, his internationally known book on Cost-Benefit Analysis with E. J. Mishan published by Routledge, UK is now in its 6th edition, 2021. The Asian edition of his *Principles of Economics* with Gregory Mankiw is now a 3rd edition Cengage published book, 2021. Professor Quah is also the only person who headed both the economics departments at the National University of Singapore, and at the Nanyang Technological University.

Chapter 36 — A Crazy Fondness for Stick-insects

Francis Seow-Choen is a colorectal surgeon in private practice. He was previously head of the Department of Colorectal Surgery at Singapore General Hospital as well as Head of Surgical Oncology at National Cancer Centre. He had been on the editorial board of many surgical journals and has honorary fellowships in many national colorectal societies. Apart from his professional work, he is an associate researcher with Lee Kong Chian Natural History Museum and the National Biodiversity Board in Singapore. He has published 10 books on stick-insects and has described and named more than 250 new stick-insect species from Southeast Asia.

Chapter 37 — Managing Seagrass Meadows for Resilience in Highly Urbanised Coastal Cities: A Singapore Case Study

Dr Siti Maryam Yaakub is a marine ecologist working across tropical marine ecosystems. She specialises in seagrass ecosystems and applications of nature-based solutions for climate change mitigation and adaptation. Dr Siti is currently the Director of the International Blue Carbon Institute at Conservation International. The institute works with blue carbon scientists and practitioners in developing projects and policies that protect and restore coastal blue carbon ecosystems. In her spare time Dr Siti leads TeamSeaGrass, a citizen science group monitoring seagrass habitats in Singapore.

Chapter 38 — The Smooth-coated Otters of Singapore

N. Sivasothi, aka "Otterman" has been immersed in mangroves and wildlife for research, education and conservation at the National

University of Singapore since the late 1980s. He also actively promotes youth development, public education and environmental stewardship. He is coordinator for NUS Toddycats, the International Coastal Cleanup Singapore, OtterWatch, and (in partnership with NParks) The Biodiversity Roundtable and The Biodiversity Friends Forum. He is an active contributor to numerous wildlife working groups, ground-up partnerships and closed-door engagements to mitigate development impact. He is now an active advocate for habitat enhancement and community participation in the OneMillionTrees movement.

Chapter 39 — Birds of Singapore

Morten Strange is a retired petroleum engineer, retired nature photographer and retired publisher. He lived in Singapore from 1980 to 1993 and again continuously since 1999. He has been a member of Nature Society (Singapore) since 1984, and is now a life member and active on and off. In 2014, Morten qualified as a financial analyst. When he is not studying capital allocation or writing about economic and environmental issues, he enjoys long walks in the woods looking at the critters, as well as spending time with his family. Check mortenstrange.com for more.

Bee Choo Strange is a former mechanical engineer and Managing Director of Nature's Niche Pte Ltd. Post-retirement from business, she helps out as the International Coordinator of the Hornbill Research Foundation (since 1992) and Program Manager of the IUCN SSC Hornbill Specialist Group (since 2017). She has been organising conferences, workshops and liaising with the international community working on hornbill research and conservation. She is also a life member of Nature Society (Singapore) and has been a member since 1987.

Chapter 40 — The Power of a Story

Audrey Tan is the science communication and outreach lead at the National University of Singapore's Centre for Nature-based Climate Solutions and Tropical Marine Science Institute. She was previously an award-winning environment journalist at *The Straits Times*, Singapore's national broadsheet, where she covered a variety of environmental issues such as biodiversity conservation and climate change for 10 years. Audrey holds a master's degree in climate science and policy from the Scripps Institution of Oceanography at the University of California San Diego, and is also an advisory committee member of the Pulitzer Center's Rainforest Journalism Fund for Southeast Asia.

Chapter 41 — The Greening of NUS Campus: From Iconic Ambience of Bukit Timah Campus (BTC) to Global Sustainability Leader

Professor Tan Eng Chye was appointed President of the National University of Singapore (NUS) on 1 January 2018. He is the University's 5th president, and the 23rd leader to head Singapore's oldest higher education institution. Professor Tan is a passionate and award-winning educator. He was a pioneer architect of the current academic system in NUS, and has seeded many initiatives such as the Special Programme in Science, University Scholars Programme, University Town Residential College Programme, Grade-free Year, and Technology-enhanced Education. He was recognised with the University Teaching Award for Innovative Teaching in 1998, and other teaching awards.

Chapter 42 — Gardens by the Bay

A pioneer in the transformation of Singapore's landscape, **Dr Kiat W. Tan** has built his career around the stewardship of nature. He served over 30 years in the public service and held many senior appointments, including founding CEO of National Parks Board in 1990. When he stepped down from the role in 2006, he continued to lend his professional expertise to steer the development of Gardens by the Bay, becoming the Gardens' founding CEO until his retirement in 2018. Dr Tan continues to devote his energies to Singapore's City in Nature vision as Advisor to National Parks Board and Corporate Advisor to Gardens by the Bay.

Chapter 43 — Resurrecting a National Heritage — The Lee Kong Chian Natural History Museum

Leo Tan Wee Hin is a marine biologist and conservationist, with research interests in mangrove regeneration and science education. He is an Advisor to the Lee Kong Chian Natural History Museum at the National University of Singapore (NUS). He chairs National Parks Board's Garden City Fund; is a Board Director of Temasek Foundation Ltd and Temasek Foundation IPC Ltd; Singapore Governor of the Asia Europe Foundation; Board Director of Mandai Park Holdings; Governing Member of the Singapore Environmental Council; Board Director of Conservation International Asia-Pacific and Fellow of the Singapore National Academy of Science. He has also served as Chairman of NParks Board, CEO of the Singapore Science Centre and Dean of Science and Director, National Institute of Education, Nanyang Technological University (NTU).

Chapter 44 — Chek Jawa

Tan Yong Soon is a former senior civil servant who served as Permanent Secretary in the Ministry of the Environment and Water Resources, and for Climate Change in the Prime Minister's Office; Chief Executive Officer of the Urban Redevelopment Authority, Deputy Secretary in the Ministry of Finance and the Ministry of Defence, and Principal Private Secretary to the Prime Minister. He is Professor in Practice at the Lee Kuan Yew School of Public Policy, National University of Singapore, where he started the LKY Senior Fellows in Public Service Programme. He coauthored the book, *Clean, Green and Blue: Singapore's Journey Towards Environmental and Water Sustainability* and edited the book, *50 Years of Environment*, as part of World Scientific series on Singapore's 50 Years of Nation-Building.

Chapter 45 — International Climate Negotiations: Reflections from Singapore's Chief Negotiator for Climate Change

Joseph Teo was appointed Singapore's Chief Negotiator for Climate Change on 2 July 2018. Prior to this appointment, Joseph has held various positions in the Ministry of Foreign Affairs (MFA), including Singapore's Deputy Permanent Representative to the United Nations in New York. In his current role at the Ministry of Sustainability and the Environment (MSE), Joseph has been a keen advocate of sustainability and climate action. Joseph is also a member of the Caritas Care for Creation Committee, Caritas Singapore.

Chapter 46 — Singapore's Blue Heart: The Sisters' Islands Marine Park

Dr Karenne Tun is Director of the Terrestrial, Coastal, and Marine Branches at the National Biodiversity Centre, National Parks Board (NParks), and her work focusses on the management and conservation of Singapore's natural areas across the terrestrial, coastal and marine environments. Her team is also responsible for managing Singapore's first Marine Park — the Sisters' Islands Marine Park. In 2021, Karenne was nominated to represent Singapore as one of 25 members of the Group of Experts for the United Nations Regular Process for the 3rd Cycle tasked to prepare the 3rd World Ocean Assessment (WOA3) by 2025.

Chapter 47 — The Battle to Save the Lower Peirce Forest

Dr Wee Yeow Chin played a significant role as a green advocate in Singapore. He was Secretary of the Malayan Nature Society (Singapore Branch) (1978–1990) and Founding President of the Nature Society (Singapore) (1990–1995). He has also served in the Nature Reserves Board, Nature Reserves Committee, Singapore Environment Council and Work-Group on Nature Conservation. He was appointed Honorary Museum Associate of the Lee Kong Chian Natural History Museum in 2012. In 2005, he started the Bird Ecology Study Group. With more than 6,000 entries, the website has become a valuable resource consulted by students, birdwatchers and researchers locally and internationally.

Chapter 48 — My Fascination with Mangroves

Yang Shufen joined NParks in 2006 as a project officer to survey natural areas in Singapore. In 2009, she managed the Coastal Protection and Restoration of Mangrove Biodiversity at Pulau Tekong with a multi-disciplinary team. She did a three-year stint in park planning and corporate development where she was part of the team that established Friends of Ubin Network (FUN). As Deputy Director (Sungei Buloh), she did wetlands management, Kranji Coastal Nature Park nature-based solutions and migratory shorebird conservation since 2016. Currently she is the Director (Sungei Buloh) managing the wetland Reserve, Mandai Mangrove and Mudflat, Kranji Marshes, Lim Chu Kang mangroves and Khatib Bongsu.

Chapter 49 — Singapore's Freshwater Habitats: More Than Meets the Eye

Darren Yeo Chong Jinn is Head of the Lee Kong Chian Natural History Museum, Faculty of Science, National University of Singapore (NUS). He is also an Associate Professor at the Department of Biological Sciences, Faculty of Science, NUS, where he leads the Freshwater and Invasion Biology Laboratory. His main research interests are freshwater ecology and biodiversity, aquatic invasions, and freshwater crustaceans, which the lab investigates through studies of freshwater ecosystems in Singapore and other parts of tropical Asia.

Chapter 50 — Protecting Migratory Birds in Singapore and the Flyway

Yong Ding Li coordinates BirdLife International's work to protect migratory birds and wetlands in Asia, and is currently closely involved in the development of the Regional Flyway Initiative with the Asian Development Bank. He taught for several years at National Junior College before pursuing a Ph.D. on conservation biology at the Australian National University. Ding Li has written several books and papers on the birds and biodiversity of Asia and Australia, including the recent *Field Guide to the Birds of Malaysia and Singapore*. He paints and volunteers for the Nature Society (Singapore) during his free time.

Chapter 1

The Built Environment in Harmony with Nature

Esther An

Will there be a winner in a war between humanity and Nature?

The world must cease its "senseless and suicidal war against nature...", United Nations (UN) Secretary-General António Guterres said in a landmark speech in 2020, "We will not have a liveable planet unless humanity acts now." His warning of the catastrophic climate effects resulting from the war humans waged on Nature has sadly become reality.

To date, at least 85% of the world's population have experienced the effects of climate change, with the past seven years being the hottest in history. One million plant and animal species are now threatened with extinction, many within decades. Air pollution claims the lives of seven million people every year — more than the COVID-19 pandemic. This is accelerated and worsened by climate change, with the effects most acute for the 70% of the global population living in cities.

Planetary health is essential for human health. Decisive action is needed to spearhead change towards a climate positive future. At the end of 2022, the COP15 UN Biodiversity Conference came to a historic agreement to protect 30% of land and water by 2030. There is indeed strong synergy between the green and blue economies in preserving the planet's resources and improving the health and well-being of people and biodiversity, on land and in the oceans.

The environment and economies are interconnected and co-dependent. It is encouraging to see more than 90% of the world's GDP spanning across borders and sectors pledge support for the "race to zero" campaign led by United Nations Framework Convention on Climate Change (UNFCCC) following COP26. With building and construction activities accounting for about 40% of global carbon emissions, the real estate sector is in a strong position to advance sustainable development. As a pioneering developer in Singapore, with presence in 28 countries and regions, City Developments Limited (CDL) has joined leading global organisations to strengthen our decarbonisation commitment for long-term business resilience.[1]

Today, the business case for integrating sustainability has never been stronger. A report from Swiss Re estimates that by 2050 global warming could reduce global GDP by as much as 14% or US$23 trillion. This does not bode well for businesses. However, with a concerted global effort, this scenario can still be mitigated.

Companies that can adopt new ways of thinking, managing, and regenerating natural and social capital will create positive impact on their organisations' financial performance and long-term growth. The COVID-19 pandemic has also pushed businesses to think beyond short-term profits to be future-ready.

CDL's Environment, Social and Governance (ESG) strategy, founded on our corporate ethos of "Conserving as We Construct" since 1995, has prepared us well in the transition to a low-carbon economy. Our

[1] Information is up to date as of March 2023.

value creation business model, anchored on four strategic pillars — Integration, Innovation, Investment, and Impact — provides us a solid foundation to mitigate and adapt to unprecedented threats and challenges. We are committed to achieving three deliverables: "Decarbonisation", "Disclosure and Communication", and "Digitalisation & Innovation".

Integration: Embracing ESG and UN Sustainable Development Goals (SDGs) Adds Purpose to CDL's Business

For close to two decades, Sustainability has been effectively integrated into our corporate governance structure, business strategy, operations, and reporting. CDL's Sustainability team, empowered to set goals and track performance, reports directly to the Board Sustainability Committee. This structure has enabled ESG to be coordinated both horizontally between the ESG pillars and functions, and vertically across hierarchical levels. To address ever-changing stakeholder expectations, tackle emerging risks, and future-proof our business, we have conducted annual materiality assessments since 2014 with key internal and external stakeholders. The top ESG issues including innovation, energy efficiency, decarbonisation, and climate resilience are integrated into our sustainability practices and product stewardship.

Addressing these issues in a holistic and integrated manner, CDL became the first real estate conglomerate in Southeast Asia to sign on to the World Green Building Council's Net Zero Carbon Buildings Commitment in 2021. We pledged net zero operational carbon by 2030 for our new and existing wholly owned and managed assets and by 2050, all new and existing assets to be net zero across the whole life cycle, including operational and embodied emissions.

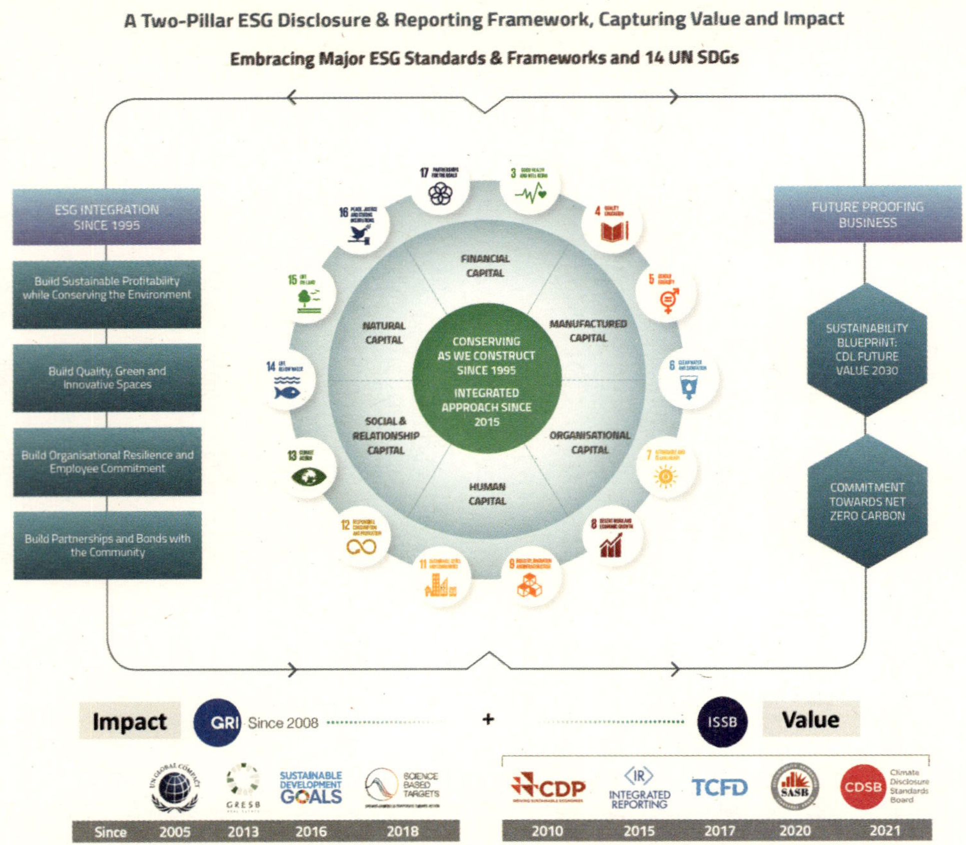

CDL's Pioneering Application of a Two-Pillar ESG Disclosure Framework Capturing Value and Impact, in its 16th Integrated Sustainability Report, *Zero in on Positive Impact*, (2023). (Photo credit: City Developments Limited)

With this pledge, we adjusted the carbon reduction targets set for the 2°C warmer scenario in 2018 to align with the 1.5°C scenario validated by Science Based Targets Initiative in end 2021.

Innovation: Applying Technologies Towards a Greener and Regenerative Economy

With our commitment to the global "race to zero", we accelerated our investments in innovation and technology through an Enterprise Innovation Committee established in 2018. To further accelerate innovation efforts, our top management decided to set up a team dedicated to green building technology application in 2020, at the peak of the COVID-19 lockdown. It aims to apply cutting-edge technologies to improve product design and operational efficiency, preparing CDL for a post-pandemic recovery that is greener and more sustainable. At CDL, we not only build bricks and mortar, but create spaces for healthy living, personal and business growth, and long-term investments. As a catalyst for change, CDL is committed to making sure our value chain adopts more sustainable and innovative practices aligned with global best practices.

In support of the Singapore Green Building Masterplan advocating for Super Low Energy (SLE) Buildings, CDL's redevelopment at 80 Anson Road was awarded Singapore's first Building and Construction Authority's (BCA) Green Mark Platinum SLE Certification for mixed development in 2022. Our Copen Grand Executive Condominium was also awarded Singapore's first BCA Green Mark Platinum SLE Condominium.

To achieve a net zero world, we need zero energy buildings. To date, CDL has built two net zero facilities using eco-friendly technologies and materials — the Singapore Sustainability Academy (SSA) and the CDL Green Gallery at the Singapore Botanic Gardens. The SSA, a BCA Green Mark Platinum-certified building, is the first in Singapore to have its timber construction materials verified from sustainable sources by the Nature's Barcode™ system.

Investment: Channelling Capital to Future-Proof Business

In the transition to a low carbon economy, companies must be willing to invest in sustainable solutions and innovations that will disrupt the status quo. According to Bloomberg, global ESG assets may surpass US$50 trillion by 2025, or one-third of the projected total assets managed globally.

CDL's strong track record in ESG performance has enabled us to tap onto the fast-rising ESG investment funds and sustainable finance. Being the first Singapore company to issue a green bond in 2017, CDL has since secured more than S$3 billion worth of sustainable finance to support our continuous pursuit of a greener built environment.

Impact — Zeroing in on Positive Impact

Today, a successful business is no longer about short-term profits. Many investors and consumers are assessing companies on their impact to the environment and communities. Being an early adopter of the UN SDGs, CDL was conferred the 2018 SDG Pioneer for green infrastructure and a low carbon economy by UN Global Compact. Embracing SDGs has helped us add purpose to our "Triple Bottom Line" — doing well financially by doing good. CDL is honoured to be listed under the Global 100 Most Sustainable

Corporations in the World by Corporate Knights since 2010, maintaining our position as the world's topmost sustainable real estate management and development company since 2020. CDL's robust ESG performance is widely recognised by 14 global ESG ratings, rankings, and indexes, including "AAA" leader position on MSCI ESG Rating since 2010.

The "race to zero" requires companies to have true conviction and engagement with all stakeholders. To tackle the climate emergency, companies should go beyond risk mitigation and turn threats to opportunities through adaptation. It is not sufficient to conserve Nature, we need to adopt Nature-based solutions for business resilience. We are piloting technologies that turn food waste to compost; plastic waste to form part of raw material for making cement walls. To lower our footprint, we are transitioning to adopt Nature-based carbon credits for prudent offsetting.

With two decades of integrating ESG into our business, we have managed to capture growth opportunities while mitigating ESG risks, enhancing long-term value for our investors, communities, and the planet.

Indeed, there is an urgency to make peace with Nature. In February this year, I was privileged to be part of the Antarctica Climate Expedition led by Dr Sylvia Earle, 88-year-old legendary marine scientist and a National Geographic Explorer-in-Residence. This icebound continent at the southern end of the world is "a natural reserve, devoted to peace and science" under the Antarctic Treaty inked between 12 countries in 1959. The Treaty also provides any member of the United Nations access and has now 52 signatories, including 28 who are Consultative Parties being original signatories or conducting substantial research there.

Antarctica is a great example of putting priority on Nature conservation. Being free from war, Antarctica has served as a protected Nature reserve for peaceful collaboration for scientific research which has contributed to the protection of the global environment. Can the Antarctic Treaty model be adapted to tackle the global climate emergency? On 5 March 2023, the United Nations inked the first ever "High Seas Treaty" in a bid to protect the oceans of the world that lie outside national boundaries. This treaty, coming after a decade of effort, reflects a greater commitment by humanity to co-exist in harmony with Nature through collaboration.

In a war between humanity and Nature, no one will win.

Esther An has been instrumental in establishing CDL's leadership in sustainability for nearly three decades. CDL is ranked top real estate company on the Global 100 Most Sustainable Corporations in the World since 2020. Named by Reuters as one of 25 trailblazing women leaders in climate 2023, Esther's pioneering ESG initiatives include publishing the first sustainability report in Singapore in 2008 and issuing the first green bond by a Singaporean company in 2017. She sits on the Global Reporting Initiative (GRI) Supervisory Board, GRESB Foundation Board and UN PRI Real Estate Advisory Committee; and chairs the World Green Building Council Corporate Advisory Board and the Asia Pacific Real Estate Association's ESG Committee.

Chapter 2

Primates of Singapore

Andie Ang and Sabrina Jabbar

Humans included, there are 533 species of primates in the world. Humans aside, primates are also one of the more visually prominent and charismatic animals. Some of these non-human primates are already familiar to us: the lemurs of Madagascar, the spider monkeys and howler monkeys of Central and South America, and the great apes like chimpanzees, gorillas, and orangutans. In this part of the world in Asia, a large part of primate diversity is attributed to lorises, monkeys, and gibbons. In Singapore, we have three native species: the Sunda slow loris, long-tailed macaque, and Raffles' banded langur.

The Sunda slow loris is a small animal with huge eyes and a layer of tissue called *tapetum lucidum* behind its retina, thus allowing it to see very well in the night. Even though they are generally slow-moving, slow lorises can actually act quickly when catching prey such as small insects. Besides invertebrates like insects, they also consume tree gum, fruits, leaves and even bird eggs. Slow lorises are the only venomous primates in the world. When under threat, they lick the glands on their forearms. The secretion from the glands mixed with saliva will produce a composite venom which is then injected through bites. Mothers may also apply a layer of venom on their infants as protection, whilst parking the little ones in the trees before going out to forage. The Sunda slow loris is considered nationally endangered given their small numbers in Singapore. There is also limited information about the lorises in Singapore, given their elusive and nocturnal nature.

The long-tailed macaque, on the other hand, is highly visible to the public given its ability to adapt and make use of different habitats including secondary forests, coastal forests and urban areas. Long-tailed macaques also prefer forest fringes, which means that we can see them near roads and walkways in the context of Singapore's urban setting. Their numbers underwent drastic changes over the years with Singapore's active management strategies. In 2012, it was estimated that there were between 1,810 and 2,166 long-tailed macaques, but between 2011 and 2013, culling reduced one-third of their population. This extreme management approach was discontinued in 2019 when the National Parks Board (NParks) took

A long-tailed macaque mother nursing her infant. (Photo credit: Sabrina Jabbar)

over the wildlife management operations of the former Agri-food and Veterinary Authority of Singapore (AVA).

In other parts of Southeast Asia, populations of the long-tailed macaque have drastically declined such that in 2022, it was classified as endangered by the International Union for Conservation of Nature (IUCN). Capture for laboratory research is listed as one of the major threats to the species. This threat, combined with habitat destruction and capture for the pet trade and entertainment industry, have resulted in some places in Cambodia, Laos and Vietnam reporting forests emptied of macaques. Recent surveys conducted in Bangladesh have found that long-tailed macaques have become extinct. In Singapore, these primates face threats from human-macaque conflicts. Through the provision of food intentionally (e.g., leaving leftover fruits along forest edges) and unintentionally (e.g., food that is unattended; trash bins that are not secured), long-tailed macaques have gradually lost their natural fear of humans and learned that human habitations are a source of food. Coupled with the closer proximity of urban areas to nature spaces, there are increased opportunities for monkeys and people to interact. If people are not aware of the do's and don'ts when encountering wild animals, the chances of inappropriate human behaviours increase and can lead to undesirable interactions and consequences.

Not all monkeys eat bananas. Long-tailed macaques are omnivorous, feeding on plants and small animals such as insects and crabs (hence their other common name as the crab-eating macaque). A study conducted in Bukit Timah Nature Reserve reported that the macaques consumed more than 250 types of plants! Most animals, like wild pigs, wait until durians fall and, in the process, split open before they can get to the fleshy seeds. Long-tailed macaques, on the other hand, begin feeding on durian flowers first, which are full of nectar. When durians start to fruit, they try to take a few "sample" bites by gnawing through the tough spiky outer layer before eventually reaping the benefits when the durians become ripe. Being opportunistic feeders, they not only feed on flowers and fruits but also insects and other small animals such as apple snails, green crested lizards, and bird eggs. The forest provides sufficient natural food resources for them. Our feeding them (including giving them our leftovers) causes health issues and results in an unnatural increase in their population size. It also takes away the macaques' role as a seed disperser in the forest, disrupting ecosystem functions.

"Its colour is chiefly black. The inside of the thighs and lower part of the abdomen are entirely white. It is not easily tamed." These were some of the descriptions made by Sir Stamford Raffles in 1822 when he was presented with a monkey roughly twice the size of the long-tailed macaque in Singapore. This black-and-white monkey was later formally described to be from Singapore and came to be known as the Raffles' banded langur. While adults are covered with mostly black fur, babies are born with chiefly white fur, with characteristic black bands across the shoulders and from the head to the tail, forming a cruciform pattern.

The Raffles' banded langur has a selective palate. Apart from a few species such as sea apple and saga trees, for the majority of their diet the langurs choose one part of each food plant, going only for leaves of rubber trees, fruits of rambutans, and seeds of petai, for instance. This vegetarian diet and a specialised multi-chambered stomach much like that of a grazing cow mean that the langurs rest plenty and exude a languid demeanour. But this does not imply that the langurs are unhurried or slow. Instead, when it comes to fleeing, they are among the fastest, escaping into the depths of the forests in the blink of an eye. Certainly not easily tamed, it takes almost forever to habituate the langurs to human presence, making field observation for research challenging and time consuming. It does not come as a surprise then, that langurs or leaf monkeys are among the least studied groups of primates, requiring exceptional patience and physical endurance to follow. As an exclusively tree-dwelling creature, the Raffles' banded langur is among the most hard-hit by forest destruction and fragmentation. Besides a small area in Singapore, it is only found in Johor and Pahang in southern Peninsular Malaysia. Their limited distribution in remaining habitats, small population numbers, and specialised diet are some of the reasons for their highly endangered status.

Primates are a part of our natural heritage. They play an essential role in the ecosystem as seed dispersers, seed predators, and animal predators, helping to regulate the abundance and distribution of different plant and small animal species. The integrity of a healthy ecosystem will therefore rely on healthy populations of its inhabitants, including the primates. We need to protect their remaining habitats and restore their connectivity to facilitate gene flow in wildlife populations. More work also needs to be done to improve public awareness and increase appreciation of our diverse natural heritage, such as through public participation in citizen science programmes. Similarly, education on appropriate human behaviour when encountering wildlife is essential for us to live in harmony with them. Singapore still has plenty of wildlife and natural areas, and it is not too late to find ways to develop sustainably and co-exist with our wild neighbours.

Andie Ang pursued her M.Sc. at the National University of Singapore (NUS), studying the ecology of critically endangered Raffles' banded langurs, before completing her Ph.D. at the University of Colorado, Boulder, USA, working on the conservation of leaf monkeys in Vietnam. She is currently the Head of Primate Conservation and Singapore Programmes at Mandai Nature. She is also a Deputy Chair in the IUCN Species Survival Commission (SSC) Primate Specialist Group. Since 2018, Andie has served as the President of the Jane Goodall Institute (Singapore), a charity organisation aimed at promoting greater awareness and protection of nature and wildlife.

Sabrina Jabbar leads the Monkey Guards programme at the Jane Goodall Institute (Singapore). Since 2013, she has been actively involved in collaborating with agencies and nature groups for an integrated approach to foster harmonious co-existence between people and macaques. Together with ACRES, the Monkey Guards project was first piloted in 2014. Monkey Guarding has since been adopted by the Macaque Working Group as one of the modern approaches to resolve human-macaque conflicts. Today she is also actively engaged in cross-border collaborations to share and exchange knowledge on smart and effective approaches to help people and macaques.

Chapter 3

Cities and Biodiversity

Lena Chan

We are embedded in Nature, which encompasses all life on Earth, together with the inanimate components like geology, water, climate, etc. that make up our planet. Biodiversity is a key component, the living constituent, of Nature.

Biodiversity, which includes all living things, at the ecosystem, species and genetic levels, is crucial for our survival. All life on earth depends on the essential ecological processes like replenishing oxygen into the atmosphere, sequestrating carbon dioxide, cleaning air and water pollution, providing food, medicines, materials for human use, etc. It has been increasingly recognised and research studies have documented that human physical health, mental and psychological well-being are intricately linked to regular connection and interaction with nature. In the meantime, the rapid rate of biodiversity loss and climate change exacerbated by human activities has affected our lives adversely. Loss of free ecosystem services, extreme weather conditions, heavy downpours resulting in floods, very hot weather, very cold temperatures, droughts, strong winds, etc., are becoming more common.

There are more people living in cities than in rural areas. By 2030, more than 60% of the world's population will reside in cities and cities will grow larger in terms of physical area and human population. It is not likely that the trend of increasing urbanisation will slow down or reverse. Hence, it is in cities that nature must thrive. Nonetheless, not all is doom and gloom as contrary to popular belief, cities are rich in biodiversity. Many cities around the world like Edmonton (Canada), Sao Paulo (Brazil), Singapore, Vitoria-Gasteiz (Spain), etc., are taking positive actions to conserve, restore and increase their biodiversity so that they can benefit from the free ecosystem service.

In cities, we can live in close proximity to biodiversity. Surveys have shown that during COVID-19, many people appreciated being able

The best of both worlds — living in a city and enjoying the ecosystem services provided by the Bukit Timah Nature Reserve for free.
(Photo credit: National Parks Board)

to connect with nature and to see nature flourish without development.

Here are some facts and figures about Singapore's nature areas that are providing ecosystem services *gratis*.

How Many?

The National Parks Board (NParks) manages four nature reserves, 84 regional parks, 317 neighbourhood parks, 371 kilometres of park connectors and 2,099 hectares of roadside greenery. In addition, other agencies that manage green and blue spaces include the Housing and Development Board (HDB), Sentosa Development Corporation, JTC, Public Utilities Board (PUB), town councils, etc. Singapore, as a city-state, would have to accommodate many competing land-uses; hence, it is a challenge to juggle the optimal proportion for numerous diverse demands.

The Senseable City Lab of the Massachusetts Institute of Technology developed a metric, the Green View Index, to evaluate and compare canopy cover. Singapore and Breda, Netherlands, jointly rank second with a score of 29.3%. Singapore's population density is 5.3 times higher than that of Breda.

How Good?

In addition to the amount of nature, other vital parameters in the evaluation of biodiversity are the quality and range of the flora, fauna, fungi, micro-organisms, etc.

Different ecosystems support unique assemblages of biodiversity. Hence, the more ecosystems there are in a city, the greater number of species diversity will be supported.

There are at least 12 different types of ecosystems found in Singapore: (1) lowland dipterocarp forest; (2) secondary forests; (3) grasslands; (4) streams; (5) urban ecosystems; (6) mangroves; (7) rocky shores; (8) sandy beaches; (9) inter-tidal mudflats; (10) seagrass meadows; (11) coral reefs; (12) sea-beds.

Conserving a wide range of diverse ecosystems is a strategy to maximise future flexibility and minimise the risk of losing substantial amounts of biodiversity in uncertain future scenarios affected by biodiversity loss and climate change.

Compared to global species diversity, Singapore's statistics show that there are more species found in Singapore despite its small physical size. Four hundred and twenty-nine (429) bird species have been sighted in Singapore — this is approximately 4% of the world's total number of bird species. On the marine front, 255 species of hard coral species, estimated to be 32% of the world's total number of hard coral species, have been recorded in Singapore's busy and crowded seas.

Not forgetting that we spend more than 90% of our time in the built environment, it is beneficial for nature to be incorporated into buildings and other green infrastructures. Skyrise greenery, a term coined in Singapore, refers to rooftop greenery and vertical greenery. Currently, there are 155 hectares of skyrise greenery in Singapore and the target is to attain 200 hectares by 2030.

How Connected?

To increase the effective functional areas of nature for plant dispersal, movement of animals, etc., it is crucial that green and blue spaces be ecologically linked. The Park Connector Network

(PCN) — comprising numerous island-wide routes, Coast-to-Coast trails, the upcoming Round Island Route and the NParks Rail Corridor — is an island-wide network of linear green corridors. These 371 kilometres of park connectors have been carefully planned to link nature reserves, parks, natural areas, etc. to places where people live, play and work. Roadside planting also serves this connectivity function through (a) Nature Ways that are planted with specific bird-friendly and butterfly-friendly trees and shrubs and (b) multi-tiered planting that emulates the structure of a tropical rainforest, hence providing multiple ecosystem services like cooling of temperatures, reducing air pollution, minimising soil erosion, providing habitats for pollinators, small mammals, birds, etc., adding colour; and many more.

The Eco-Link @BKE is a bold overhead ecological link above the Bukit Timah Expressway (BKE) that provides connectivity for wildlife to move between Bukit Timah Nature Reserve and the Central Catchment Nature Reserve. Camera traps have shown that the Eco-Link is functioning well as an ecological link for both flora and fauna.

How Close?

As mentioned above, there is a growing number of research literature providing evidence that proximity and accessibility to nature are positively related to human physical and mental health. While proximity measures the straight line distance of households living within a stipulated distance from a park or green space, accessibility measures the actual walking distance from a park or green space. The latter measurement is a better indicator. NParks is committed to planning a target that 100% of the population will be within a

10-minute walk or 400 metres from a park or nature reserve or green space by 2030.

How to Measure?

In 2009, Singapore mooted the idea of developing an index for cities to measure their biodiversity conservation efforts at the Ninth Meeting of the Conference of the Parties (COP-9) to the Convention on Biological Diversity (CBD). This was to ensure that we could track biodiversity conservation efforts in cities. What one cannot measure, one cannot evaluate or monitor. At the CBD's Tenth Meeting of the Conference of the Parties (COP-10) in Nagoya, Japan (2010), the Singapore Index on Cities' Biodiversity (SI) was formally endorsed by the Parties under Decision X/22 on the Plan of Action on Sub-national Governments, Cities and Other Local Authorities for Biodiversity, which supported the involvement of cities in the implementation of CBD decisions and encouraged the use of the SI as a monitoring tool. Many cities, including Singapore, have applied the SI to evaluate and monitor their biodiversity and biodiversity efforts.

Global Obligations

Nature and biodiversity do not recognise national boundaries; hence, it is important that many of the problems are addressed cooperatively at the global level and implemented at the local level. The city level is probably the most effective level.

An illustration of Singapore as a global citizen is in the phenomenon of global migration of birds. Migratory birds use Sungei Buloh Wetland Reserve and Mandai Mangrove Nature Park. Singapore is an active member of the East Asian–Australasian Flyway. We now have evidence that many migratory birds fly through the whole of Singapore and that they have benefited from Singapore's paradigm shift in transforming from a City in a Garden into a City in Nature by greening Singapore more ecologically. This adds a broader nature-based dimension to biodiversity conservation in cities.

Global Trends

The Fifteenth Meeting of the Conference of the Parties (COP-15) to the CBD was held in Montreal from 7 December to 19 December 2022. The Kunming-Montreal Global Biodiversity Framework (KMGBF), a landmark agreement that was intensely negotiated for over four years, was adopted on 19 December 2022. Two COP-15 outcomes that pertain specifically to cities are (1) Target 12 of the KMGBF that aims to "Significantly increase the area and quality and connectivity of, access to, and benefits from green and blue spaces in urban and densely populated areas sustainably, by mainstreaming the conservation and sustainable use of biodiversity, and ensure biodiversity-inclusive urban planning, enhancing native biodiversity, ecological connectivity and integrity, and improving human health and well-being and connection to nature and contributing to inclusive and sustainable urbanization and the provision of ecosystem functions and services"; and (2) the adoption of decision 15/12 that pertains to "Engagement with subnational governments, cities and other local authorities to enhance the implementation of the Kunming-Montreal Global Biodiversity Framework." Both outcomes attest to the importance of the role that cities can and must play in the conservation of biodiversity.

Biophilia and What You Can Do

Biophilia means a love of living things. Humans have biophilia, an intuitive and deeply engrained love for nature that has been evolutionarily imprinted into our DNA, as biodiversity is crucial for our survival. Living in cities, many of us have become disconnected from nature. Hence, it is essential that we consciously make efforts to immerse ourselves and connect with nature. Taking daily walks, visiting nature parks and nature reserves periodically, volunteering in nature-based activities, photographing or drawing nature — plants, animals, birds, butterflies, etc., would help us maintain our health, appreciate nature and cultivate our love for nature in a peaceful city.

Lena Chan is Senior Director of the International Biodiversity Conservation Division, National Parks Board, Singapore. Her duties include being the National Focal Point for the Convention on Biological Diversity and a Governing Board member of the ASEAN Centre for Biodiversity. She has published papers on ecology, parasitology, and book chapters on urban conservation biology. She co-authored the *Handbook on the Singapore Index on Cities' Biodiversity* and co-edited a journal supplement on a comprehensive biodiversity survey of the Bukit Timah Nature Reserve.

Chapter 4

Business and Our Natural World

Jessica Cheam

From the small window of the propeller plane where I sat in freezing temperatures, the landscape that greeted me below seared into my memory. A modern-day Mordor — barren, charred, marked with pools of murky water as far as my eye could see, with miniature steel structures, oil rigs, smoke chimneys, and Caterpillar trucks providing specks of colour.

It was 2008. I was flying into Fort McMurray, in Alberta, Canada, where in the past few decades the country's boreal forests have made way for the controversial oil sands industry. I was a young journalist then covering the energy beat, and I was invited by Shell to visit their operations.

The Athabasca oil sands, also known as tar sands, are home to the largest deposits of heavy crude oil in the world and because it exists in a mixture of bitumen, sand, clay minerals and water, it is expensive and dirty to extract.

Billed as the world's dirtiest fuel due to its ecological impact and high emissions, the industry's growth had been driven in the aftermath of the 1970s oil crisis and amid energy security concerns. As I interviewed the workers and surveyed the operations on the ground, it was clear the industry provided a key source of livelihoods for locals — for many, never mind the high-profile environmental protests, it was even a source of pride. By opening its operations to journalists then, Shell wanted to demonstrate how it extracted this fuel in a responsible manner. While I was persuaded of the high standards of safety and worker welfare, that entire experience — from feeling the tension between communities, understanding the trade-offs involved, and witnessing the devastated landscape — became for me a deeply-imprinted manifestation of the unprecedented impact that humans have on the planet.

That assignment formed part of a special report I eventually wrote for *The Straits Times*. Headlined "*The heat is on: Once the domain of dreamers, the development of clean, green energy is now more critical than ever*", it investigated the changing forces shaping our energy systems. I became hooked on the topic, writing stories exploring the relationship between business and our natural world whenever my editors would let me.

The era we live in now has been termed by scientists as the Anthropocene, in which humans have become the dominant force shaping Earth's bio-geophysical composition and processes, including climate change and its consequences such as sea level rise, extreme weather events, the effects of plastic pollution on marine and terrestrial processes, unprecedented rates of biodiversity loss and extinction, and the changing chemical composition of soils, oceans, and the atmosphere.

As I reflected on how the Industrial Revolution has yielded cheap and abundant energy driven by the mass extraction and burning of fossil fuels — and in turn fuelling the rise of capitalism — it became crystal clear that we were only starting to comprehend its extraordinary impact on the planet and our ecosystems, and that we desperately needed to find new ways of sustaining humanity.

Within the year, with the blessings of my editors, I started cooking a first-of-its-kind news platform that would allow journalists to write and publish stories on these undercovered, complex issues. I was grateful for the initial seed funding provided by the British High Commission and the Singapore Environment Council then, and with a loan from my mother, Eco-Business was launched in November 2009 just prior to the landmark United Nations Framework Convention on Climate Change (UNFCCC) meeting, or COP15, in Copenhagen, Denmark.

*

People often ask me about the inspiration for Eco-Business's name, and many assume it simply means "eco" as in "environment" and "business". In fact, the name is the combination of "*ecology*" and "business". Looking at the etymology, "ecology" is a term derived from Greek, meaning learning about "logos" or the ecosystems, while "eco" comes from the Greek word "oikos", meaning "household".

In other words, ecology is the study of the relationships among living organisms, including humans, and their physical environment, at the individual, population, community, ecosystem, and biosphere level. Eco-Business was set up to investigate the interactions of our ecosystems with one another, and it is still the north star that guides the company's coverage, advocacy and thought leadership activities throughout the region.

It was extremely tough in the early years to gain traction, as few really understood what we were trying to do. In more than a decade since, it has been gratifying to see the issues that we cover now at the top of international agendas and being debated extensively. Sadly, it is also due to the fact that the climate crisis has made its presence felt more acutely across the world. But encouragingly, global attention on this issue has gained momentum and in 2015, the United Nations (UN) adopted the 17 Sustainable Development Goals (SDGs) to provide a framework for humanity's development that looks after that of future generations. Later that year, 196 nations under the UN adopted the Paris Agreement, which, for the first time, provided a global treaty to address climate change.

Eco-Business has since grown from a small Singaporean operation to have a presence in the Philippines, Malaysia, Indonesia, Hong Kong, China and India, and hopefully even more countries in the future. Every single day, the issues we cover continue to fascinate me. This complex relationship between the role of business and our ecology deserves our attention, and we need to have informed debates and constructive dialogue with each other to chart a way forward that continuously improves how we live.

*

Some years after Eco-Business was launched, I was invited to author a book to commemorate the 40th anniversary of the then-Ministry of Environment and Water Resources (MEWR) in 2012 and more broadly, Singapore's environmental journey. Published by Straits Times Press, the result of that effort, *Forging a Greener Tomorrow: Singapore's Journey from Slum to Eco-city,* for the first time dived into the archives to document Singapore's environmental challenges during its pre-independence days and its subsequent journey over the decades.

I was grateful for that endeavour, which provided valuable access to former ministers, permanent secretaries, agency CEOs, rank and file officers and a diverse set of stakeholders including UN officials.

I interviewed more than 100 people for the book and these interviews provided me with rich history lessons on the twists and turns in the journey of a young nation state seeking independence, economic success and long-term sustainability.

As I wrote then, many today will look back on Singapore's early post-independence kampung days with nostalgia and memories of a simpler village life. But those living in the 50s and 60s will also recall how water supply was frequently disrupted, toilets were outdoor huts with a hole in the ground that housed a night soil bucket, streets were choked with rubbish and Singapore's waterways were open sewers. While these days we worry about the next unknown virus that could cause a pandemic, back then it was the fear of catching mundane diseases such as typhoid, malaria and cholera.

In a few short decades, Singapore has earned an international reputation for its innovation in water recycling, and as a clean and green city — it was a vision articulated by Singapore's founding Prime Minister Lee Kuan Yew, who declared in his memoir *From Third World to First: 1965–2000*: "After independence, I searched for some dramatic way to distinguish ourselves from the other Third World countries. I settled for a clean and green Singapore."

Former Prime Minister Goh Chok Tong once joked that Singapore's cabinet must be the only one in the world that read the minutes of a garden city committee.

The journey to where we are today was however not without plenty of sacrifices and trade-offs where nature is concerned. While the island's green cover has been increasing to over 40% according to latest figures, only 0.3% of an island once entirely forested is now classified as primary forest. As Singapore's natural landscapes made way for gleaming skyscrapers, industrial buildings and public housing projects over the decades, there were some small conservation victories. Some examples of rare policy reversals include the preservation of Sungei Buloh Wetland Reserve in 1986, Lower Peirce Reservoir in 1992, and Chek Jawa in Pulau Ubin in 2001.

Meanwhile, ongoing development chips away at the edges of what remains. Perhaps one silver lining of the COVID-19 pandemic was that, when millions of residents on the tiny island became involuntarily trapped, it catapulted into Singapore's collective consciousness the value of nature and open spaces.

The pandemic prompted a quadrupling of visitors to Singapore's nature parks and some environmentalists commented on how visiting Sungei Buloh Wetland Reserve for a bird-spotting competition gave them the feeling of being in "just another crowded shopping mall". While there was visible concern on the impact of the overwhelming visits, there was also hope that Singapore's renewed appreciation for nature would continue to be preserved in the future.

In 2021, increasingly nature-conscious citizens were up in arms when a developer flattened a piece of woodland in Kranji that it was not meant to. Photographs juxtaposing Singapore's historical railway flanked with luscious green woodland against those of the cleared, barren land shocked the public. The incident triggered an ongoing criminal investigation. These acute tensions between nature and development, citizens and government are still playing out today in the debates around the Cross Island Line, which will controversially run directly under Singapore's largest nature reserve, and in the debates on how much of Dover Forest should be left alone.

*

It has been a decade since that book was published. MEWR has now been renamed the Ministry of Sustainability and the Environment as a reflection of the times, and Singapore has had to confront a different set of challenges. Prime Minister Lee Hsien Loong in his milestone 2019 National Day Rally identified climate change — for the first time — as an existential "life and death matter" for Singapore, pledging S$100 billion to shore up our defences. The country has since declared a net zero emissions target by 2050 and launched the Singapore Green Plan, an updated national blueprint to guide our sustainable development journey.

There have been a few hits and misses along the way. We missed the opportunity to electrify our transport systems earlier — despite Singapore's ideal small size and tech-savviness, it took more than 10 years of being in what I term "perpetual pilot mode" before regulators made the call to support this shift; Singapore's resource consumption rates, along with its carbon footprint per capita are among the highest in the world, while its recycling rates remain abysmal despite repeated national campaigns. But Singapore has also shown leadership in being the first Southeast Asian country to declare a carbon tax; its regulations are among the highest in environmental standards, and there is a recent palpable momentum in building a resilient, competitive green economy, including fostering renewable energy trading, carbon services and sustainable finance activities in the region.

While the government provides the legislative framework and national budgets to spur the transformation needed to achieve the Paris Agreement and SDG targets, businesses play an even more critical role. They have an outsized footprint on our ecology, yet often overlook the fact that nature provides services worth at least US$125 trillion per year globally, providing all that we need and facilitating global trade and livelihoods for billions of people. It seems that we are, as UN Secretary-General António Guterres said recently, "waging a self-defeating war on nature".

The fundamental role of business has been the subject of a lot of recent debate. It has been three centuries since Adam Smith's 1776 book, *The Wealth of Nations*, defined gross domestic product (GDP) — the monetary value of final goods and services produced in a country in a given period of time — and provided the foundation for classical economics and capitalism. Milton Friedman went on to popularise the doctrine that the social responsibility of business is solely to increase its profits.

These definitions are outdated. We urgently need to redefine them and create a new set of metrics that are fit for purpose in this century. Encouraging conversations are happening, such as the rise of "stakeholder capitalism", which prioritises all stakeholders rather than only shareholders, and the increasing global importance of environmental, social and governance (ESG) strategies in investment decisions. The latter movement was borne of a seminal report *Who Cares Wins* in 2004 led by the late then-UN Secretary-General Kofi Annan to better integrate ESG considerations into finance.

Other promising signs include the European Parliament's Beyond Growth 2023 forum which is aimed at "challenging conventional policy-making in the European Union and to redefine societal goals across the board". Will we see such a conversation in Singapore? It is my hope that the next generation of leaders will put this on our national agenda.

Meanwhile, my work continues to take me to far-flung corners of the globe. From the Antarctic to the Arctic, the Himalayas to the Sundarbans, my mission on every journey has been to document the wonder of our natural world, to explore the impact of humanity and to provoke awareness and action. Antarctica was a particularly unforgettable realm — it is the only place on Earth relatively untouched by man, thanks to a global treaty (which is to be reviewed in 2041) that preserves it for science and peace. The scale of its mountain ranges, glaciers, wildlife, and its all-encompassing sublime beauty makes you feel simultaneously inspired and in awe, yet acutely insignificant and ephemeral.

I yearn for and chase experiences with these majestic natural landscapes. That adage "*you can't protect what you don't know*" rings true. At the same time, I have realised while we have witnessed unprecedented biodiversity loss and the degradation of natural ecosystems, fixing climate change and all the ills of not living within our planetary boundaries is more about ensuring our own survival. Nature will march on its timeless, relentless path — whether humans survive or not.

At home, on this little red dot, I seek the pockets of nature that provide a healing and thinking space whenever I can. There are many if you look for them. I intentionally live next to a forest on a hill with a road flanked by luscious trees — here we encounter monkeys, bats, snakes, and all sorts of wildlife which provides learning opportunities for my kids on the nature that is at our doorstep. Four nature parks surround us, and we seek out Singapore's coastal parks on weekends too, for that wide horizon and calming presence of the repeated ocean waves lapping onto its shores.

These days, the sight that greets me from an airplane window whenever I return home is an expanse of the Singapore Straits dotted with vessels, trees hugging the coastline against blocks of flats, and reclamation and construction works. Wherever we cast our eyes, there are splashes of green. As our country continues to evolve, it is my hope that we will always remember this of nature — we can never have enough of it.

One of my favourite places on the coast of Sentosa.

Jessica Cheam is the Founder and Managing Director of Eco-Business, Asia-Pacific's leading independent media and business intelligence organisation dedicated to sustainable development. She is recognised as a sustainability pioneer with two decades of experience in media, sustainable development and ESG issues globally. She serves as an independent, non-executive director for two Singapore-listed companies Wilmar International and ComfortDelGro. She is a regular columnist for national newspapers and is an ESG committee member of the Singapore Institute of Directors. She is accredited with INSEAD's Certificate of Corporate Governance, the CFA Institute Certificate in ESG Investing, and specialises in advising boards on sustainability strategy.

Chapter 5

From Plant-blind to Botanist

Chong Kwek Yan

There is often the assumption that people who love nature or whose work involves nature must have nurtured such interests from young. This was not true in my case; there was not much in my upbringing that could have brought me close to nature. My first impressions from nature were from children's encyclopedias, which showed mostly domesticated animals and temperate trees and vegetation that I could not relate to. On the rare occasions when we were allowed to watch television, I do remember choosing to watch nature documentaries, but these almost invariably featured the African savanna. While cheetahs, elephants, and lions are always interesting to young children (and adults alike), as ecosystems far away, they were, again, unrelatable to my immediate experiences. Poisonous periwinkles (*Catharanthus roseus*) and pong-pong (*Cerbera odollam*) were mentioned in primary school textbooks but, as far as I can recall, the science curriculum then did not teach us about the tropical forests that we had and still have.

It was probably a third-year undergraduate course I attended at the National University of Singapore (NUS) that, botanically speaking, began to change the trajectory of my life. After two sessions of learning about plant morphology and function in a teaching laboratory, the third session was a visit to the Singapore Botanic Gardens with our teaching assistants to see the plants growing outdoors. I cannot pin down what exactly it was about the field trip experience that impressed me so much but by the end of it, I decided that I wanted to work on plants for the Final Year Project of my upcoming Honours year and approached the course coordinator, Associate Professor Hugh Tan, of the Department of Biological Sciences, for his supervision.

This project involved, as a first step, the compilation of a checklist of all the vascular plant species that have ever been recorded in Singapore, including those that were introduced and cultivated, "escaped" into the wild or naturalised, as well as those that were originally found here, or "native". Vascular plants refer to the set of plants that includes ferns, conifers, and flowering plants. This was a list of 4,180 species and their sub-specific varieties from 243 plant families. I was informally co-supervised by Professor Richard Corlett, who was then based in Hong Kong. At the end of my Final Year Project, I was very familiar with *spelling* the names of these species and families, which were mostly derived from Latin or Greek...but was still quite clueless as to what plants the vast majority of those names referred to.

Another part of the project involved data analysis. To do this, I sought the advice of Professor Yap Von Bing from the NUS Department of Statistics and Data Science, who is also a botanist by hobby. He was looking at my results when he asked me about the "Rubiaceae". Seeing my blank look at that name, he followed up with, "Opposite leaves, interpetiolar stipules? The coffee family?" My blank look continued.

After my Honours year, I went straight on to postgraduate studies. In my first couple of years trying to figure out my postgraduate research topic, I had several conversations with Richard who had taken up a position here in Singapore. In one of these conversations, Richard was explaining to me how the characteristics of fruits suggested likely modes of dispersal and gave the example of *Terminalia catappa*. Seeing my blank look at that name, he followed up with, "The sea almond? The large tree outside our building that you pass by every day?" The same blank look continued.

It is a paradox that plants make up most of the living matter that surrounds us and yet, for most people, seem to be subconsciously filtered out from our vision and other senses. James Wandersee and Elisabeth Schussler coined the term "plant blindness" for the inability to notice and appreciate plants and recognise their importance in our lives. One manifestation of plant blindness is surely our ability to recognise cheetahs, elephants, and lions from a faraway continent, and our inability to match a name to a plant that we pass by every day or those that are found on our plates or cups. Wandersee and Schussler had originally proposed that plant blindness had a physiological or evolutionary basis. Other research has also shown that, culturally, there are groups less plant-blind than others. Whether biological or cultural, one *can* train oneself to open a "third eye" for plants, and overcome plant blindness.

As postgraduate students on scholarship, we serve a number of hours as part-time teaching assistants for undergraduate courses. I signed up to help with a new course on forest ecology coordinated by Richard. My allocated lesson was to bring students into the forest patch in the middle of the university's Kent Ridge campus and teach them to set up a "plot" — a standardised area where they would make measurements and *identify the plants* within the plot. Pulling raffia string to demarcate a square plot or reading numbers off equipment, those I could do. But for me to teach them how to identify plants was surely going to be a situation of the plant-blind leading the plant-blind. The forest in Kent Ridge campus was of the *Adinandra belukar* vegetation type, arising from soil conditions exhausted by past unsustainable agriculture and in terms of trees, dominated by a single (native) species, the tiup tiup or *Adinandra dumosa*, that could tolerate the poor soil. The term "belukar" is the Malay word for regenerating — or in ecological terms, "secondary" — vegetation. I was told that *Adinandra belukar* as well as mangrove swamps were good places to start in learning to identify plants because they were relatively depauperate in plant species. Even so, there were at least 20 plant species that could be commonly found in and around a typical patch of *Adinandra belukar*, and I could recognise almost none of them.

In the front part of Edred John Henry Corner's classic work, *Wayside Trees of Malaya*, there is a section titled "How to identify a tree" where he listed four methods. His first method can be paraphrased as, essentially, to take a specimen of the tree and bring it to ask a trained botanist. He wrote: "This is the surest method." It is probably also the fastest method. Desperate to avoid embarrassment in front of scores of undergraduate students, I went to look around the edges of the forest patch that I was supposed to bring students to, and took a specimen of any plant that looked like a different species from the others. I then brought them back to my seniors in Hugh's laboratory to tell me what they were. These plants were then kept sealed in a Ziploc plastic bag to keep them relatively fresh for some time — a simple and common botanising practice. Every day for two weeks before my first lesson, I would take the previous day's plants out of these bags and try to remember their names, specimen by specimen. For those whose names that I managed to recall confidently, I could discard; for those that I could not, back they went into the Ziplock bag to test myself again the next day. I would then go out for another round of botanising to try to find and collect plants that I thought I had not collected before or could not recognise yet, to add to the Ziploc bag. This is no different than using flashcards to teach young children. On the occasions where I collected more than one of the same plant species and found that they were the same, I learned about the morphological variation that could be found *within* a species that was important to grasp in order to be able to tell *between* different species. Within two weeks I had reached what ecologists call the "plateau" of a "species accumulation curve" for the *Adinandra belukar* and was reasonably confident to take students into this tiny corner of the botanical world.

The plant third eye takes effort to open for the first time, but once opened there are whole new worlds to see. I then started turning my attention to "weeds" growing on lawns and in "wastelands". Who knew that there were several species from the dandelion family hidden among the grass? Who knew that grasses were a different family from superficially similar-looking sedges? That some of the traditional remedies we take to ward off a cold or sore throat, available as pills or drinks in stores, were growing in cracks along the walls and between the tiles of pavements? Who knew that much of the "wild" vegetation we see in pockets around expressways and on vacant land awaiting development were a mix of runaway species from the Americas, Africa, and Australia, in addition to other parts of Asia, and that their ancestors had never encountered each other in the past few million years? With the plant third eye open, weeds become wildflowers, and wastelands become "novel ecosystems".

Finally, I ventured into the forests of our nature reserves where the plant third eye needs additional training to see into its beauty and secrets. The branches of larger trees are more often out of reach.

With a pair of binoculars, we can try to match fallen leaves on the ground to those that are on trees. We also have to learn to use tree barks, branching patterns, presence of buttresses, exudates, or even smells as clues for identification. Tropical forests are famous for being rich in species, which makes the task of plant identification from so few clues extremely challenging; there could be many close-related, similar-looking species occurring in the same place. For a jogger or hiker passing by on the forest trail, the sight of someone peering intently into the crown of a tree, squatting to look through leaves on the ground, and then stepping to the tree to smell its bark must look like the practice of some secret shamanistic art. But once this craft is honed, we will be able to read the story of a forest through its trees and other plants.

I finally left university academia in 2021 and joined the Singapore Botanic Gardens as one of its researchers. Stepping into my new workplace on my first day of work felt surreal: This was a metamorphosis that I would never have anticipated as a student on a field trip years ago. Nonetheless, learning about the plants around us is an endless process — one that I am confident shall continue.

Dr Chong Kwek Yan is a Senior Researcher at the Singapore Botanic Gardens, National Parks Board (NParks), where he coordinates a Tropical Forest Ecology Research Programme. This programme is anchored by a Long-Term Forest Ecological Monitoring project that maintains a network of permanent research plots in Singapore's nature reserves and parks. His main research interests are in vegetation ecology, urban ecology, and invasion ecology.

Chapter 6

Coral Reefs in the Urban Seascape

Chou Loke Ming

For over 150 years since the founding of modern Singapore in 1819, early naturalists have described Singapore's coral reefs as rich and vibrant. The full beauty of this colourful habitat was enhanced by the clear waters and incredible abundance of life. Many species new to science were collected, documented, and kept in established natural history museums in Britain and Europe. These reefs, especially those fringing the western and southern shores of the main island were right by our doorstep and easily accessible. You could, until the early 1970s, walk over to these intertidal reef flats at low tide after a short bus ride. Reefs fringing the numerous offshore islands could be reached quickly by a fast boat. Singapore was at peace with coral reefs, but not for much longer.

Economic development was prioritised after Singapore gained independence in 1965 and the pace of urbanisation accelerated to transform the island state into a modern metropolis. Infrastructure and land were needed to support economic growth and human population expansion. Extensive land reclamation from the 1960s started to change the situation and by the 1990s, over 60% of the country's coral reef habitat was lost forever. Waters turned murky as the sediment load kept increasing from coastal development projects that were implemented without environmental impact considerations. Underwater visibility of 10 metres in the 1960s decreased to less than two metres by the 1980s. Sediment reduced sunlight penetration through the water and corals at lower depths died, deprived of adequate light. Shallower-depth corals still received sufficient sunlight, but sediment rejection meant that a fair amount of their energy was exhausted, which could have otherwise been diverted to support growth. Sediment deposited over the reef floor made it less suitable for coral larvae to settle and survive. This was a rough time for coral reefs. No agency was responsible for their protection or management. It was a battle that coral reefs simply had no chance of winning.

The coastal development mantra was to get rid of reefs if they were in the way of safe navigation, and a couple of reefs were blasted out of existence. Also, during this period, collection of reef organisms for the aquarium trade intensified without any regulation. Marine aquarium shops sprouted along Pasir Panjang where access to the southern islands' reefs was fast and direct, and they profited from the export of reef organisms in the thriving international marine aquarium trade. There were also people hacking off entire coral colonies and exporting the skeletons in the marine ornamental trade. Anemones, anemone fish, giant clams, and many other creatures were exploited one after the other depending on international demand, denuding reef biodiversity from reefs already strained by heavy sedimentation. Such wanton exploitation underscored the tragedy of the commons as it proceeded openly. Regulations were outdated and largely inadequate. Surveillance and enforcement were ineffective because of the lack of a specific management agency.

Most of the concern during this period came from the ground up with civic groups leading the conservation call and drawing attention to the sorrowful plight of our coral reefs. Academics supported the cause with scientific data as research began to reveal the important contribution of coral reefs to society. A noteworthy initiative by civil society is the "Singapore Reef and Marine Conservation Project" in 1988. In this collaborative effort between the Singapore Institute of Biology (which provided the academic input), the Singapore Underwater Federation (which provided the scuba divers), and the Republic of Singapore Yacht Club (which provided the boats), over 150 volunteer divers were trained to survey reefs in what was possibly the largest citizen science programme then. Surveys of almost all coral reefs of the southern offshore islands were completed within two years and the results defined four general clusters of reefs that required protection.

The perception that the Government did not want to talk about reef conservation was prevalent, but response was not entirely lacking. Singapore became a Party to the Convention on International Trade in Endangered Species of Wild Fauna and Flora (CITES) in 1986. This helped immensely to ease exploitation pressure on the reefs for the aquarium trade. Environmental Impact Studies (EISs) began to accompany projects from the late 1990s. Construction of the Semakau Landfill project marked, for the very first time, active intervention to minimise damage to coastal habitats; and coral reefs adjacent to the development footprint were protected by sediment screens.

All natural habitats utilise solar energy to generate high productivity, but coral reefs are extremely proficient with their unique plant (unicellular algae) and animal (coral) partnership. The algae remain inside the coral tissue and nutrient recycling between plant and animal stays optimal. The diverse array of shapes of different coral species provides structural complexity which in turn provides shelter to a host of other reef species including visiting species. Reefs are an ideal feeding and nursery ground to numerous species because of the rich biodiversity that they support. They are, by far, the most colourful habitat on earth. Reefs protect shores from powerful waves and contribute material to nourish sandy shores. Global coral reef fisheries are estimated to be worth US$6.8 billion per year and the livelihoods of 30 million people in developing countries are dependent on coral reefs.

Urbanisation left a legacy of sedimented waters that reduced underwater visibility. The clear waters of the 1960s are gone for good. But a new coral reef management phase emerged from the late 1990s. While Singapore does not have a law mandating Environmental Impact Assessment, development agencies are now required to initiate an Environmental Impact Study (EIS) with attention directed at minimising impact on the natural environment. This includes relocation of corals that would otherwise be destroyed. The EIS is then presented to selected stakeholders including nature groups.

A boost to marine biodiversity management came with the formation of the National Biodiversity Centre in 2006, which enabled the National Parks Board (NParks) to oversee the technical rigour of the EIS and adequacy of the recommended mitigations. Development projects now also require an "Environmental Monitoring and Management Plan" with real-time monitoring to ensure that impacts remain within tolerance limits identified in the EIS throughout and after project completion. The development agency conducts the monitoring and logs all the data. Work is halted as soon as the threshold of any environmental parameter is breached. These measures are helping to contain further sediment loading and unnecessary loss of marine habitats.

As urbanisation continues and potentially affects more marine areas, is coral reef conservation and restoration relevant? The answer, backed by science, is yes. Research has shown appreciable reef resilience to the decades-old urbanisation impacts. Reef biodiversity remains high, mass spawning of corals is seasonally consistent, larval supply is self-replenishing, and settlement and growth of larval recruits are persistent. The reefs have also withstood three major bleaching events triggered by elevated sea surface temperature. Response to urbanisation and climate-change impacts is seen in changes to reef community composition as species that are less tolerant of the new conditions are replaced by those that are more tolerant. But what is important is that the reefs have not undergone ecological phase shifts where, for example, corals die out and the reef gets overgrown by algae. Research also indicated that reef restoration in our highly sedimented waters is viable. It can not only rehabilitate degraded parts of reefs, but also create reef communities in non-reef areas. The latter is crucial considering that over 60% of Singapore reefs have been lost. The 2018 deployment of purpose-built, artificial reef structures that extend through the water column in the Sisters' Islands Marine Park offers 1,000 square metres of new space for the development of corals and reef-associated organisms and will essentially boost reef biodiversity.

Civil society remained active in pushing the coral conservation agenda. One group produced the first Singapore Blue Plan in 2001. The second Blue Plan in 2008 included more scientific data and resulted in the five-year Comprehensive Marine Biodiversity Survey launched in 2010. It was coordinated by NParks and the National

University of Singapore. Establishment of the Sisters' Islands Marine Park in 2014 gave a clear signal of the Government's commitment to coral reef conservation. Furthermore, a "Friends of the Marine Park" initiative involving stakeholder participation in responsible use of the park demonstrates a new management approach in which the public has a say.

Our experience shows that despite physical space limitations, coral reefs can co-exist with the urbanised marine seascape. Institutional arrangements for their management and protection remain extremely relevant. Reef restoration is useful for enhancing reef area and biodiversity. During the first four decades (1960 to 2000) of rapid urbanisation, management and protection were lacking and the conservation call came mostly from civil society. In the next two

High coral species richness present in Singapore reefs despite heavy sedimentation. (Photo credit: Reef Ecology Study Team, National University of Singapore)

decades (2000 to now), commitment from the Government increased significantly. Bottom-up advocacy is now matched by positive top-down management responses. Such synergy is setting the stage for concerted and sustained action to conserve and enhance Singapore's coral reef habitat. There is now renewed hope for this natural heritage that we call our own. We can and should live in peace with coral reefs.

Chou Loke Ming is Emeritus Professor at the National University of Singapore (Department of Biological Sciences). He devoted much of his research career to the study of marine biodiversity, specifically coral reefs. He is a Fellow of the Singapore National Academy of Science and an Honorary Fellow of the Singapore Institute of Biology. In recognition of his contributions, he was given the "Green Leaf Award" from the Ministry of Environment in 1994, the "SeaKeeper of Singapore Award" from the International SeaKeepers Society in 2016, and the "ASEAN Biodiversity Hero Award" from the ASEAN Center for Biodiversity in 2022.

Chapter 7

Working with the IPCC: A Singapore Boy's View of Climate Change

Winston Chow

A Boy Growing up in Singapore

I was born in the 1970s, and grew up as a kid in the 80s in Bedok and the East Coast. I still call the East side of the island as my home. I have spent my entire life in Singapore living, playing, going to school, and relaxing in the East. There is a "chill" vibe here, one that comes from being by the coast and enjoying the sea breeze, spending the evenings playing football with friends, and having easy access to excellent food with family and loved ones.

In some ways, being an East kid also made me appreciate nature, and helped stoke my interest in the environment. Growing up, I read issues of *National Geographic* that my father brought home from work every month, and regularly watched nature documentaries back when Channel 12 was on air before the advent of cable TV and the internet. I remember, for show and tell in Primary School, haltingly speaking to my classmates about this notion of "global warming", which I had learned would be a future issue of concern, as opposed to the then-topical issue of ozone depletion.

I guess that East Coast mentality helped spur my subsequent interest in studying environmental geography, leading to my eventual Ph.D. in Geography, and my current job as a University Professor of Urban Climate. Little did I know, as an 11-year-old schoolboy talking about global warming in school, that it would also eventually culminate in an invitation from the Intergovernmental Panel on Climate Change (IPCC) to lead a chapter in their climate change assessment reports.

What Does the IPCC Do?

The IPCC is the United Nations (UN) body tasked with advancing scientific knowledge about anthropogenic (or human-caused) climate change. Formed in 1988, it is an inter-governmental organisation governed by the 195 UN member states. It is considered the authoritative body of knowledge about global warming science and its impacts, as well as discerning pathways to adaptation and mitigation. Every five to seven years, the IPCC compiles a set of three comprehensive reports authored by global climate experts assessing all relevant scientific literature on climate change in the preceding years. For the Sixth Assessment cycle, which concluded in 2023, IPCC authors examined over 88,000 scientific documents in their reports. These documents provide policy-relevant information to help policy makers (and increasingly, other stakeholders) act on climate change.

Being invited as an author to formally draft the IPCC report is an honour and privilege, as these are among the most rigorously reviewed and widely-read scientific documents with enormous impact. However, for 700 IPCC colleagues and myself, the already difficult challenge of authorship was greatly affected by the COVID-19 pandemic from 2020, which significantly delayed the writing of the report and its approval processes as we could not regularly meet face-to-face. Instead, online meetings between authors held at odd hours of the day (usually during the evenings or past midnight in Singapore!) were the norm.

One final thing — IPCC authors are not paid for their work. Several of my colleagues have incurred significant financial costs working many hours *pro bono* on authoring these documents, as well as when taking part in the often-tedious report approval process to UN member states which can last for weeks. While unfair, it is justified as authors must be objective and neutral in their assessments, and not viewed as paid agents or in the employ of particular organisations. This objectivity is one reason why such reports are treated as authoritative assessments of the science underpinning climate change.

A Clear Set of Messages About Climate Change

The three reports from this assessment cycle totalled more than 11,000 pages in combined length. The executive summaries — termed the Summary for Policymakers — are a "mere" 40 pages for each report. Despite the voluminous content, there is a clear set of messages about what we know about climate change and what can be done to stop it. I will attempt to summarise them in eight parts:

- Human-caused climate change, resulting from Greenhouse Gas (GHG) emissions such as carbon dioxide via burning fossil fuels and deforestation, has led to global temperatures increasing by about 1.1°C from temperatures measured from the 1850s.

- These increased emissions have destabilised the climate system, resulting in observable changes in weather extremes such as more frequent heat waves, more intense rainfall events and regional drought conditions, and more severe tropical cyclones. Unsurprisingly, most of these extreme weather events are likely to be more frequent and intense as more GHGs are emitted.
- These weather extremes expose vulnerable natural and human systems to climate-driven shocks, several of which are beyond physical adaptation. For instance, more frequent yearly or biannual marine heatwaves result in warm-water corals dying from intense bleaching events, and these ecosystems — which usually take decades to evolve — are unlikely to cope at such short timescales.
- Regardless of adaptation, the economic and social costs will be higher in a warming world, especially for cities that will be affected by climate risks extending beyond their physical boundaries. Here in Singapore, we can develop and finance infrastructure to locally protect against regional flooding and drought conditions. However, such protection may not be present in farms from which we import our food that are subject to the same drought conditions, or at neighbouring ports vulnerable to floods where we import essential goods. In both cases, there is a higher price to pay from importing food and goods subject to more severe climate hazards.
- Presently, humanity adds an additional 50 billion tonnes of GHGs per year into the atmosphere, which will very likely result in Earth's temperature exceeding the Paris Agreement threshold of 1.5°C early in the 2030s. Notably, even during COVID-19 lockdowns, global GHG emissions only dropped by about 5%.
- Worryingly, even with recent commitments from governments in ramping up their ambitions to cut GHG emissions, we are on

course to reach warming levels close to 3°C by the end of this century, with severe consequences likely ensuing.

- Despite these warnings, there still exists a narrow window of opportunity for action to keep warming levels to 1.5°C. This involves extensive investment in climate adaptation of vulnerable systems, combined with rapid global GHG emissions cuts to net-zero by 2050 or sooner, as well as conserving biodiversity which enhances removal of carbon dioxide, and lastly enabling a systemic, whole-of-society transformation aligned with the 17 UN Sustainable Development Goals.
- The IPCC terms this pathway to 1.5°C as "climate resilient development". This involves sustained investments in approaches which reduce societal vulnerability, enhance knowledge transfer of climate solutions (such as renewable energy technologies), and increase equality of opportunities through regional and international cooperation and finance — all of which accelerate GHG emission reductions towards net-zero.

What Can Singapore Do?

My role in the IPCC was to lead assessments on urban related issues, such as climate impacts and adaptation into settlements and their key infrastructure, as well as evaluating these for coastal cities like Singapore.

I see elements of climate resilient development within the Singapore Green Plan 2030. It is a long-term framework allowing for the transformative, whole-of-society approach needed to reduce risks, like the 30-by-30 plan to reduce food insecurity. The plan also drives behavioural change through policy and education, such as phasing out the internal combustion engine for electric vehicles, and focussing on sustainability education in schools at all levels.

There is also provision in adapting to relevant climate risks in the plan, with the support of academic research in reducing urban heat exposure, or developing coastal protective infrastructure against impending sea level rise. The plan also involves an energy reset in cutting domestic GHG emissions, through expanding renewable energy generation and its imports, in order to reach net zero around 2050 or as soon as possible thereafter.

From my perspective, it appears that the Green Plan's tenets are promising — a good step forward; however, is the plan both urgent and expansive enough? Even if we succeed in implementing the Green Plan and reach net-zero by around 2050, our small emissions profile — about 0.1% of global annual GHG emissions — amount to little in the larger picture.

However, this should not be a reason for inaction as there is significant scope for upscaling actions within the Green Plan framework beyond our Little Red Dot. Financing regional renewable energy technologies, or supporting knowledge transfer of best industrial practices — such as local corporations minimising Scope 3 emissions from international supply chains — can have discernible, knock-on impacts in reducing emissions beyond Singapore's borders. It is a goal worth pursuing to expand the effectiveness of Singapore's GHG emission reduction goals.

Fear vs Hope

Even a place as "chill" as the East Coast has seen warmer temperatures, periodic flooding, and — most worryingly — the slow but inexorable rise in sea levels that have eroded a good part

The author with his grandmother at East Coast Park, circa 1980, when mean sea levels were about 10 centimetres lower than today.

of the beach where I used to play in (see picture). I fear that the place where I have strong roots in will either be unrecognisable or will disappear sooner rather than later, no thanks to a changing climate that is beyond saving.

But that fear is tempered by hope from the work I have done. The IPCC assessments are clear that even if we exceed the 1.5°C threshold over the next 10 years, a rapid reduction of GHG emissions to net-zero by 2050 will allow global temperatures to drop back to 1.5°C by 2100, and substantially reduce the worst risks humanity faces. That should give us all hope in driving urgent climate action to grasp this opportunity.

Dr Winston Chow is a Lee Kong Chian Research Fellow and an Associate Professor of Urban Climate in Singapore Management University's (SMU) College of Integrative Studies. He is a Co-Lead Principal Investigator in the ongoing Cooling Singapore Initiative, leading research into how a digital urban twin enables climate-resilient urban design, and assessing how Singapore's urban heat risks can be minimised under a warming climate. In SMU, Dr Chow teaches interdisciplinary courses on climate change and urban sustainability. Lastly, Winston was a Lead Author for the Intergovernmental Panel on Climate Change's 6th *Assessment Report on Impacts, Adaptation and Vulnerability* on urban climate issues.

Chapter 8

My Personal Journey with Nature

Chua Ee Kiam

After graduation, I decided to explore beyond my comfort zone. Armed with an analogue camera, I was stupefied on my first nocturnal visit to the forest — a serendipitous encounter. I was delirious as I had stumbled upon a world of critters and other creatures. That was in 1988. The forest became my outdoor classroom. I thought of the many people who were less adventurous, who were afraid of the dark and who were limited in their abilities and decided to document and share the magic of the forest with them. My journey had just begun; the mission became an obsession. I was adventurous, inquisitive but naïve.

Unlike the present digital era of photography, there was none of the instant gratification for I had to wait patiently for the slides to be developed. There was no chance of a repeat moment. Exposures were challenging and even as low as an ISO (International Organization for Standardization) 400, the images were grainy and only limited to 36 exposures in a roll of film. Current auto-focus lenses are considered a vast improvement but I had to be content with manual focus lenses back then. There were no social media platforms to share information and I had to rely on sheer luck and only known locations for the journey.

While trying to photograph some wild ducks at a pond in Marina South (it was a remote place with vast areas of grassland then) I encountered a horrifying experience. Alone, I was surrounded and attacked by more than 10 dogs looking for an easy meal that morning. Luckily I was able to stave off their ferocity with a tripod. To this day, my tripod remains with me in all my outings. My first book *Ours to Protect* was released in 1993, epitomising my passion for the wild.

Whilst on a tour, my travel guide in Sabah saw the book and understood that he was dealing with an audacious Singaporean and offered me a life-changing experience in Kadazan country. I travelled with two other enthusiastic greenhorns. Nocturnal rambles in the forest were not for the faint-hearted. Leeches were queasy, sand-flies were nasty and any exposed skin was not spared. The ubiquitous rattan thorns tore at our skin. Rain is often a dampener for any work to be done — the rainforest is so called, not for nothing. The humidity saps one's energy and spirit and we were away from civilisation for the most part of our time in the forest. The rainforest in Sabah is extensive compared to Singapore's miniscule pockets of fragmented forests.

Unlike the African open plains, roaming wild elephants are only noticed at closer distances, hence the danger; for they can easily outrun us. For our safety, the rangers provided us, the naïve Singaporeans, with thunderflashes to use in times of danger. Clouded leopards on the prowl can be deadly; a ranger showed us his abdominal scars. We had high hopes of photographing a Sumatran

Rhinoceros, but the long-serving rangers had never seen one before. Orang-utans at the sanctuary grappled with our belongings, and we were no match for their strength.

Photography demands much more time compared to trekking. Under-estimating the travel times can have serious repercussions as forests get very dark after twilight. Compounded by heavy camera gear, getting out of the forest at night can be a chilling experience. Blocked mountain roads due to fallen rocks/gravel make navigating the narrowed roads harrowing. Once, our vehicle was stuck in mud at an isolated area. Fortunately, a passing vehicle helped extricate us or else we would have to spend the night in the wilderness. Against potential large mammals and the marauding mosquitoes, we could only imagine the potential discomfiture.

Crested Terns in Layang Layang (a dive resort) rained their claws or droppings at us when we got too near their nesting sites. We had to constantly watch where we placed our feet; the island is their sanctuary. Navigating river streams was unsettling as submerged, fallen logs were not obvious. Our boat nearly overturned when a foolhardy boatman went too fast. Luckily, we held on tight to our photographic gear.

To place my nose next to an exquisite *Rafflesia* bloom was a sublime experience. The long-distance treks we took over undulating terrain just to view large pitcher plants were worth every step. And Mount Kinabalu was a formidable challenge. Even carrying minimal photographic gear drained our energies. The various tribes (including head-hunters) were a cultural revelation. I was exposed to both montane and tropical rainforests and am still awed by their magnificence. *Borneo's Tropical Eden – Sabah* (2005) was created to pay tribute to the experience; albeit slightly delayed.

The experience in Sabah paved the way for my direction in nature photography. What I saw endeared me to the wilderness. But before my sojourn in Sabah, there was parallel work done in Singapore. I spent many weekends in Pulau Ubin and explored it in detail as my fascination with the laid-back island was reminiscent of my childhood years in Malaysia. The sand-flats of Chek Jawa drew much attention from Singaporeans who were suddenly awakened to see a nature area soon to be obliterated. I learnt how to photograph intertidal areas without an underwater camera. Like-minded enthusiasts (especially Ria Tan) rallied to document whatever that was still left. Despite the no-entry signs in the area, we walked for miles during unearthly hours (there was no taxi service during those hours), hell-bent on photographing whatever that was left (even after the salvage team had removed whatever that was needed). I remember that a heavy *Tembusu* branch fell on us during the wee hours but we managed to scamper when we heard the rustle of the falling branch. We could only look at each other in utter disbelief at the close shave. Two books were produced — one on *Pulau Ubin* (2000) and another on *Chek Jawa* (2002). There was more work to be done on our shores around the island. There were more unearthly hours to brave through and more salt to wipe from our cameras. I was always fearful of the spines of hidden stonefish. *Singapore Splendour – Life on the Edge* (2007) was the outcome of this endeavour. We were fortunate to have teams of nature lovers who fanned out to spot creatures for us, for there was only a window period of about two hours before the waters returned. Once we had to swim to an island when the boat was unable to land — triple-wrapped plastic bags protected our gear but we were hopelessly drenched. I ran for my dear life en route to the toilet when I was chased by an alpha male long-tailed macaque at Sisters' Islands.

It was a dreadful encounter. Despite the adversity, I can only marvel at the denizens at low tide.

Singapore lies along the East Asian–Australian Flyway and the chance to see migratory birds at our mudflats was the highlight between September and March. So I gravitated towards Sungei Buloh. Avian photography requires long lenses that are heavy; it took a toll on my back and shoulders. Use of improper boots in the mud can be a fatal experience. Fortunately friends helped to extricate me from sinking further. The experiences recounted further augment the importance of never travelling alone. With help from Wang Luan Keng, *Wetlands in a City* made it to the bookstands in 2010.

It came full circle when I decided to work on the forests of Singapore. With support from National Parks Board (NParks), work went on a quicker pace and much ground was covered. Besides weekends, most of my leave was consumed for this project. I salute the vision of the past and present CEOs of NParks to document the biodiversity of whatever nature areas that are left. *Rainforest in a City* (2015) was the culmination of those efforts. Pulau Ubin received renewed attention from the government in terms of conservation efforts to ensure the rich biodiversity continues to flourish on the island. Again, more time was devoted to the island. *Footprints on an Island – Rediscovering Pulau Ubin* was published in 2016 together with two co-authors, Wong Tuan Wah and Chia Mui Eng. The COVID-19 pandemic curtailed everybody's movements for the next two to three years but my restless spirit prevailed. Digging into my archives I found enough material to produce the next coffee-table book *Moments* (2022). The book captures the many behavioural moments that I learnt along the way and subscribes to the mantra "expect the unexpected". Many wildlife experts helped shape my understanding of nature and they are instrumental in the production of my publications.

Static images are no longer challenging. Coupled with new technology, easily capturing images of creatures flying, diving, capturing prey and their interactions, has become the new norm. Fine details of subjects can now be recorded using new optics. The new dimensions in photography have challenged photographers to advance their craft. Photography is a never-ending learning journey. Yet it does not mean that with every outing there is something to show.

My fascination continues and the journey seems infinite, for there is more for me to uncover despite already having scoured most of the island. The production of a number of coffee-table books highlights my intimacy with nature. Most of the proceeds from the sales of the books funds nature causes or nature organisations.

Gray-headed Fish Eagle at Pandan River.

Hopefully, readers can marvel at the miracle of life and the importance of nature, and future generations can continue to venerate its existence.

I have found my inner peace. I know my existence is not in vain.

Dr Chua Ee Kiam is a Senior Consultant with the National Dental Centre, Clinical Associate Professor with Duke-NUS and Honorary staff member of the Lee Kong Chian Museum. He still finds time to excel in his favourite past-time — nature photography, focussing on the tropical rainforests and intertidal areas. He has written award-winning books on nature, including *Nature in Singapore – Ours To Protect; Pulau Ubin – Ours To Treasure; Chek Jawa – Discovering Singapore's Biodiversity; Borneo's Tropical Eden – Sabah; Singapore's Splendour – Life on the Edge; Wetlands in a City; Rainforest in a City; Footprints on an Island – Rediscovering Pulau Ubin; Moments of Wonder.*

Chapter 9

Singapore and the Protection of the Marine Environment

Tara Davenport

The oceans cover more than 70% of the Earth's surface. They support the world's economy ranging from international trade and shipping, to fishing and tourism. The oceans provide an essential source of food, and are home to nearly 250,000 known species. The oceans also help us breathe and regulate the climate, playing a vital role in absorbing 31% of the carbon dioxide emissions released into the atmosphere. Due to the intensification of human activities, the oceans face a variety of threats including overfishing, marine pollution, habitat destruction, and climate change impacts such as ocean warming, ocean de-oxygenation, ocean acidification and sea-level rise. The inter-related nature of the oceans means that these threats pose unprecedented risks to the multi-faceted benefits provided by the oceans and will inevitably undermine the social and economic security of states (and their populations) that rely on such benefits.

Singapore is a tiny island and maritime city-state. From time immemorial, the oceans have been critical to Singapore's survival and success. From its colonial history to its independence in 1965,

Singapore has always been a vital conduit for maritime trade due to its strategic location, connecting the Indian and Pacific Oceans through the Straits of Malacca and Singapore (SOMS). Today, Singapore is a major global maritime hub — it is the world's busiest container transshipment port, the top bunkering port, and has the fifth largest ship registry. Singapore's small size has also meant that our coastal and marine areas are necessarily heavily urbanised to support our population and economic growth, with extensive land reclamation further entrenching the interface between land and sea. At the same time, Singapore's coastal waters, while small, are rich in marine life and biodiversity, with more than 100 reef fish species, more than 200 species of sponges and 255 species of hard corals which accounts for more than 25% of the world's coral species. Singapore is keenly aware of the careful balancing act it must undertake to ensure that it can continue to utilise the oceans in a sustainable manner and mitigate the most severe impacts of human activities. In this regard, Singapore has demonstrated its commitment to the protection of the marine environment and marine biodiversity in several ways.

First, Singapore has played an instrumental role in multilateral efforts to establish binding international legal rules on the protection and preservation of the marine environment and marine biodiversity. The international legal framework for the protection of the marine environment was established by the 1982 UN Convention on the Law of the Sea (UNCLOS), which has been described by Ambassador Tommy Koh as the "Constitution" for the oceans. UNCLOS is the only global treaty to address all matters relating to the protection of the marine environment. Part XII of UNCLOS, amongst other things, establishes general obligations on the protection and preservation of the marine environment and on measures to prevent, reduce, and control pollution of the marine environment. It sets out prescriptive and enforcement rights and obligations of states in relation to specific sources of pollution (including pollution from land-based sources; seabed activities subject to national jurisdiction; deep-seabed mining; dumping; vessels; and from or through the atmosphere). Unlike other environmental treaties, UNCLOS contains robust compulsory third-party dispute settlement mechanisms which allow states to unilaterally refer disputes on the environmental provisions in UNCLOS to a court or tribunal having relevant jurisdiction. Singapore played an active role in UNCLOS negotiations. Indeed, Ambassador Tommy Koh was President of UNCLOS negotiations from 1980 to 1982 and is widely credited for its successful adoption. Similarly, the negotiations of a new implementing agreement to protect marine biodiversity beyond national jurisdiction under the auspices of UNCLOS was helmed by another Singaporean, Ambassador Rena Lee, and a text has been agreed upon on 4 March 2023 after several years of negotiations. This is a testament to Singapore's commitment to developing a legal order for the oceans that places prime importance on the protection of the marine environment and marine biodiversity.

Second, in the context of the 17 Sustainable Development Goals (SDGs) adopted by all United Nations Member States in 2015, Singapore has undertaken 33 voluntary commitments in order to help achieve SDG 14 on the conservation and sustainable use of the oceans, seas and marine resources. While the targets of SDG 14 are not all directly applicable for Singapore, it has made voluntary commitments that will help meet, *inter alia,* the SDG 14 targets of protecting and restoring ecosystems; conserving coastal and marine areas; and increasing scientific knowledge, research and technology for ocean health. Some of these initiatives have been taken in relation to Singapore's maritime transport sector; the protection of the marine environment and biodiversity of Singapore's coastal waters and marine research programmes and will be outlined below.

Third, Singapore has taken significant steps to facilitate the sustainable development of its maritime transport sector to reduce its impact on the marine environment, which applies to both vessels that fly the Singapore flag (applicable to 4,400 ships that sail around the world) and all vessels plying Singapore waters, including in the SOMS. Singapore is the only State in Southeast Asia that is a party to all the main shipping instruments on the prevention of pollution from ships adopted by the International Maritime Organization (IMO), which is the competent intergovernmental organisation regulating international shipping. This includes the International Convention for the Prevention of Pollution from Ships (MARPOL 73/78) and its annexes that govern different sources of pollution from ships; the 2001 Anti-fouling Convention; the 2004 Ballast Water Convention; the IMO Conventions on Preparedness, Response and Cooperation and the conventions addressing liability and compensation from oil pollution damage. Singapore has adopted national legislation that implements its obligations under these international conventions including the Prevention of Pollution of the Sea Act and relevant subsidiary legislation. The Maritime and Port Authority of Singapore (MPA) has also launched the Maritime Singapore Green Initiative in 2011 to reduce the environmental impact of shipping and related activities, which includes a pledge of S$100 million to support programmes that incentivise companies to adopt green shipping practices beyond what is required by the IMO Conventions. This encompasses efforts to spearhead the transition towards the supply of environmentally friendly ship fuel, as well as encouraging shipowners to switch to energy efficient technologies.

Fourth, Singapore has made efforts to protect the marine environment of its coastal waters overseen by the National Parks Board (NParks). Singapore has adopted an Integrated Urban Coastal Management framework in order to manage the diverse uses of coastal areas and conserve marine biodiversity, developed in collaboration with the Partnerships in Environmental Management for the Seas of East Asia (PEMSEA). The framework facilitates Singapore's coastal management by enhancing coordination between governmental stakeholders and promoting coherence in coastal management governance. Singapore has established the Sisters' Island Marine Park in 2015 as Singapore's first marine park spanning 40 hectares, which is home to a wide range of marine habitats including coral reefs, sandy shores and seagrass areas. In addition, one of the key activities under Singapore's Marine Conservation Action Plan is species recovery, and Singapore has initiated recovery programmes for marine turtles, giant clams, Neptune's Cup Sponge and other local hard and soft coral species.

Fifth, Singapore, cognizant of the importance of data and scientific knowledge for marine environmental protection, has committed to research projects that aim to enhance our understanding of the oceans. This includes allocating a proportion of its budget to the field of marine science and technology in order to fund the work of St. John's Island National Marine Laboratory, as well as other research projects on Marine Climate Change Science, the sustainable management of marine fish populations and the use of solar energy to facilitate coral growth.

Singapore, like all states heavily dependent on the oceans, must grapple with the persistent tension between utilising the oceans for a variety of activities that support economic development (and ultimately the well-being of its people) and ensuring that such activities cause the least harm to this vital resource. While the developments described above are a mere snapshot of Singapore's efforts to achieve this balance, it underscores Singapore's increasing recognition that these two ostensibly competing imperatives, in fact, go hand-in-hand. While there will inevitably be more that can be done, Singapore has taken vital steps in the long march towards the sustainable development of the oceans.

Dr Tara Davenport is currently an Assistant Professor at the Faculty of Law, National University of Singapore (NUS) where she teaches Principles of Property Law, Law of the Sea, and International Regulation of Shipping. She is also co-head of the Oceans Law and Policy Team at the Centre for International Law (CIL) at NUS, Deputy Director of the Asia-Pacific Centre for Environmental Law (APCEL), member of the Executive Council of the Asian Society of International Law, and member of the Editorial Board of the *Asian Journal of International Law and Ocean Development*, and *International Law Journal*.

Chapter 10

The Importance of Birds to Humanity

Vinayagan Dharmarajah

Birds have always been a part of our consciousness. Over time they have inspired civilisations, philosophers and poets, whilst their all-pervading presence has influenced and guided life's journeymen. Even as we marvel at the abilities of the Arctic Tern to travel from pole to pole, the Bar-headed Goose to rise majestically above the Himalayas or the Peregrine Falcon to speed unrivalled through our skies, we must acknowledge the broader contributions birds make to our lives. This essay explores how birds have left an indelible mark on our existence and profoundly shaped the world we live in.

Symbols of Our Existence

Birds have variously inspired song, dance, art, superstition and reverence whilst serving as totemic representations of our values and aspirations. Across Asia the crane is associated with divinity, happiness, longevity, fidelity, wealth, tranquillity and grace. Its presence in our midst is venerated and celebrated. The vulture in India is celebrated for its loyalty to the Hindu god, Ram, whilst the Parsi community has historically disposed of human remains by offering them to vultures. Garuda the mythical eagle of Asian lore features prominently in Indonesian, Thai and Cambodian iconography and heraldry. The Peacock Throne is almost as much a symbol of Mughal grandeur as the Taj Mahal whilst ravens were viewed as guarantors of good fortune both by Norseman pillaging the British Isles and by the more contemporary guardians of the Tower of London. Falconry, the keeping of cagebirds and the hunting of ducks and pheasants for sport, whilst controversial, all suggest that birds are central to the way people view themselves and their place in this world.

The Bald Eagle, the national bird of the United States, has come to symbolise American power, reach and its love for freedom. When Neil Armstrong landed Apollo 11 on the moon, his words the "eagle has landed" represent both the limitless reach of American endeavour and innovation, and the triumph of American exceptionalism. As Indonesia contemplates moving its capital to Kalimantan, the Javan Hawk Eagle, as its national bird and designated manifestation of Garuda, reminds us of the historical epicentre of its national life. The less-than-judicious reference to Singapore as a *little red dot* has resulted in some in the city-state embracing the industrious Crimson Sunbird as a symbol of national resilience and hope.

In commerce and popular culture, brands, titles and references draw inspiration from birds, even as they capitalise on their ability to tug at our heartstrings. The majesty of birds, their ubiquitous presence, their ability to make amazing journeys, their role in nurturing their young and their penchant for conversing in staccato bursts have inspired brands from industries as diverse as airlines, the media and those producing food and beverage. Equally, in popular culture, Han Solo's avian-inspired *Millennium Falcon* will always represent the speed, agility and chivalric purpose required to save a desperate princess from a dark lord.

Multilateralism, a Shared Heritage and the Legacy of Conflict

Narratives around national heritage often emphasise the superiority of national characteristics, ideologies and accomplishments, resulting in a rejection of globalisation and a suspicion of multilateralism.

By flying across borders, birds represent a shared natural heritage whilst the sites and routes they use on their journeys across nations represent a shared ecological landscape. Preserving such a common heritage — and addressing global challenges more generally — can only be accomplished through peaceful engagement, collective action and by embracing the diversity of the people, cultures, and political systems of the world. Birds bring joy and wonderment to the different communities they pass through. They remind us that our exhilaration at seeing them is shared by people who look and sound different and who partake in prayer and politics in diverse ways. The contribution of each to their salvation is equally vital and the effort of one no more worthy than that of the other.

The accordance of World Heritage status to critical migratory bird sites along the Yellow Sea demonstrates how Chinese leadership can benefit a broader community of nations bound not by agreements but by a shared ecological heritage founded on an invisible pathway in the sky. This mutual love is also seen in collaboration among scientists from the United States, China, Japan and Russia even as geo-political tensions persist. Similarly, the conservation of Asia's threatened vultures benefits from scientists from India, Pakistan, Nepal and Bangladesh setting aside rivalries and suspicions spawned by the dissolution of the British Raj. Working for the common good of birds can help unite a sometimes broken world. In so uniting, to borrow generally from a Maori aphorism relating to the amazing migration of godwits, we become flocks of gods driven by a common purpose.

Doves have historically symbolised peace just as carrier pigeons have helped facilitate communications during war. Birds continue to be relevant as metaphors in understanding conflict. The division of the Korean peninsula and the establishment of the de-militarized zone (DMZ) have come to represent the ambiguity, distrust and discord that continue to pre-occupy statesmen and threaten us with nuclear Armageddon. Many birds — including the Cinereous Vulture, Golden Eagle and White-Naped and Red-Crowned Cranes — and other wildlife have, however, chosen to live and flourish in the DMZ. To some they represent the peaceful resolution of differences and a shared future we should work towards. To others they represent the ability of birds, unencumbered by the vagaries of politics and life that bedevil us, to find opportunity, solace and sanctuary amidst our struggles. Perhaps we too can find spaces of peace and joy in our lives even as we are compelled to deal with the intensity and uncertainty that are symptomatic of our contemporary existence.

Canaries in the Coal Mine and Harbingers of Hope

Birds are indicators of the state of the planet's health. When migratory birds arrive at unusual times, or fail to arrive at all, that could be the result of how climate change or unsustainable development has impacted their habitats or behaviour. If common birds begin to disappear, that could indicate increased pesticide use, industrial pollution or a reduction in the green spaces that cool our cities, oxygenate our air and address our recreational and spiritual needs. When waterbirds disappear, that could result from toxic effluents contaminating the rivers and lakes we rely on for water, agriculture and fishing.

Conversely, birds manifest themselves in our visions for a healthy future. In Europe, efforts to address the impact of industrialised agriculture on the population of farmland birds represent a preference for a more artisanal approach to farming complete with its delightful quirks, greater neighbourliness and melodious birdsong.

Efforts to promote Crane-friendly farming in Cambodia and Bhutan reflect a broader recognition that the willingness of these birds to traverse our agricultural landscapes (and share our food) symbolises the health and vitality of our own ecosystems. To this end birds represent a true measure of both human well-being and a civilised existence. A civilisation defined, not by ancient ruins, but by a time-honoured balance with the natural (and feathered) world. Similarly, local people in Bangladesh welcome the migratory Pallas Fish Eagle through the festival *Raio Uutshav* as they deem the birds to be co-participants in the working wetlands that they rely on.

In Singapore, the presence of hornbills and parakeets in human landscapes, to some, validates a development trajectory that is well considered, balanced and sustainable. Birds, by living and thriving amongst us, provide affirmation and legitimacy to the policies and approaches we have chosen to pursue, and serve as proxies for the green growth that we crave.

In this regard, the Asian Development Bank, with the support of BirdLife International, has employed the East Asian–Australasian Flyway as an organising principle to finance climate resilience and economic development in a revolutionary project called the Regional Flyway Initiative. This initiative will see loans and grants being disbursed to finance investments at wetlands frequented by migratory birds that also support livelihoods and provide green infrastructure. It recognises that birds, over millennia, have identified the healthiest places on the planet not just for themselves but for humankind as well and that we should be guided by them in the investments we make.

Saving Us

As the late father of biodiversity, Thomas Lovejoy, noted, "If you take care of birds, you take care of most of the environment problems in the world." This in large part is due to the critical ecosystem services birds deliver.

As we grapple with the climate emergency, the conservation and restoration of forests has been presented as a panacea for absorbing and sequestering atmospheric carbon. Yet it is birds like hornbills (through seed dispersal) and sunbirds (through pollination) that help maintain the health and functionality of forest ecosystems, giving us a real shot at mitigating the impacts of climate change. Similarly, coral reefs are strengthened by the droppings of sea birds whilst some shorebirds in North America reinforce coastal ecosystems by consuming voracious plant-eating snails.

The role of birds in agriculture is also vital. Some species of banana, papaya and nutmeg benefit from bird pollination. They are also instrumental in eliminating agricultural pests. Swifts play that role in relation to insects whilst kites and owls play a similar role in eliminating rodents.

Birds also help guarantee human health. Vultures provide vital sanitary services through the consumption of carcasses. In South Asia, the crash of vulture populations has resulted in domestic dogs taking over these same sanitary services. The consequent increase in dog populations has also seen a spike in rabies. The Asian Koel, reviled by some for its loud calls, is a cuckoo that lays its eggs in crow nests which helps keep crow numbers at manageable levels.

COVID-19 and the movement restrictions that resulted meant that people were unable to leave their homes and neighbourhoods to engage and interact. Birds visiting people's gardens and apartments enabled humans to embrace the sound, colour and vibrancy of a world that was otherwise denied to them and to deal with social, economic and psychological extremes imposed on them. The role of birds in delivering mindfulness and mental health must be valued and promoted.

Finally, birds feature in biomimicry, or the design of products and systems based on a replication of adaptations found in the natural world. The manoeuvrability of eagles and falcons, the ability of owls to fly silently and the ability of geese to save energy by flying in formation have all inspired aviation engineers. The ability of hummingbirds to hover has been employed in drone technology whilst shock-absorbing technology has benefitted from the study of woodpeckers and their ability to pound away relentlessly at trees. Speed trains in Japan have been inspired by the ability of kingfishers to slice through the air just as the humble zipper has been inspired by interlocking feathers. It is ironic that the adaptations developed by birds over millennia are shaping our own evolution.

Understanding Ourselves

Birds also remind us of who we are and what we are capable of experiencing as a species. Birdwatching, bird photography and bird spotting competitions (or bird races) have become increasingly popular pursuits in many parts of the world. In addition to generating revenues for communities, the emotions that these hobbies generate often reflect the broader spectrum of impulses and responses that collectively fashion humanity.

The joy of spotting a bird, the sense of anticipation generated in seeking one out, the disappointment of not seeing one and the envy that accompanies acknowledging the success of others all represent vicissitudes of the human condition. The competitive spirit that drives people to spot rare birds or seek better photographs is a pivot to our individualism and adventurism. Equally, birdwatching, in bringing people together, facilitates our more visceral need to

Asia's Vultures. (Photo credit: Bjorn Olesen)

connect as a species. When we go birdwatching with those we cherish, we love even as we pursue beauty. When we share sightings, images and insights, this reflects our instinctive need to coalesce around issues we value and to barter relentlessly in an information marketplace. However, most importantly, even as we compete, connect, marvel — and of course, tweet — in their name, birds help us find that elixir of life that often eludes us — inner peace.

Vinayagan Dharmarajah (Vina) is the Regional Director (Asia) of BirdLife International. He oversees the delivery of BirdLife's Strategy in Asia which includes the conservation of threatened avian species including hornbills, migratory shorebirds, bustards, vultures and cranes, and promoting the important roles they play. He also serves on the board of SAVE (Saving Asia's Vultures from Extinction), a consortium addressing the threats faced by Asia's vultures. Vina has a degree in law (LLB) from the University of Bristol and an LLM in International Business Law from the Sorbonne-Assas International Law School. He serves concurrently as BirdLife's Head of Governance.

Chapter 11

Greening Singapore: From Garden City to City in Nature

Kenneth Er and Leong Chee Chiew

Transformation of Singapore's Landscape

> "The forests that now form my delight will gradually give place to man and his habitations, but they are more interesting to me in the present state. Flora here luxuriates in endless varieties, where she finds soil, climate and everything, congenial."

This was in a letter penned by William Jack, the botanist who had accompanied Sir Stamford Raffles to Singapore, to Nathaniel Wallich, the Superintendent of the Calcutta Botanic Gardens, in 1819 (Gage, A.T. et al. (1916). Jack's Letters to Wallich, 1819–21, *Journal of the Straits Branch of the Royal Asiatic Society*, 73: 178). Jack anticipated the degradation of the lush vegetation found in Singapore with the arrival of the British. Prior to that, in the early 1800s, short of a few settlements near the mouth of rivers, Singapore was almost entirely covered in lowland mixed dipterocarp forest, with permanent open habitats confined to coastal cliffs and beaches and most of the coasts lined with mangrove forests. This landscape of flourishing and vibrant vegetation led Thomas Oxley, an Irish surgeon and botanist, to describe Singapore's landscape as an "unceasing verdue" and "an eternal spring" (Oxley, T. (1850). The Botany of Singapore, *Journal of Indian Archipelago and Eastern Seas*, 4: 436–40).

Jack's forewarning unfortunately rang true. With the establishment of the British colony upon the arrival of Sir Stamford Raffles, Singapore's landscape underwent tremendous changes with the primeval vegetation giving way to timber extraction, plantations and agricultural crops such as gambier, pepper and pineapple. Growing and processing these crops led to the decline of the lush and verdant forest cover inland, while the mangrove forests that once lined the coasts were badly degraded by over-exploitation, and reclamation to form the newly-founded town and harbour at the Singapore River. This dismal state of the forests and its potential impact on precipitation alarmed the British administration who, in the early 1880s, commissioned Nathaniel Cantley, Director of the Singapore Botanic Gardens, to prepare a report on the state of the forests in the colony, and make recommendations for its preservation, in which he remarked quite scathingly:

> "It is apparent that no sufficient attempts have been made to conserve the Government forest lands…it is hard to conceive a more short-sighted policy than that which has suffered these Settlements to drift into their present condition of scarcity of forest and forest produce." (Cantley, N. (1883). *Report on the Forests of the Straits Settlements*, Singapore Printing Office, Singapore).

Following Cantley's recommendations, the British administration wasted no time in designating forest reserves. Forest reserves amounting to 11% of the land area were established in 1884. However, it was a little too late as it was estimated that less than 7% of the primary forest remained by then, with the rest replaced or degraded.

Singapore's Greening Journey

Amidst this backdrop, Singapore achieved self-governance in 1959 and independence in 1965. The newly established government promptly set forth to urbanise and modernise the small island nation with no hinterlands. This led to the replacement of plantations and kampungs for public housing estates, canalisation and damming of rivers for reservoirs, and further land reclamation.

Despite this, the Singapore government under the leadership of founding Prime Minister Lee Kuan Yew, recognised the importance of greenery in an ever-increasingly urbanised city-state. While the rationale often cited for greening Singapore was to attract foreign investors and visitors, a lesser known motivation was environmental justice. Lee saw greening as a social leveller, where all Singaporeans had equal access to greenery and green spaces. Underpinning this was the social belief that nature will uplift the human spirit, as revealed by Lee in 1995:

> "I have always believed that a blighted urban landscape, a concrete jungle destroys the human spirit. We need the greenery of nature to lift up our spirits." (Lee, K.Y. Speech delivered at the opening of National Orchid Garden, 20 October 1995).

With that, in 1963, Singapore's greening journey began with Lee, also affectionately known as Singapore's Chief Gardener, launching the first nationwide tree-planting campaign by planting a Mempat sapling at Farrer Circus. This grew into a greening movement that continues today. As Lee's Garden City vision evolved into a City in a Garden, and now a City in Nature vision, the underlying intent throughout was to provide a quality living environment. This has become even more critical with the existential threat of climate change and the need for nature-based solutions to future-proof the city-state.

Becoming a Garden City

As a young nation, the focus was to green Singapore as quickly as possible to provide shade and soften the concrete landscape. Lee took an active role in urging government agencies to achieve this by forming the Garden City Action Committee to coordinate efforts and to build professionalism and expertise. In a memo to the committee in 1975, he wrote:

> "The objective is a city pleasant, green and cool, and safety and convenience for the pedestrian. Trees and vegetation need air, … , to breathe. We must get the right trees, shrubs, creepers, and ivy for the right soil, exposure of sun, humidity of soil, etc."

Initially, hardy and fast-growing species were selected, but over time, colour was introduced through the addition of flowering trees and shrubs to the planting palette. Concrete structures such as flyovers and overhead bridges were planted over with climbers and creepers, while expressway viaducts were built with spaces in between to allow sunlight to filter down onto the plants growing in the gaps. Parks were also created to provide respite and recreational opportunities. In 1975, the passing of the Parks and Trees Act ensured that planting provision is imposed on any proposed land development, and that land is set aside for tree-planting along roadsides, in carparks and housing estates.

With this commitment to greening, Singapore solidified its global reputation as a Garden City for international visitors and residents alike.

Evolving into a City in a Garden, then a City in Nature

The Garden City vision evolved into a City in a Garden vision in the 1990s through to the 2010s to make greenery more accessible for all. This was done through strengthening the island-wide network of green spaces, such as by creating a network of park connectors as greenways for recreation, and curating parks with thematic identities, like East Coast Park as a coastal beach park and HortPark as a one-stop gardening hub.

Building on the Garden City and City in a Garden visions, the National Parks Board is now transforming Singapore into a City in Nature by restoring nature into the urban ecosystem, in light of the challenges of urbanisation and climate change. Through four key moves, it is hoped that the City in Nature vision will strengthen ecological, climate and social resilience:

- **Conserve and extend our natural capital.** Conserving the nature reserves as core biodiversity areas, the plan is to then establish nature park networks and corridors to buffer the nature reserves and ensure ecological connectivity between the core areas. Collectively, this network of nature parks and corridors will also provide new recreational opportunities.
- **Intensify nature in our gardens and parks.** New and existing parks will take on a more natural landscape with native vegetation curated to bring about greater human well-being. Waterbodies and waterways will be naturalised to enhance flood protection, while supporting rich biodiversity. Therapeutic gardens will be developed for enhanced well-being and nature playgardens introduced for children to connect with nature.

- **Restore nature into the urban landscape.** To bring nature closer to people, more skyrise greening will be implemented, while industrial estates will be greened up to mitigate the urban heat island effect.
- **Strengthen ecological connectivity between our green spaces.** Designed to mimic the natural structure of forests, streetscape greenery is transformed into Nature Ways to facilitate the movement of animals like birds and butterflies between green spaces, and cool our environment even more. More recreational greenways, such as the Round Island Route and Coast-to-Coast trails, will be added to provide Singaporeans with greater access to nature and create a sense of space on the island.

City in Nature: Conserving and extending our natural capital in Singapore. Aerial photo of Hindhede Nature Park. (Photo credit: National Parks Board)

The success of City in Nature depends on community participation and stewardship. To bring the community onboard the greening efforts, community programmes have been rolled out, including the OneMillionTrees movement that aims to plant one million more trees across the island by 2030 in close partnership with the community, as well as the well-loved Community in Bloom programme that seeks to set forth a culture of gardening in Singapore.

As Singapore transformed from a Garden City to a City in a Garden through the decades, the idea has been to ensure that Singapore continues to be highly liveable. Moving forward, the City in Nature vision will ensure that Singapore's living environment continues to be the best that it can be through balancing development with conservation. By restoring nature into the urban ecosystem through the extension of natural capital, softening the urban landscape matrix and strengthening ecological connectivity, Singaporeans will have convenient access to greenery and can reap the benefits that nature has to offer. Truly, we will be at peace with nature.

Kenneth Er is the Deputy Secretary (Planning) at the Ministry of National Development. Formerly the Chief Executive Officer of National Parks Board (NParks) from 2014 to end May 2023, he played a key role in the conceptualisation of the City in Nature vision, one of the five pillars under the Singapore Green Plan 2030, and led NParks to realise the vision by conserving and extending Singapore's natural capital island-wide. As the lead agency overseeing greenery and biodiversity conservation of our City in Nature in Singapore, NParks manages more than 400 gardens and parks, four nature reserves, island-wide Park Connector Network and streetscape greenery. NParks also oversees veterinary services. His research interests are in conservation biology, forest ecology, and avian ecology.

Dr Leong Chee Chiew joined the Singapore Botanic Gardens in 1983 as a research officer. In 1990, he was appointed Deputy Executive Director of the National Parks Board (NParks). When the Parks and Recreation Department merged with NParks in 1996, he became the Deputy Chief Executive Officer (Specialist Services Department). He is currently the Commissioner of Parks and Recreation; Director-General, Plant Health; Director-General, Wildlife Trade Control; and also Executive Director (National Parks, Gardens & Nature Reserves Cluster).

Chapter 12

Speaking up for Nature

Geh Min

When I became a Nominated Member of Parliament (NMP), many of my friends and family were surprised, but no one more so than I. Politics had never been of particular interest to me, and was largely limited to the TV series "Yes Minister". However, as I discovered, a political agenda can appear unexpectedly and galvanise the most politically inept and apathetic into action. The catalyst was Nature, so you could describe my foray into Parliament as "Green" in all senses of the word.

Nature lovers like myself joined the Nature Society (Singapore) (NSS) to enjoy, appreciate and study Singapore's rich natural heritage but found ourselves catapulted from hobbyists to lobbyists by the rapid disappearance of many valuable nature areas in the name of urban development. Of course we benefitted and recognised the need for public housing, roads and other developments for our economic survival and success. But many of these were achieved with apparent disregard for what was destroyed in the process and, worse still, since mandatory Environmental Impact Assessments (EIAs) were not required, the developers seemed totally unaware of this. When highways were needed, planners chose the fastest and straightest routes, thereby destroying valuable biodiversity sites like Khatib Bongsu (a rich wetland for migratory birds) or endangering their future survival, like the Bukit Timah Expressway (BKE) which isolated the Bukit Timah Nature Reserve. The reasons given seemed spurious: "We want Singaporeans to have a seamless travel experience", and "If Singaporeans want to enjoy nature they can go across the Causeway".

The problem was not that policy makers and planners were not "green" but that their interpretation of greening was significantly different. So while nature reserves were degazetted, many roadside trees were planted and new golf courses proliferated (23 in total at one point). Even more worrying was the absence of any protection for coastal and marine ecosystems. Valuable wetlands and mangroves were described as "mosquito-ridden swamps" and destroyed during land reclamation while marine ecosystems had no protection at all.

The mantra that used to upset me most was "Singapore has no natural resources", when we had some of the richest terrestrial and marine biodiversity in our tiny "red dot" worthy of comparison with large continents. The science of ecology and ecosystem services was still a young one but the efficiency, thoroughness and speed of development was so acute that we feared all our natural heritage would be destroyed in the name of economic development, before their value became evident to policy makers.

The official Green Plan of Singapore, inspired by Mr Lee Kuan Yew, was decidedly First World, urban, economic and anthropocentric in concept. It had become a branding exercise for Singapore's Garden City, was copied by other progressive leaders in the region and admired globally. The NSS' biocentric conservation approach was viewed askance as Third World, regressive and anti-development; the sentimental agenda of "Tree huggers". This polarisation of views and hardening of stereotypes was exacerbated by a lack of trust which resulted in no dialogue or sharing of data, which then continued this cycle of increasing hostility. The media, by labelling our issues as "hot-potatoes" and reporting every confrontation between the NSS and the government as a battle, made it difficult for either side to back off.

When I became President of the NSS, our Patron, Prof Tommy Koh, arranged for meetings with key individuals in the National Parks Board (NParks) and the Urban Redevelopment Authority (URA); and I discovered that the differences were often not as stark or extreme as imagined. And much could be resolved by quiet negotiation, which I personally preferred to open confrontation. This was not favoured by our more militant members but was key to our success in keeping Chek Jawa, where much of the negotiating was done out of the public eye.

My experience with Chek Jawa convinced me that continuous negotiation, sharing of information and building of trust were key to saving our biodiversity and nature areas; not heroic confrontations that pushed the other party into a corner, even if they generated more publicity and demonstrated that we were active defenders of nature. This is when I decided to take the plunge and continue the conversation in Parliament.

A key deciding factor was the growing conviction that nature conservation was not the obsession of a minority of Singaporeans but was supported by a growing majority. While Chek Jawa demonstrated this by the crowds that flocked there spontaneously to see the fascinating marine life, there was the other side of the coin where Singapore suffered from choking pollution from forest fires in neighbouring countries, and came to the realisation that the natural environment was closely linked with economic development and had serious social consequences that could be regional or even global in their reach.

A survey by the Singapore Environment Council in 2001 strengthened this conviction and also showed that it was the younger and more educated Singaporeans who indicated that they were more likely to visit nature areas. This was borne out by my personal experience when, as President of the NSS and later NMP, I gave numerous talks to schools and universities. The level of interest, concern and knowledge on issues such as biodiversity conservation and climate change shown by students and teachers was truly heartwarming and inspiring.

From Marginal to Mainstream

Parliamentary procedure was far from being a TV drama and in fact could be extremely dull. It was also not an ego trip and I soon realised that this was not a race for glory where you claimed to be the first with an issue or motion or tried to better the Minister in a fiery debate and get reported in the media. It was often better to bring up an issue quietly in a non-confrontational manner but backed by sound reasons and as much collaboration as possible. We were all working as a team, not as adversaries, and our goal was the shared interest and future of Singapore.

I raised many issues such as solar energy, green buildings and transport, a carbon tax, a green GDP, more cycling tracks and nature parks, better protection against flooding in the event of rising sea levels, especially of our reclaimed lands and underground facilities, an eco-link to restore the connection between Bukit Timah Nature Reserve and the Central Catchment, better protection for our biodiversity, particularly our marine life and the setting up of Marine Protected Areas. Most did not get a positive response then and some were met with scepticism or ridicule. “We have not experienced any floods in Singapore since 1965” or (in the Members’ lounge) “how are your constituents — the bugs and slugs?” But our job was to push the envelope of possibilities; the policy makers had the far more challenging task of creating a functioning whole from these myriad diverse bits. However, I felt that every suggestion was given due consideration and the fact that these have finally had successful outcomes is a testimony to the fact that seeds of ideas can, with patience, grow into sturdy trees of standard practice

Whose Big Picture?

Concepts such as Natural Capital, Environmental Sustainability and Ecosystem Services were still relatively new then, though they have become today’s clichés, and I had a hard time framing my questions and issues to demonstrate their relevance to Singapore and Singaporeans, and to prove that I did not just represent a narrow interest group, but all Singaporeans.

Singapore’s policy makers have always prided themselves on not only seeing the Big Picture but taking a long-term view. However, their lens is a socio-economic one. Trying to convince them that the biggest picture and longest view is an environmental one, was challenging, partly, I suspect, because I was not regarded as an “expert” but a “tree-hugger”. However, I made sure that I worked and consulted with as many experts as I could, both local and international and, being in Parliament, albeit as a lowly NMP, was immensely helpful in making useful contacts who patiently filled my knowledge gaps. Fortuitously, the Parks and Trees Bill (55/2004) was debated in January 2005 in the first week of my entering Parliament, and I had the opportunity to speak at length:

> "Singapore sees itself as a city-state...Our laws were designed to protect our greenery within the limits of this image. While this was sufficient, even forward-looking 30 years ago, this is no longer the case today. I urge the government to see Singapore as a country with a hinterland. Our seas, our off-shore islands, our nature areas, are not just space for our city to expand; they are repositories of our valuable biodiversity...Our laws should protect them as our natural reserves, in the same way as we protect our fiscal reserves."

I also proposed the introduction of mandatory EIAs for nature areas:

> "In the past, speed and cost-cutting were given priority. Today, increasing land scarcity and the escalating value of disappearing natural ecosystems requires a paradigm shift....
>
> Insufficient consultation and planning at the conceptual stage will result in short-term, narrow objectives to the detriment of long-term sustainability. Everyone will be the loser, not just our biodiversity."

I continued to view civil society and younger Singaporeans, including future generations, as the people I spoke for, and found many students were far more informed and concerned about Climate Change which was rarely, if ever, mentioned in Parliament then. I therefore used the Budget debate in 2006 to push for more attention and action on this by the government:

> "The question is no longer 'Is climate change happening?' but 'What are we doing about it?'...How is Singapore playing its part in this global challenge? What are our present and future strategies for improving energy efficiency and reducing greenhouse gases? How does the Government see its role in the local, regional and global arena? Will Singapore be a leader, a follower or a freeloader? The Minister Mentor (MM)'s vision of a clean and green Singapore

> as good for business, good for people and good for the environment pre-empted the Triple Bottom Line...But while visions are timeless, their interpretation and implementation must be regularly reviewed to remain relevant to new challenges. In today's context of global warming...clean and green requires new mindsets, policies and practices."

Being an NMP was a milestone in my life but, like marriage, motherhood and medical practice, I feel I could have done much better if I could do it all over again. However much one reads or is taught or advised by others who are more experienced, the real learning is by actual doing. Areas where I regret not having been more effective or successful are many, but I will mention two:

(1) Mandatory EIAs are still not required and this has resulted in many unforeseen or accidental losses and damage to nature areas.

Even when required, they are often compromised, improperly executed or even ignored. Clearly the laws on protecting what little nature we have need to be strengthened, more widely implemented and effectively enforced.

(2) Climate Change is now recognised as "an existential threat" and the government is tackling this challenge on many fronts. My regret here is that I was not sufficiently effective as an advocate to get the government to do more earlier. But this is speaking with the benefit of hindsight and even I would not have expected such an acceleration of climate events. In fact, this is one area I had hoped to be proven wrong in rather than right!

Now that Nature has become a mainstream topic, both within and outside of Parliament, my greatest satisfaction is to say, not "I did this on my own", but "We achieved this together". Constructive collaboration, I have learnt, is the most sustainable and happiest path to both conserving our Nature and our Nation.

Dr Geh Min is an Ophthalmologist with a strong interest in environmental issues. She served as President of Nature Society (Singapore) from 2000 to 2008 and as a Nominated Member of Parliament (2005 to 2006). She was a recipient of the inaugural President's Award for the Environment (2006), the Stellar Awards — Celebrating Women (UNIFEM) (2006), the Honorary Watermark Award (2007), the SMA Merit Award (2007) and the Patrons of the Arts Award (Friends of the Arts Award) (2017 and 2018). She currently serves on several boards and advisory councils including Nature Society (Singapore), World Wide Fund for Nature (Singapore) Limited and BirdLife International (Asia).

Chapter 13

The Role of Financial Institutions and the Environment

Piyush Gupta with Helge Muenkel

Birdwatching is my passion. In addition to the mental and physical health benefits of getting out from behind a desk and into the great outdoors, birding has helped me to connect with nature. While waiting for an oriental pied hornbill to emerge from the canopy, you start paying closer attention to nature and gaining a deeper appreciation for how each bird species interacts with a complex web of other animals, plants, and their physical surroundings.

Being connected to nature has also allowed me to gain a deeper understanding of the wealth of ecosystem services that nature offers, which help humans to survive and thrive. These include food, water, medicine, materials for shelter, and even natural cycles such as climate and nutrients.

This dependence on nature makes it deeply troubling to witness the severity of nature loss and degradation, which has been caused by human activity. According to the United Nations Environment Programme (UNEP), we are currently using the equivalent of

1.6 Earths to maintain our current way of life, and nature's ecosystems cannot keep up with our demands.

The Intergovernmental Science-Policy Platform on Biodiversity and Ecosystem Services estimates that one million of the world's approximate eight million species of plants and animals are threatened with extinction, and 66% of the ocean area is impacted by human activities, such as fisheries and pollution.

The resultant effects are stark. Nature loss and degradation exacerbate climate change, undermine food security and put people and communities at risk. UNEP estimates that around 3.2 billion people are adversely affected by land degradation, and close to US$600 billion in annual global crop production is at risk from pollinator loss. If declines in nature and biodiversity continue at the current rate, it will undermine progress towards a large number of targets as established by the United Nations' Sustainable Development Goals, across poverty, hunger, health, water, cities, climate, oceans and land.

I believe that banks have a critical role to play in reversing nature loss and degradation, as well as in tackling other sustainability challenges across a large number of inter-connected environmental and social concerns. Given the complexity of this task, I believe that no one can tackle all these challenges alone. Instead, we need collective resolve and action; we need ecosystem-wide change to re-wire the way we organise our economies and societies. This ecosystem comprises governments, regulators, the private and finance sector, with all of us embedded in the community at large. And each part of this ecosystem has specific and complementary roles to play.

Banks for instance will be instrumental in the re-allocation of capital towards more sustainable activities, and by doing so, tilting the cost of financing and changing the relative economics of investing in lower carbon and nature-positive activities compared with those that pollute.

At DBS, we want to do more, so much more, and also be at the forefront of innovation. For example, we are a founding shareholder and partner of Climate Impact X (CIX), a Singapore-headquartered but globally operating carbon market and exchange. CIX established platforms that facilitate the buying and selling of high-quality carbon credits, which support global capital flows towards nature-based and technology-based decarbonisation solutions. In 2022, CIX successfully concluded its first major auction, which sold 250,000 tonnes of carbon credits from the Delta Blue Carbon Project in Pakistan, the world's largest mangrove restoration project, at US$27.80 per tonne. The capital raised via this auction will be instrumental in supporting the preservation of this very important natural ecosystem.

All our efforts to tackle sustainability challenges are underpinned by a strong sense of purpose. As Southeast Asia's largest bank by total assets, we feel that we have a unique responsibility to foster inclusive growth and prosperity, and to enable a fair and just transition that will benefit people across the region in which we operate. DBS started as the Development Bank of Singapore in the 1960s, with the express intent of helping in the industrialisation and development of Singapore. For the longest time, this idea of being sustainable, being relevant to society, doing real things for real people, and therefore having a purpose, has been deeply rooted in our DNA.

Fast forward over 50 years, and we are a very different kind of bank. Over the last decade, we focussed on pervasive innovation and digital transformation to improve our offerings for a better customer experience. We have been named the world's best bank five years in a row since 2018. And while doing all this, we have maintained our strong sense of purpose, and developed our new mission which is to be the Best Bank for a Better World, the latter part encapsulating our approach to sustainability.

Based on this, we have consistently refined and expanded our sustainability agenda, which is principally centred around three pillars: (i) Responsible Banking, which not only aims to empower our clients to be more sustainable but also addresses the important issue of financial inclusion, i.e., banking the under-served, (ii) Responsible Business Practices, which defines how we conduct ourselves as an organisation and (iii) Impact Beyond Banking, which supports social entrepreneurship as well as a variety of community causes.

Our approach is to weave environmental and social considerations into the fabric of our business across all three pillars.

Being conscious about the urgency of climate action, and how climate is inter-connected with other sustainability challenges such as nature loss and social inequality, we have materially accelerated our climate agenda in recent years.

In the run-up to COP26 in 2021, and as part of our Responsible Banking strategy, we became the first bank in Singapore, and among the first 100 globally, to sign up to the Net Zero Banking Alliance (NZBA). By doing so, we committed to aligning our lending and financing activities with net zero by 2050. In 2022, we then published a new report, which we called *Our Path to Net Zero — Supporting Asia's Transition to a Low Carbon Economy*. In this report, we described in great detail how we selected science-informed decarbonisation pathways, and interim 2030 decarbonisation targets for a large number of sectors. At the time of publication, and still today, this is among the most comprehensive and ambitious sets of decarbonisation targets among banks globally.

Additionally, as part of our Responsible Business Practices strategy, we achieved carbon neutrality in our own operations in 2022. One example of our comprehensive efforts to accomplish this was the retrofitting of a 30-year-old DBS branch, DBS Newton Green. It became the first net zero building of a bank in Singapore. In our design thinking, we are committed to not only eliminating greenhouse gas (GHG) emissions, but also to creating additional positive impacts on nature. Over 50% of the building's perimeter façade is covered with living plants, which serves a dual purpose of lowering the internal building temperature by reducing urban heat gain and providing refuge for native butterfly and bird species such as the magpie robin, bulbul and flowerpecker. DBS selected the plants in collaboration with the Nature Society of Singapore.

Reflecting again on my passion for birdwatching, I have taken many of the lessons I have learnt from observing nature into the boardroom. For instance, nature teaches you the importance of balance that enables each organism to live and thrive as part of the larger ecosystem. As a business leader, I equally need to be mindful of balancing trade-offs given that there are 17 UN Sustainable Development Goals (SDGs) across environmental, social and economic dimensions. It is when this balance is tipped, that we all start feeling the effects.

Piyush Gupta while bird watching.

Nature has been a huge source of inspiration for me. And I think it can also inspire others. You just need to bother to look.

Piyush Gupta has been the Chief Executive Officer and Director of DBS Group since 2009. He was previously Citigroup's CEO for Southeast Asia, Australia and New Zealand. Piyush is Chairman of the Board of Trustees, Singapore Management University; Vice-Chairman of the Institute of International Finance; and Vice-Chairman of the Executive Committee, World Business Council for Sustainable Development. He has a keen interest in nature, and serves as Co-Chair of BirdLife International's Advisory Group, a global conservation NGO.

Helge Muenkel is the Chief Sustainability Officer at DBS. He is responsible for developing DBS' overarching sustainability framework and driving sustainability initiatives across the bank. He acts as Secretary to the bank's Board Sustainability Committee (BSC), and chairs its Group Sustainability Council. Helge also represents DBS in several global and regional working groups, is alternate director in Climate Impact X Pte Ltd, and sits on the Impact Advisory Panel of the Asia Impact First Fund. Helge holds a Master's Degree in Economics from Munich University (major in Development Economics) as well as a postgraduate degree in sustainability from Cambridge University. He is also a Chartered Financial Analyst (CFA).

Chapter 14

SUNGEI BULOH

R. E. Hale

In 1986, having recently returned to Singapore after a long absence, I found that some of my former favourite birdwatching spots had been lost to development and was looking for possible new pastures. It was a hot, cloudy, late morning that tended to rain as I passed Kranji Dam and parked on a bumpy track. Nothing moved, nothing called. I pressed on, on foot, coming to a halt after a while at a small cluster of attap kampong houses, sheltered by trees, on the bank of what I later learned to be the Sungei Buloh. The opposite bank was a scrub-infested bund, intersected by a sluice gate. The water, a turbid muddy stream, seemed motionless in the heat. No dogs barked. Chickens scratched in the dust. It was not a promising place.

I waited, eating my sandwiches. After a while a small flock of Redshank from the Johore Straits way off to my right whirred past, swerving to the right as they came level and disappearing over the sluice gate. The tide, it seemed, was on the turn, the brown water now starting to flow slowly upstream instead of down. As the mudflats in the Straits became covered by water, more waders flew past and disappeared over the sluice-gate. The clouds massed and

I beat it back to the car, my mind made up that the ground beyond the river must be investigated.

We had no GPS in those days, and the official road map of the island of Singapore showed but a vague indication of the tracks in use but, over the course of the next three weekends, I found my way to a land of enchantment. The area had been developed for prawn and fish farming. Lagoons of varying sizes, formed by the building of mud bunds and which could be flooded or drained as needed, stretched into the distance. Waders on migration were there in abundance, rising in whirling flocks at my approach. Redshank, Greenshank, Snipe, Whimbrel, Sandpipers, Plover were present in hundreds if not thousands. A large heronry added variety. This was an isolated "island" covered with trees rising 40 feet or so above the mud, of which every branch seemed to hold a messy nest of sticks. Grey and Purple herons seemed to have agreed to divide it between them while Night Herons filled any gap they could find. Mangroves of several species flourished along the coastline and the small offshore island of Pulau Buloh boasted a magnificent undisturbed forest.

For many weeks most of my free time was spent there and when, much later, I met other birdwatchers, I was amazed to find they did not know of this "El Dorado". Of course, they then wanted to come and see it with me and all agreed that this was somewhere special.

It was with alarm that a few weeks or months later I read in *The Straits Times* that the authorities had plans to reclaim the whole area for "high-tech agriculture" and realised that, by hook or by crook, we had to do something to preserve this microcosm. Friends in the Malayan Nature Society (Singapore branch) derided our chances. Too many other important sites had already been lost to development despite protesting letters to the papers but a small group of five of us, with help from Chris Hails who was employed by the Government "to bring back the birds to town" decided that a different approach must be taken. Official "Face" had to be saved.

The first stage was to prepare an illustrated booklet laying out our proposal, describing the site, listing the 142 species of birds seen there, and setting out why, in our opinion, a nature reserve was vitally needed.

A total of 318 hectares was suggested and our proposal sought to provide:

1. In liaison with the Science Centre and school teachers, broad-based educational facilities for students and others undertaking field studies in biology, geography and other environmentally-related disciplines.
2. Areas of habitat especially managed to increase their attractiveness to the wide variety of flora and fauna already found there, and to increase this variety, with special emphasis on the birdlife.
3. Promotion of the concept of environmental conservation among the general public of Singapore.
4. An attraction to a type of tourist already numerous in Europe and the Americas who are interested in birds and other wildlife in their natural habitat rather than in captivity.

The proposal was printed in illustrated booklet form in December 1987 under the names of Dr Ho Hua Chew, Dr R. Ngim, R. Subharaj and myself, assisted by C. Briffett and Dr C. J. Hails. It was sent, if my memory is correct, to every Member of Parliament, Permanent Secretary and persons we thought to have some influence in the

A proposal for a
nature conservation area
at
SUNGEI BULOH
Prepared by the Bird Group Conservation Committee of the
MALAYAN NATURE SOCIETY (Singapore branch)

higher reaches of the civil service or society. Bravely or perhaps foolishly, putting our necks on the line, this stated:

> "The plans proposed are for the initial stages only and it is confidently expected by the writers that recurrent costs and most capital expenditure can be financed under corporate donations and sponsorship."

We talked about our idea to anyone who would listen and, to our surprise, found a ready audience. Various people asked to see the area. The Member of Parliament for that constituency was amazed. The President of Singapore Dr Wee Kim Wee came with two bodyguards (who spotted more birds than we had ever done) and the birds themselves, apparently knowing that this visitor was important, responded by putting on the best display ever. The President was delighted.

Some months later, on 8 April 1988, to our great delight and the astonishment of the many pessimists in the Nature Society (Singapore), it was announced by Mr S. Dhanabalan, the Minister for National Development, that 85 hectares of land at Sungei Buloh would be set aside as a bird sanctuary. Although less than a third of the area we had suggested, it was a splendid start and in later years the preserved area was extended along the coastline. To help plan the reserve, the Ministry recruited an expert on ducks and geese from Slimbridge in England. He was happy to have input from members who knew about the habits of shore birds here. Some members thought the Society should have a major role in running the reserve but this was not to be. As Mr Dhanabalan explained personally to this writer, enthusiastic volunteers are fine until they leave or lose interest and are then difficult to replace. It would be better to have paid, supervised, qualified management and this has proved to be a wise decision. We did, however, need to spend much time explaining to officialdom that a bird sanctuary was not the same thing as a public park. It was not to be a second Jurong Bird Park; no captive flamingos, no camp site in the middle. If, as they hoped, thousands of visitors would descend on the place each weekend, the birds would not remain. It was to be a place primarily for the study of birds *in situ*, their habits, migratory patterns as well as for botanical and other studies.

All went well despite minor hiccoughs, and Sungei Buloh opened to visitors and scientists. Many years later it was officially gazetted as a Wetland Reserve, with certain areas open to the public and others limited for research purposes. Prawn farming ceased (a pity to this writer). Bushes and trees were allowed to grow along the bunds to provide cover for watchers and the Reserve became known worldwide not just for tourism but also for the research carried out and published.

It was pure chance — or fate — which led me to the bank of the river just when the tide was turning, and at the right season of the year when the migrants were present. How glad I am for that. I thank all the many people who helped or gave their support to the project, and those in the National Parks Board (NParks) who have carried it forward so successfully.

Sadly, the flocks of waders have diminished over the years, as have migrants down the flyway. Reclamation of former wetland sites along coastlines, which were vital resting and feeding places for the birds as they migrate twice a year, has had inevitable consequences; this has made Sungei Buloh an even more important world resource in the challenges of meeting the unintended consequences of economic development and progress.

As a well-known naturalist declared, we should do all we can to help birds which, unaided, undertake journeys of thousands of miles while we, humanity, need a jumbo jet aeroplane or equivalent to do so. The Sungei Buloh Wetland Reserve does this. I pray that it will be allowed to continue to do so for many, many years to come.

R. E. Hale's career with HSBC was spent mainly in Hong Kong, Japan, Malaysia, and in Singapore where he was the first recipient of the Singapore Green Leaf Award in 1991. Retiring from commercial banking in 1995, he was elected director of various public companies. Apart from birdwatching and a general love of nature, he is a dedicated philatelist. He also researches Singapore's 19th century commercial history and the people who made it happen. His 2016 book *The Balestiers* was followed by *Fraser's Hill and Lewis J. Fraser of Singapore* in 2018 and *The Pioneer Merchants of Singapore* in 2022.

Chapter 15

From Engineering to Diplomacy

Hazri Hassan

Sometimes when I look back, I always wonder how I ended up late one night in a small room in the Bundeshaus, in the former West German capital of Bonn. It was the year 2000, and I was in a business suit and seated elbow to elbow with negotiators from across the world. Only less than a year before, my work was in a totally different setting. The business suit was a far cry from the hard hat and construction boots I used to don at my landfill rehabilitation project in Lorong Halus.

My transition from engineering to international policy in the then-Ministry of the Environment (ENV) was a quick one. I had to learn the ropes of international relations, negotiations, diplomacy and protocol, fast. The Bonn meeting was one of a series of meetings to negotiate an internationally binding treaty to control persistent organic pollutants (POPs) — chemicals that are carcinogenic. The small room was the venue of a "contact group" formed to resolve the issue of dioxins produced from waste incineration. Over the years, similar committees would spring up to consider many other pressing global environmental issues such as ozone depletion, transboundary movement of hazardous waste, heavy metals, and the hot topic right now — plastic pollution.

Domestic Imperatives and International Interests

What was an ENV officer, usually associated with waste operations and public hygiene inspections, doing in international negotiations? Although the Ministry's focus was on the domestic environment and the well-being of Singaporeans, international cooperation constitutes an integral part of the Ministry's work.

The key driver of the Ministry's international engagements is the simple fact that environmental issues do not recognise national boundaries. The quality of the air and water around us depends not only on our domestic efforts but also on the actions of our neighbours. A clear example is how slash-and-burn practices in the region have caused transboundary haze. Greenhouse gas emissions in countries far away have an impact on the global climate, which affects all of us. Being reliant on other countries for 90% of our food supply, any disruption in food production overseas or the supply chain would be disastrous to Singapore. It is not good enough to do well locally; we need to encourage others to do likewise, and raising our common concerns at various international platforms is necessary.

At the same time, there is a need to adopt a global mindset when handling local issues that have international implications. A case in point is how Singapore quickly set up a licensing regime with a view to control hydrofluorocarbons (HFCs) in domestic legislation when global concerns emerged that HFCs, while viable alternatives to ozone depleting substances, were potent greenhouse gases.

The Path to Sustainable Development

The search for international cooperation to resolve global sustainability problems has become a central concern of international diplomacy. This was evident to me in 2002 when I was involved in my first major global summit — the World Summit on Sustainable Development (WSSD) in Johannesburg in 2002. There was acknowledgement that the global environment continued to suffer and that resource disparities posed a threat to global stability, security and well-being. There were calls for more support for multilateralism and collective international responsibility. Sustainable development was reaffirmed as a critical objective. Agenda 21, an unprecedented global plan of action for sustainable development adopted at the 1992 UN Conference on Environment and Development (UNCED), was upheld.

Singapore subscribes to the sustainable development concept. The Singapore Green Plan (SGP) was our first domestic blueprint, first published in 1992 and circulated at the UNCED. It was refreshed into the SGP 2012 in 2002 and presented at the WSSD. The SGP 2012 highlighted Singapore's on-going national efforts towards sustainable development, and Singapore's desire to do more for the global environment through collaborative efforts with others. I was happy to be involved in its public consultation phase.

Sustainable development came to the limelight once again in the many months leading to the adoption of the 2030 Agenda for Sustainable Development (2030 Agenda) in 2015, an ambitious long-term global development framework that includes a set of 17 Sustainable Development Goals (SDGs). I made many trips to the UN Headquarters (UNHQ) in New York City to negotiate on what the SDGs should encompass. Negotiations were long drawn. While the SDGs are not legally-binding, they serve as a guidance document for global development, and are used as a global benchmark to assess a country's developmental progress, economic and environmental sustainability, and social inclusivity.

To track progress on the achievements of SDGs, countries present Voluntary National Reviews (VNRs) where they share their experiences and lessons learnt in implementing the SDGs. I took part in Singapore's presentation of our first VNR in 2018 at the UNHQ. This year, I plan to take part again when Singapore presents our second VNR. The centrepiece will be the SGP 2030 unveiled in 2021 as a whole-of-nation movement to advance Singapore's national agenda on sustainable development. I hope our second VNR will be as well-received by the international community as the first.

Good Neighbourliness

On the regional front, Singapore recognises the importance of working closely with our neighbours. Transboundary haze pollution arising from land and forest fires remains the most prominent and pressing environmental problem facing ASEAN. Many would remember the haze crisis in 2013, when the region experienced high levels of transboundary haze pollution, unprecedented since 1991.

There was a need to hold accountable those that were responsible for causing the haze. I was heavily involved in the drafting of a bill, designed to hold accountable, and deter, entities responsible for causing or contributing to serious haze pollution affecting Singapore. A key feature is its extra-territorial effect, which covers the operations of all entities whose activities outside of Singapore contribute to haze pollution in Singapore. It is a novel piece of legislation that incorporates applicable international principles and norms of law. Under international law, States have the sovereign right to exploit their own natural resources but bear the responsibility to ensure that activities within their jurisdiction or control do not cause damage to the environment of other States. My work on transboundary haze pollution continues to this day.

Trade–Environment Nexus

Apart from fellow officials from environment ministries, many of my international counterparts are foreign service officers. Increasingly, I have been working with trade negotiators too. This corresponds with the growing linkage over the years between trade and sustainability issues.

With the concept of sustainable development gaining wide acceptance, many of the Free Trade Agreements (FTAs) that Singapore enters into contain specific environmental obligations. I was involved in a small way during negotiations of the United States–Singapore FTA — Singapore's first FTA with environmental obligations being part of the core text. Subsequently I played a larger role as Singapore's lead negotiator for the environment-related chapters of the Trans-Pacific Partnership and European Union–Singapore FTA. I had an even larger role when I was appointed Co-Chief Negotiator for the Singapore–Australia Green Economy Agreement (GEA). It was a first-of-its-kind agreement and touted as a model for rules and standards in advancing trade and sustainability in future agreements. I am proud to have played a part in concluding the GEA within a year of negotiations, made possible by the excellent working camaraderie between the Australian and Singaporean teams.

Bilateral Cooperation — Helping Each Other

A key part of my job is to work closely with foreign counterparts bilaterally. Such collaboration enables closer ties to be forged, with the firm belief that caring for the environment is in everyone's interest regardless of which country we are from. Only by sharing our expertise with other countries and theirs with us — and helping each other care for the environment — are we then able to manage global problems.

Maldives, like Singapore, is a member of the Alliance of Small Island States (AOSIS). Maldives was one of the countries which bore the brunt of the Indian Ocean tsunami and earthquake disaster of December 2004. In February 2005, Singapore donated a portable desalination plant to provide drinking water to the tsunami-affected residents. I was honoured to be part of the Singapore delegation which officiated the handing over of the plant to the Maldives. It was an eye-opening experience visiting the temporary settlement camps for islanders displaced by the tsunami.

The roles could easily have been reversed. In our early years of nationhood, Singapore was able to overcome many difficulties by constantly learning from our more advanced counterparts and adopting technologies to suit our local context. We should continue to learn and adapt, given the increasingly complex and dynamic landscape, and the fact that there are other countries which are more advanced in particular areas. Besides the hard aspects of technology, the softer side of environmental culture could also be learnt from other countries.

Diplomacy in Nairobi

Of all the places I have been, Nairobi is the most memorable. It is where the United Nations Environment Programme (UNEP) is seated. Formed in 1972 — the same year that ENV was formed — UNEP is the leading global authority which sets the environmental agenda for the world. I recall making my first trip there in 2001 to attend the Global Ministerial Environment Forum, a precursor to the UN Environment Assembly (UNEA) where strategic decisions are made on the work of UNEP. I was responsible for the substantive aspects and administrative arrangements for the delegation, led by a political office holder then. The logistics were challenging as I was not familiar with the place. But despite the logistical issues, and memorable incidences, my first trip to Nairobi itself was an eye-opener to the challenges faced by developing countries in balancing economic growth, social development, and environmental protection.

There was no way of knowing then that 15 years later, I would be appointed as Singapore's first Non-Resident Permanent Representative to UNEP in 2016. At the Fourth UNEA in 2019, I was elected to represent the Asia Pacific Group as a Bureau member and served as Rapporteur. In this capacity, I had the honour to preside over a few sessions, gained the experience as an office bearer in a major UN meeting, and from the podium, observed the proceedings from a different lens.

Saving the Planet

I had started this essay with my involvement in international negotiations on a POPs treaty. I had the utmost satisfaction of seeing it through and adopted as the Stockholm Convention on Persistent

Organic Pollutants, which Singapore ratified in 2005. Singapore also acceded to the Rotterdam Convention on the Prior Informed Consent Procedure for Certain Hazardous Chemicals and Pesticides in International Trade. These are just two multilateral environmental agreements out of many others such as the Montreal Protocol, the Basel Convention, and the Minamata Convention.

The world's attention right now is on plastic pollution. Plastic pollution, especially in the form of marine litter, is a global problem, spoiling our environment and causing harm to wildlife. However, plastics have many important uses and continue to be essential in many aspects of our daily lives. While the world shares a common global problem of plastic pollution, we do not necessarily share a common solution. Every country has a different context, characterised by unique circumstances. This is not unlike the many other issues that the planet is confronted with. The journey towards a universally acceptable solution will be fraught with difficulties and obstacles, but I am optimistic this can be achieved.

Reflections

Singapore has managed its environment well, despite certain natural limitations as a city-state. However, many issues are not constrained by national boundaries alone, but interdependent on the larger global arena. The optimal way to deal with them is through the collective effort of the global community. This is where Singapore should make its mark.

As I reminisce about the small room in Bonn where it all started, it is a source of pride for me that I have been given the opportunity to represent Singapore and make our voice heard on the world stage.

March 2023, in Manhattan, New York to attend the UN Water Conference.

And it has been deeply satisfying to know that I have a part in making the world a better place.

Hazri Hassan joined the Ministry of the Environment in 1990 as an engineer focussing on solid waste management and public health engineering. At present, as Divisional Director of International Policy at the Ministry of Sustainability and the Environment, his job entails formulating strategies and approaches for bilateral, regional and international issues to advance Singapore's efforts in the environmental and sustainability space. Hazri was appointed as Singapore's first non-resident Permanent Representative to the United Nations Environment Programme (UNEP) in 2016, where he takes part in international decision-making on the best means to resolve pressing global environmental issues.

Chapter 16

Our Water, Our Life, Our Future

Eugene Heng

Water! We often take our water for granted in Singapore.

While we are clearly not totally self-sufficient in our own water resources, it is conveniently available and on tap in modern Singapore. Many, however, take for granted that our clean water is freely abundant. It is fair to say most do not fully comprehend where our drinking water comes from or how intricate and challenging it is to keep this "source of life" potable and in healthy supply.

I founded the Waterways Watch Society, a non-governmental organisation and non-profit organisation in 1998. The motivation behind its founding and the catalyst behind the systemic management and care of our precious waterways was the publicly shared vision of our late Prime Minister and Mentor Lee Kuan Yew. He envisioned the complete transformation of a dirty foul-smelling Singapore River into one that is clean enough to sustain aquatic life. It took the government 10 years and a huge clean-up cost to turn vision into reality. It was to become an enduring pride of the Central Business District (CBD), the heart of the nation. We need to learn to be at peace with nature by better understanding and appreciating our waters. In my years working in the CBD, I developed a close relationship and vested interest in the river.

The Waterways Watch Society had its humble origins in a small "kampong-like" group of volunteers, the "kaypohs" (busybodies) of Singapore who took it upon themselves to patrol faithfully every weekend, the now-cleared Singapore River. Its initial founding objective was to help clear flotsam, report indiscriminate discharge of all nature of garbage and sightings of general pollution, etc., to ensure the three-kilometre Singapore River remained clean and unpolluted, especially as it ran along our main CBD.

However, the initial mission objective to keep our rivers clean and picturesque took on greater national importance when our late Prime Minister Lee Kuan Yew made the decision to dam up the Singapore River and transform the area to become our 15th reservoir, now known as the Marina Reservoir.

The Marina Reservoir has evolved into the largest catchment area amongst our 17 reservoirs today, and has now become one of the most important and largest sources of potable water. Many of the 48 waterways and catchment areas spread across the island through a network of 8,000 kilometres of drains and canals would eventually flow into the Marina Reservoir.

While the Marina Reservoir was a significantly positive development in Singapore's history, it also meant that upstream pollution from streams and drains (often referred to as "longkangs"), from both urban and rural areas, would find its way into the Marina Reservoir, where our future drinking water would come from.

The Waterways Watch Society, located along the Kallang Basin of the Marina Reservoir, suddenly took on a bigger and more critical role. Our initial group of concerned and enthusiastic community volunteers who helped to clean the waterways for mainly aesthetic reasons now needed to assume a greater responsibility to keep our network of rivers and drains relatively free of pollution before their final discharge into the Marina Reservoir.

With the creation of Marina Reservoir and the push for increasing Singapore's self-reliance on water, the Waterways Watch Society saw itself tasked with the enormous responsibility of educating the people of Singapore and the general public on the paramount importance of keeping our entire network of waterways, which now empties itself into the Marina Reservoir, free of pollution. The value of our finite water sources has to be brought home through educating the masses on how our waterways can be easily polluted through ignorant and irresponsible social behaviour and disrespect of our environment. Needless to say, it was and still is a major challenge to achieve this goal. Today, we still see huge tonnes of rubbish collected every single day from our prominent source of drinking water. During the COVID-19 pandemic and post-COVID, irresponsibly disposed masks were prevalent in our waters. On our first weekend patrols for 2023, we managed to scoop-up over 45 kilograms of litter from our waterways. Bad habits appear not to have changed and our 70,000 cleaners bear evidence of this.

Environmental change takes time, and so do mindsets. This year (2023), the Waterways Watch Society celebrates its 25th Anniversary since its establishment. Yet we still see littering and pollution today, despite our strict laws. The Society believes that education is the only sustainable way forward to foster greater stewardship for our waters. This requires the direct involvement of the Ministry of Education. Perhaps we need to introduce a new course on Social

Graces and Environmental Responsibility and emphasise its importance in moulding a truly first-class nation with first-class citizens.

While the world continues to focus and champion for the greater environment, the Society still faces the core struggle to entice and encourage people from all walks of life, the young and the old to come visit and join us in our Values-In-Action (VIA) activities, designed to inculcate basic values of good environmental behaviour and instil the correct mindset on the infinite value of clean drinking water. While the Singapore Government has pushed for initiatives to ensure water security, and has built and established our Four National Taps, ensuring the sustainable supply of clean and safe drinking water is a national responsibility that every citizen should undertake. It is in the hands of every individual's daily actions, and not just the sole responsibility of the Government or our public cleaners.

It is disheartening to see how "picking up litter" is no longer seen as a social pride in the eyes of many. It is a constant challenge to make litter-picking activities attractive for people, especially youths, and is made more difficult by overly-protective parents. It is also difficult to relay and convince institutions and companies that the organisation of these clean-up activities will definitely incur costs. Indeed, it was difficult for us to convince schools and corporations to set aside a budget for these initiatives.

To generate a willingness to care for our environment and to increase active participation in cleaning our waterways calls for a mindset change which undoubtedly takes time. Fortunately for the Society, we were able to receive good support from some schools and educational institutions (only some) who took an important step forward and supported our outdoor learning programmes. They understood the importance of understanding the challenges Singapore faces as a water-scarce country, and were willing to be the change agents in their own community.

We fervently believe that the investment of our time in educating youths from various schools is well worth the effort, as we see some encouraging signs in the increasing number of young citizens becoming future advocates of the values we teach. We recognise that every youth we engage is an investment into our future. The true challenge, however, is whether such youths have the stamina and grit to sustain their beliefs and take it forward.

As a non-profit and non-governmental organisation, financing is always a huge challenge for the Society.

In 2020 and 2021, with the restrictions and lockdowns during the COVID-19 pandemic, the Society was badly affected much like many other organisations. Though we did not reduce our staff, we had to utilise our reserves as our activities came to a stand-still. With restrictions in place, the Society was only allowed to accommodate a limited number of participants in each activity. While we believe in engaging small numbers at a time to allow a more holistic learning experience, this was an immense strain on cost and manpower. Fortunately, as the nation moved forward in the post-pandemic in 2022, we were fortunate to have more corporations coming forward (local and foreign) to sign up for our environmental programmes as part of their Corporate Social

Responsibility (CSR) pillar. We look forward to welcoming more schools and educational institutions to participate in our VIA programmes in the years ahead.

Sponsorships and special one-off grants from government bodies remain very much lacking and slow to materialise, as education about the sustainable environment remains an intangible product, and we are unable to see results in the short term (within the project timeline or even within four years). A successful mindset change and social behaviour will inevitably take at least one if not two generations. We are, indeed, in for the long haul.

From Land or Water, the litter is always the same. Waterways Watch Members help to clear the "daily litter" every weekend. (Photo credit: Waterways Watch Members)

On this note, we continue to fervently believe in what we do and we view this as a national goal befitting a First World Nation. On a brighter note, we are also pleased to share that in 2022, we managed to conduct over 400 programmes with schools and corporations.

Hopefully, this promising trend will continue in the years ahead.

Water is Life. Let us not take it for granted!

Eugene Heng, JP, BBM, is the founder and CEO of Waterways Watch Society. He started his environmental journey in the 1980s, first as an environment coordinator at the foreign bank he worked for. Eugene was later appointed to the Government Parliamentary Committee (Environment) from 1995–2000. He went on to serve in several advisory committees relating to environmental issues in Singapore, including the Water Focus Group, the Policy Study Workgroup on Physical and Environment Sustainability and the Singapore Green Plan 2012 Coordinating Committee. He also served as a PUB board member from 2001–2005 and was a pioneer member of the Public Hygiene Council.

Chapter 17

The Battle to Conserve Nature in Singapore[1]

Ho Hua Chew

Introduction

In the 21st century, there is an upsurge of nature appreciation and conservation concern among the general public in Singapore, as can be seen by the tremendous popularity of the Tree-top Trail, which is reflective of the increasing awareness pertaining to the emergency situation of the environmental crisis constituted by run-away global warming and the loss of biodiversity.

At the beginning of this century, this pro-conservation trend was manifested in Singapore in the widespread and vehement outcry among the general public against the plan to develop Chek Jawa, an inter-tidal habitat at Pubin Ubin. This was subsequently followed by the surging push for conservation of unprotected forest habitats, as evident through the many petitions mounted around the second decade of the 21st century for such forest patches at Bukit Batok, Dover, Clementi and Tengah that are subjected to development. These conservation campaigns are initiated by conservationists

[1] The views expressed here are from a personal perspective and do not necessarily coincide with that of the Nature Society (Singapore).

outside the Nature Society (Singapore) and have garnered an impressive amount of signatures from supporters — the petition to conserve Dover Forest had over 50,000 signatures, which is the largest number so far for nature conservation in Singapore.

What these show is that Singaporeans — other than members of the Nature Society (Singapore) — are very appreciative of their remaining unprotected natural habitats and wildlife; and their support of these petitions gives an expression of their sympathy and desire for nature conservation in areas apart from the already established parks and nature areas.

However, over the past decades, despite the increasing advocacy and clamour of conservation proponents, more and more forests and wooded areas outside of nature reserves and public parks in Singapore are being overwhelmed by or designated for development — be it for housing, industries, road networks or other institutional structures at forest-rich areas such as Dover, Kranji, Tagore, Tengah, Senoko, Bidadari, Bukit Batok, etc.

The Singapore Green Plan

At this stage, the United Nations' COP15 Biodiversity Conference on December 2022 (at Montreal) has raised the benchmark to at least 30% for the protection of the planet's land and marine natural habitat by 2030. This is an increase of 3% from the previous benchmark of 27% in the basic thrust of the UN Convention's Strategic Plan for Biodiversity (2011–2020), which is that by 2020, "at least 17% of terrestrial (including inland water areas), and 10% of coastal and marine areas, especially areas of particular importance for biodiversity and ecosystem services be set aside and integrated into the current system of protected areas". Singapore ratified the

1992 UN Convention on Biodiversity (CBD) in 1995 but so far, the country is still lagging far behind the CBD's 2020 benchmark for both land and marine areas.

Singapore has at most only 10% of land areas under its Green Plan, of which only 5% fall under the "Nature Reserve" category (Bukit Timah, Central Catchment, Labrador, Sungei Buloh), which enjoys legal protection from other development claims. The rest are labelled as "Nature Areas", which are areas identified as relatively undisturbed by human activity and rich in biodiversity and are to be kept as they are, as long as there is no need for their development. In terms of marine areas, Singapore has only the small Sisters' Islands protected as a marine park so far, which is shockingly negligible by the CBD's benchmark of 10% for protected marine areas.

The CBD's benchmark is "fair and square" for every nation as it is a cut in proportion to the total area size of the nation. Based on a 2011 satellite study done by the National University of Singapore's Centre for Remote Imaging, Sensing and Processing (CRISP), Singapore at this stage still harbours 29% of land designated as "spontaneous greenery", which is comprised of natural habitats such as primary and secondary forests, mangroves, scrublands, marshlands, etc. This is almost one-third of Singapore's land area, although since CRISP's 2011 study, it has been somewhat reduced as a result of forest clearance for developments, some of which have been mentioned above. Fortunately, there are still existing nature areas that can be included for some level of protection under the Singapore Green Plan.

In the past few decades, a huge positive move on the government's part includes setting up the following buffer parks to the forested Central Catchment Nature Reserves: (1) Zhenghua, (2) Hindhede, (3) Springleaf, (4) Windsor, (5) Dairy Farm, (6) Chestnut, (7) Thomson and (8) Rifle Range. However, it must be noted that these buffers are interim parks on a leasehold basis and that there is no certainty that they will be permanently protected like the Nature Reserves. Also in the positive direction is the National Parks Board's Ecological Profile Exercise, a plan by the government to establish island-wide ecological connectivity. This has been initiated at the Tengah Nature Way running mainly along the new Tengah Forest Town to link up the Western Catchment nature area and the Bukit Timah Nature Reserve. Also mooted is the marking out of the Clementi Nature Corridor linking up the Nature Reserve and the Southern Ridges. All of these are great steps forward, but it is still uncertain as to how to define the existing forest patches and the extent that these will be preserved as ecological linkages or stepping stones.

The Singapore Green Plan 2030 states that 1,000 hectares of "green spaces" will be added to the existing green spaces (7,800 hectares), with more new parks to be created and some existing parks to be enhanced ecologically. This is roughly a shift to 12% from the existing Green Plan's 10%, which is a big step forward in Singapore's contribution to the CBD's benchmark. However, it is still not clear as to what exactly these forthcoming "green spaces" are, and whether they will be restricted to natural habitats of biodiversity value like Clementi, Tengah, Bukit Brown and other such areas advocated by local conservationists. However, more can be done to come close to the CBD's 2030 benchmark of 30% whether for land or marine areas.

Nature Society (Singapore)'s Push for Nature Conservation in Singapore

It must be said that from Independence to about 1991, there was hardly any effort by our national government to set up any new areas for nature conservation; economic development was the top priority until the push for the conservation of Sungei Buloh by the

Nature Society (Singapore) in the mid-1980s. Sungei Buloh was designated as a "nature reserve" in 2002. Prior to this, the existing nature reserves (Bukit Timah, Central Catchment, Labrador), were set up by the British colonial government.

Following the success of Sungei Buloh, the Nature Society (Singapore) formulated the *Master Plan for Nature Conservation in Singapore* in 1990 in which many nature areas of conservation significance that were not protected in any way were demarcated and recommended for conservation. This landmark document from

Nature Society (Singapore)'s 1990 Master Plan for conservation as published then by the Singapore Branch of the Malayan Nature Society.
(Photo credit: Nature Society (Singapore))

a non-governmental organisation (NGO) was followed by a series of detailed conservation proposals for specific sites — like Marina South, Senoko, Sentosa, Ubin, Kranji Marshes, Khatib Bongsu, Kent Ridge, Bukit Brown, etc. Many of these sites were incorporated into the inaugural Urban Redevelopment Authority's Singapore Green Plan (1992) as "Nature Areas". Although these "nature areas" have no protection on a permanent basis in the long term, it is nevertheless a big step forward for whatever the level of protection they can get in view of the dominating emphasis here for economic development through the decades since Independence.

The Thrust of Nature Society (Singapore)'s Conservation Efforts

The thrust of the Society's conservation effort has gone beyond just being a watchdog for whatever has been protected like the Nature Reserves, as manifested in the campaign against the planned Lower Peirce golf course in the 1990s.

The Society's conservation efforts through the past decades have embraced a wide range of unprotected areas outside the Nature Reserves, whether this be an intertidal mudflat, mangrove, freshwater marshland or regrowth forest. The rationale or justifications for this wide-ranging conservation advocacy are:

(1) To secure buffers and habitat extension for forest wildlife in the central forested nature reserve (Bukit Timah and Central Catchment) such as at Mandai Lake Road, Bukit Brown and Tagore Forest.
(2) To preserve important forest habitats for all forms of resident forest wildlife such as at Pulau Ubin and Dover Forest,
(3) To preserve important wetland habitats for native wetland wildlife such as at Kranji Marshes and Marina South,

(4) To preserve important havens for migratory birds such as at Sungei Buloh, Khatib Bongsu and Senoko, and
(5) To establish stepping stones and wildlife corridors for wildlife dispersal between established parks such as at Alexandra and Pang Sua.

Concluding Remarks: The Issue of Land Scarcity in Singapore

It has been countered by the government authorities and other pro-development proponents that in the case of Singapore, we are unable to adhere to the CBD's benchmark because we are land-scarce. It is urged by such proponents that there are other competing demands like housing and economic development that have to be considered as national priorities.

But this mantra of land scarcity in Singapore sounds unpersuasive in view of the fact that so much land is used for golf courses — a total of 1,500 hectares which is 1.5 times the size of Pulau Ubin! The government's degazetting of four of these golf courses (Keppel, Jurong, Marina East and Raffles) is definitely a move in the right direction but this is a small dent in the over-supply to cater to the need of a small minority.

As for housing, it is pertinent to query whether the pressure to build more Housing and Development Board (HDB) apartments can be eased by reverting to the original policy of HDB housing strictly for residential need, that is, as an affordable home rather than as a vehicle for investment. As HDB is subsidised housing, the destruction of any natural habitat to give way for it, like at Tengah and Dover, would amount to the subsidised destruction of nature at all tax-payers' expense. Given these considerations, any claim that HDB housing for Singaporeans should override nature conservation is debatable, particularly in view of the current increasing demand among Singaporeans for more nature areas like Clementi, Bukit Brown, Tengah, etc., to be protected as environmental assets which will benefit all Singaporeans — whether as carbon sinks, natural air-conditioners, outdoor arenas for de-stressing activities, havens for Singapore's remaining wildlife, etc.

Recently, it was indeed most heartening to hear a parliamentary speech by a Member of Parliament from the dominant People's Action Party (PAP) Ms Carrie Tan, questioning the rampant push for more materialistic progress and economic growth, and urging for a slowing down of economic development — so that a less stressful and more sustainable standard of living that is in harmony with environmental limits can be achieved for all Singaporeans. This is a most remarkable speech coming from a PAP MP — a timely wake-up call to all Singaporeans and decision makers, which is in harmony with and a boost to the voice of local conservationists calling for ecological sustainability.

Ho Hua Chew (M.Sc. – Landscape Ecology, Design & Management (Imperial College); M.Sc. – Applied Ecology & Conservation (East Anglia); Ph.D. – Philosophy (University of Washington)) is past Chairman of the Nature Society (Singapore)'s Conservation Committee and helped formulate its conservation proposals for various nature areas as well as its Master Plan for the Conservation of Nature in Singapore (1990). He continues to help in coordinating NSS' conservation activities and projects, including feedbacks to the government on land-use and development plans, biodiversity surveys, etc. He was awarded the Outstanding Advocate of Our Time (2016) by The Singapore Advocacy Awards.

Chapter 18

Insects of Singapore: The Uncountable that Counts

Hwang Wei Song

We may have lost most of our large mammals and birds to over 200 years of continual human development, but Singapore is still remarkably rich with wildlife. This may not be apparent to most people, since the highest diversity of animals left in Singapore happens to exist among the tiniest of creatures: those that we call insects. Easily ignored, they go about their active lives in their bustling version of Singapore, in as much as we do ours. Discounting the handful of insect species that have adapted so well to the human environment that they have become labelled as global pests, the majority very much prefer their natural habitats in the wild, and would rather not bother us. And so it is that we have two parallel cosmopolitan worlds of very different sizes, living on one fateful equatorial island. Nevertheless, as we mature as a nation, assessing our needs as a society and charting our futures ahead, there also comes a greater need to pay attention to this other world — these six-legged Lilliputians living amongst us — as our destinies are inextricably intertwined.

Given our paths do not often cross, where can we find these insects? Most of them are residing in our nature areas, where familiar habitats have existed for millennia. They do not take up much space: A single leaf can be shelter for a batch of newly-hatched stink bugs, a mango tree twig can be the nest for a small raider ant colony. But what they lack in size, they overwhelmingly make up for in numbers. A single giant forest termite (*Macrotermes carbonarius*) colony can have thousands of workers, and in a healthy lowland rainforest, there can be hundreds, if not thousands, of such colonies. When accounting for living organic matter, insects rank second only to trees in tropical forests. It is no wonder that the late biologist E. O. Wilson remarked that insects are "the little things that run the world".

How many species of insects do we have in Singapore? Frankly, we do not have an accurate figure, not even a close estimate. We know that there are about 2,654 native plant species, almost 460 birds, 138 herptiles (reptiles and amphibians), 102 freshwater fishes, and 91 mammals (including locally extinct species) found in Singapore. For some better studied groups of insects, we have a pretty good idea too. There are around 330 butterfly species, and 118 dragonfly species present in Singapore. Recently, the first checklist on the ant diversity of Singapore reported 409 species present, but with more awaiting discovery. This is just the tip of the insect diversity iceberg. Estimates of the overall insect diversity in Singapore range from 40,000 to as much as 100,000 species! Taking the lower estimate of 40,000, it is still more than 10 times higher than all the known plant and vertebrate (animals with backbones) species found here.

Naturally, when we talk about our terrestrial biodiversity in Singapore, we have to consider that insects actually take up more than 90% of our species diversity. That is a very significant proportion of our wildlife that we simply cannot ignore. In Science, we like to identify knowledge gaps, to guide us towards filling them up, in order to provide a more complete picture of the world around us. In this case, the lack of knowledge on our local insect diversity is, at the very least, a very wide gaping hole.

What role does each of these insect species play within our forest ecosystem? Which insect is a key pollinator of our native plants? Who is responsible for the highest decomposition rate in our leaf litter community? Beyond knowing the existence of a species, knowing what it is doing in our forests is even more critical. The questions requiring answers are many, as we seek to understand how our green areas function, so that we can better manage and more effectively help with any restoration efforts.

Why have we not figured out all the insects living in Singapore? To be fair, the problem we face is global, and applies to all of biodiversity as well: We don't have a good handle on the overall species diversity on Earth yet, despite more than two centuries of biologists embarking on expeditions worldwide — collecting, discovering and naming species. Insects, being a significant proportion of global biodiversity, disproportionately suffer the challenge of too many species, not enough biologists, and not enough time. If any country can figure out their total insect diversity at the national level, we should be one of them, given our small land area. And this is where it gets exciting.

In 2019, we had an opportunity to intensely survey a plot of secondary forest adjacent to our Central Catchment Nature Reserve to take a closer look at our insect diversity. In just a month's worth of samples, we found more than 2,800 species of insects (and other terrestrial arthropods), living in an area roughly the size of our Botanic Gardens. Typically, to be able to identify that many species requires more than five years of hard work, by a team of dedicated insect specialists. We accelerated the process by using the latest DNA molecular sequencing technology to generate a small genetic sequence for each individual sampled. These were thereafter analysed collectively to determine the approximate overall diversity. Most of these species sampled are new to Science, and have not been described nor given a name. For instance, we recorded more than 800 species of Cecidomyiidae, a group of gall-forming flies, which are notoriously understudied. In the whole of Southeast Asia, only about 600 species have been described, with the true diversity estimated to be easily a hundred times more.

At the Lee Kong Chian Natural History Museum, a few fellow entomologists and I curate the entomological collection, which houses insect specimens of all shapes and sizes, kept in an assortment of glass jars or neatly pinned within wooden drawers. Our insect collection serves as the depository of specimens collected by various researchers over more than a hundred years, with each specimen serving not only as evidence of scientific research conducted or as a species record, but also as a miniscule time capsule, providing snippets of valuable information of the world it lived in. Pollen found on a historical bee specimen can be identified using a scanning electron microscope to belong to a flowering plant that is no longer found locally, providing evidence of a changing landscape. Molecular sequencing indicates more than one pygmy grasshopper species that can swim in our forests, suggesting a wetter landscape in the past. We may not know what new knowledge that technological advancements in the future will bring us, but we know it is our duty as caretakers of the insect collection to make sure that these specimens remain available for research well beyond our lifetimes.

Our role as custodians of our insect collection is not limited to keeping historical specimens for future use, as we continue to sample our natural environment, and share our discoveries with the rest of the world. Our collection has also embarked on a digital journey to improve access, by providing digitised specimen data to the Global Biodiversity Information Facility (GBIF), a global repository of biological information that is used by international scientists to address global challenges. Together with the contributions of other museums, our specimens provide scientists with a more comprehensive insight into how species are responding to environmental changes, which is useful in our preparations for the climate change happening now.

Back in our Museum's shelves, we made space for the insect specimens from our local forest insect survey, now safely stored in glass vials, muslin bags, and clip-top jars in a Russian-doll fashion. One of our present challenges is to find a way to efficiently document and describe all the as-yet undiscovered insect species found in Singapore and the surrounding region, numbering in the thousands. The latest DNA sequencing technology is certainly a helpful boost, but not the complete solution, as a formal description including a means to identify the unique species, and the anointment of a scientific name, is also needed. Species discovery has taken on an unprecedented, technologically-fueled, pace in recent years, as we hasten to get a better understanding of our biological world in the face of mounting extinctions — and leading the charge are entomologists from all over the world.

A thread-legged assassin bug nymph from our forest looking for prey at night.

The Singapore landscape has transformed tremendously in the last two centuries — by the early 1900s, more than 90% of Singapore's original forests had already been cleared, and only 0.28% of our land area now is considered as primary rainforest. An unknown number of our insects went the way of the tigers and became locally extinct. Others clung on to a precarious existence, seeking refuge in the remaining forest remnants. As agricultural lands were abandoned, and active re-greening efforts became national policy during the post-independence years, more suitable habitats returned, and a slow recovery began. We no longer have the Indo-Malayan tiger in our forests, but our woods are still teeming with tiger beetles, our parks and gardens with the blue glassy tiger butterfly, and our grasslands with the day-flying tiger moths, along with their countless six-legged relatives.

The thriving return of the insects in such great numbers in Singapore is a testament of the resilience of these little critters. It is a strong message to us that if left alone, and with the right management practices, it is possible to have a city in nature, and a very vibrant one, full of insect life as well.

Hwang Wei Song is Curator of Entomology and Senior Lecturer at the Lee Kong Chian Natural History Museum, National University of Singapore (NUS). His research work includes improving insect biodiversity knowledge through species discovery and creating better access to species information, especially for Singapore and Southeast Asia. He specialises in True Bugs (Hemiptera), particularly the predominantly predatory assassin bugs (Reduviidae). As an educator, Wei Song teaches for the NUS College and mentors students and interns from all walks of life, and anyone who is interested in insect biodiversity, museum curation and science communication.

Chapter 19

History of Sustainable Energy in Singapore and Its Future Role

Edwin T.F. Khew

In mid-1993, I was requested by the Ministry of Environment (ENV) to meet with Khoo Chin Hean, the Director of ENV, and Khoo Seow Poh, the Head of International Relationships and Policy to discuss starting a new association to represent Singapore's companies that provide environmental services and products. I was told that Environment Minister Dr Ahmad Mattar wanted this association to be started to develop environmental business and services in ASEAN. I was persuaded to lead this as I was already heading an environmental services committee in the Singapore Manufacturers' Association (SMA) and leading trade missions to some ASEAN countries. I was assured that the ENV would assist and support in setting up the association and help recruit new members. The Singapore Association for Environmental Companies (SAFECO) was launched in February 1994 by Environment Minister Mr Mah Bow Tan. Professor Tommy Koh and Dr Ahmad Mattar attended.

In the 12 years of its operations, SAFECO helped its members open markets into the ASEAN region with missions led by Minister Mah and Dr Mattar. SAFECO also facilitated and encouraged many of its members to develop their own environmental technologies and, jointly with ENV, facilitated discussions between Singapore's various Institutes of Higher Learning (IHLs) and SAFECO members. Many members were acting as agents or representatives of European or US system and technology providers, developing and opening markets for these foreign companies in Asia and Southeast Asia. We all agreed that this was not a sustainable business model, and this was the point when Singapore accelerated its focus on water and wastewater research and development (R&D) including various other environmental technologies within our IHLs.

The waste management and recycling industries left SAFECO to form the Waste Management & Recycling Association of Singapore (WMRAS) in 2001, and the water treatment industries formed the Singapore Water Association in 2004.

SAFECO was left with energy efficiency services companies (ESCOs), solar companies, environmental lab services companies and several environmental consulting and carbon trading companies which numbered around 35. After much deliberation, SAFECO's Council decided to close SAFECO and start a new association representing the clean and sustainable energy sector. We anticipated a growth of both the energy efficiency and solar energy sectors in Singapore because of climate issues, as there was as yet to be a sustainable energy association (representing energy efficiency, solar energy and other clean energy systems) in Singapore.

The Sustainable Energy Association of Singapore (SEAS) was launched in July 2006 and officiated by the Minister of Environment & Water Resources (MEWR) Dr Yaacob Ibrahim and Senior Parliamentary Secretary Dr Amy Khor as Patron of SEAS. Many companies in the solar, energy efficiency, carbon development sectors and environment consultants had remained and grown with SEAS to some 200 corporate members today. Members now include financial institutions and large corporations keen to learn and develop sustainable energy practices and solutions in their organisations and supporting organisations including e-mobility, grid providers, energy storage, etc.

SEAS developed this platform to allow its members to discuss, collaborate, and undertake viable projects locally in Singapore and regionally in Southeast Asia and the Asia-Pacific. I believe that this was the start of the Singapore Sustainable and Clean Energy story.

Energy Efficiency (EE) is an important part of sustainable energy and was the focus of the Government as early as 2008 when SEAS started its first seminar on energy efficiency for the process industries. Process industries consume more than 40% of the energy generated in Singapore. To meet Singapore's net zero targets, we had to help these industries improve on their use of energy. Most could reduce their energy consumption by at least 20–30% and needed the help of Energy Service companies or ESCOs, which made up more than 20% of SEAS members when we started. SEAS also ran the first Energy Efficiency Investment Forum to encourage investments in EE and demonstrate the returns industries can derive from investing in improving their efficiency in energy consumption.

Unfortunately, energy was still relatively cheap in the early 2000s, so except for large industries, many of the small and medium-sized enterprises (SMEs) did not have strong incentives to invest in new and more efficient machines and equipment. This prompted the government to start the SME Energy Efficiency Initiative (SMEE) in 2013 which was developed by SPRING (Standards, Productivity and Innovation Board) and managed by SEAS. This programme ran for four years and with proper education through seminars and workshops run by SEAS and the training of energy managers and engineers through the Singapore Certified Energy Management (SCEM) programme, many SMEs did take advantage of the SMEE grant. SEAS continues to run the SCEM courses, and because of the high cost of energy over the last few years, these classes are fully subscribed.

The solar initiative in Singapore started with the launch of the Solar Energy Research Institute of Singapore (SERIS) in April 2008, supported by the National University of Singapore (NUS), the National Research Foundation Singapore (NRF), the Singapore Economic Development Board (EDB) and the Energy Market Authority (EMA). Their representatives served on the supervisory board of SERIS. At its launch, the Minister for Trade and Industry, Mr S. Iswaran, said, "…the Government has identified the Clean Energy industry, with emphasis on solar, as a key growth area for Singapore. As a sign of our commitment, the government has allocated a total of S$350 million of public funding, including S$170 million from the National Research Foundation, to develop R&D capabilities and manpower for this sector." I continue to serve on the SERIS Supervisory Board since its inception in 2008 till today.

SERIS conducts research, development, deployment, testing and consulting on solar energy technologies and their integration into urban infrastructures, buildings, and power systems. SERIS is globally active (one of the top 3 Solar Research Centers globally), focussing on technologies and services for tropical regions (e.g., using lighter and thinner glass solar modules as these modules are not required to withstand the weight of snow), for Singapore and Southeast Asia. This serves the nation's need for solar adoption and industry development, and supports our government's pledge to reduce the nation's carbon emissions.

To accelerate the deployment of solar photovoltaic (PV) systems in Singapore, EDB and the Housing and Development Board (HDB) launched the SolarNova programme in 2014 as a Whole-of-Government effort to help Singapore adopt solar energy. To date, HDB has launched its seventh SolarNova tender and awarded the tender in October 2022, generating a total of 380MWp from HDB estates since the launch of SolarNova — HDB is well on the way to meet its projected target of 540MWp by 2030.

To expand its horizons and revenue streams, SEAS developed training programmes for energy efficiency, solar installation proficiency and maintenance as well as:

(1) An annual conference and exhibition, the Asia Clean Energy Summit (ACES), to be Asia's leading event on clean energy technologies, policy and finance; supported by leading Government agencies, research institutions, and industries in Singapore and abroad.
(2) The first Sustainable Energy Center of Excellence (SECOE) with the Asian Development Bank (ADB), to train and build capacity for senior energy officials within ADB's many developing country members.
(3) An MOU between JTC and SEAS to develop sustainable energy solutions throughout JTC's industrial estates. This opens opportunities for our members to bid for projects and sell their solutions to industrial lessees under JTC.
(4) Joint programmes between the Ministry of Foreign Affairs (MFA), the German Agency for International cooperation (GIZ) and US State Department to train third countries in energy management and financing. These programmes were again curated by SEAS members and various Singapore government agencies, and allowed many SEAS members to

gain access to government contacts in countries that they were assigned to train.

(5) Training programmes to cross-train, upskill and upgrade professionals, managers, engineers, and technicians (PMETs) for jobs in the sustainability energy sector. SEAS promoted this Sustainable Energy Development Programme with the National Trades Union Congress (NTUC) as SEAS is a U Associate (UA) member of NTUC. This was done during the pandemic to open job opportunities for many who lost their jobs in other sectors.

To further promote the sustainable energy sector and its presence in Singapore and the ASEAN region, SEAS and its members have written a number of white papers, including "Renewable Energy-Singapore", "Accelerating Singapore's Decarbonization", and "Creating a Level Playing Field for Electric Vehicles in Singapore". These papers have been developed by SEAS members with the support of various government agencies and have been quoted by members of Parliament in their various deliberations. These papers can be found on the SEAS website www.seas.org.sg.

SEAS membership has also been expanded to include companies in the business of processing/manufacturing and/or supplying micro and smart grids, renewable fuels such as hydrogen, ammonia, and sustainable aviation fuels (SAF), battery energy storage systems (BESS), carbon capture, utilisation, storage (CCUS) systems, nuclear power generators, wind turbines and systems, and other clean energy systems. This will allow SEAS to truly represent and be the voice of the sustainable energy sector in Singapore and provide these clean energy technologies and solutions not only for Singapore but also for the whole Asian/ASEAN region.

Future Focus for the Sustainable Energy Sector

To ensure that Singapore achieves its net zero targets by 2050, we must seriously consider importing clean or renewable energy from our neighbouring countries as they have land and natural resources like wind, hydro, and geothermal that we do not have in Singapore. The next phase for developing Singapore's renewable/clean energy capacity and supply to replace our current supply of electricity from natural gas is to develop generating capacity of renewable energy (RE) from within the ASEAN countries. Both SEAS members and EMA are exploring such projects in Indonesia, Peninsular Malaysia and even as far as away as Laos, Cambodia, Sarawak and Sabah, and to look at importing renewable energy via the ASEAN Grid or via subsea cables to Singapore. Indeed, I am in the midst of negotiating with the Indonesian Government on behalf of a number of SEAS solar members who have formed consortiums to bid for and develop a number of large solar projects on Batam and Riau to export RE to Singapore. This process is complex and challenging as it involves various government authorities that require licences and approvals from the Navy and Maritime Authority in Indonesia, as the RE needs to be exported through subsea cables to Singapore. Some of this energy will be used locally by industries in Batam and Riau, such as Data Centers and manufacturing industries that want their products to be sustainable within a supply chain that they are part of globally. The Consortia of SEAS members must also commit to TKDN (Tingkat Kemampuan Dalam Negri) or local content requirement which requires solar modules, energy storage batteries, and various components in a PV solar generating system, to be manufactured and supplied from Indonesia. What is also requested by the Indonesian government is that Singapore considers transferring knowledge through the setting up of a solar R&D institute in Indonesia.

I am glad to report that during the writing of this chapter, on 16 March 2023, at the annual Leaders Retreat between the Indonesian President Jokowi and Singapore's Prime Minister Lee Hsien Loong, Indonesian Coordinating Minister for Maritime Affairs and Investments, Pak Luhut, signed an MOU with Senior Minister Teo Chee Hean on the development and export of renewable energy from Indonesia to Singapore. This concluded more than six months of discussions and negotiations that I led, with a small team of the SEAS Solar Consortia supported by EMA. (See picture below) - https://www.theedgesingapore.com/news/sustainability/singapore-indonesia-sign-mou-develop-renewable-energy-domestic-use-and-export

Photo credit: Ministry of Communications and Information

On the import of RE, Singapore has imported 100 MW of hydropower from Laos through the ASEAN grid which will bring green electrons through the grids of Thailand and Malaysia into Singapore. This was done by Keppel Infrastructure (a SEAS member) as a pathfinder test-bed using the ASEAN grid. Many more of such projects will be developed including the Indonesian projects.

Singapore will continue to play a major role in the supply of sustainable/clean energy technologies, and fund and develop renewable energy systems in countries within ASEAN. It will also provide the necessary skills, training, and engineering designs to build, operate and maintain the various RE systems and be the hub to digitally monitor and control all of such RE systems. SEAS, SERIS, EMA and the various IHLs will also play a major role in supporting, promoting, and showcasing the best sustainable energy technologies in the world and their interconnections, to allow a seamless generation and distribution of clean renewable energy throughout ASEAN, so that by 2050 and beyond, all of ASEAN will hopefully operate on clean and sustainable energy.

Er Edwin T.F. Khew, PBM, is a former Nominated Member of Parliament (NMP), Singapore, and currently the Chairman of the Sustainable Energy Association of Singapore (SEAS), President of the Plastics Recycling Association, Singapore (PRAS), Emeritus President of the Institution of Engineers, Singapore (IES), and a Supervisory Board Member of Solar Energy Research Institute of Singapore (SERIS). He has an Executive MBA from the National University of Singapore, a Bachelor's in Chemical Engineering from the University of Queensland, Australia, and is Honorary Fellow and a Chartered Engineer of the Institution of Engineers, Singapore.

Chapter 20

Butterflies of Singapore

Khew Sin Khoon

It was a hot and balmy afternoon when I got home after school. As I changed out of my school uniform, I looked out the window and saw a large black-and-yellow butterfly fluttering around the rambutan tree in the garden. With great excitement, I grabbed my butterfly net, rushed out to the garden and immediately chased after it, hoping to capture it and add it to my modest collection. I managed to net it — it was a Golden Birdwing (*Troides aeacus thomsonii*) and something new for my collection. That encounter — which occurred almost five decades ago in my family home in Malaysia — seems ages ago, but its memory remains etched in my mind as though it happened just yesterday.

I still experience those same feelings of excitement, delight and awe in encountering a new butterfly species today, although it is now through the preview screen of my digital camera rather than a net. The beauty of Mother Nature's amazing creations never fails to evoke a sense of admiration and wonder — and for me, these flying jewels have always created feelings of joy and happiness.

Butterflies have always been a source of fascination and adventure for me. My interest in them was nurtured by my supportive teachers and family, and became more than a fleeting hobby that continued into my adult life. My early years in Singapore were spent on my academic and work pursuits and after a 10-year hiatus from butterflies, I was invited by a close friend to participate in a survey for the National Parks Board (NParks) in the mid-1990s. These surveys reignited my passion for butterflies and I started on a journey of documenting, researching and sharing information about them with the nature community in Singapore.

Singapore has the benefit of being very conducive for biodiversity research, in that nature is very accessible — a 30-minute drive will bring you from any part of the city to the nature-rich forest reserves. Singapore is also relatively safe and not easy to get lost in, with its forests highly navigable, unlike that of its neighbouring countries.

Over the past 30 years, I have gone on numerous weekend outings to various green areas in parks, gardens, nature reserves and offshore islands, observing and learning about butterflies in our little city state. It has been an enriching knowledge-acquiring process, and I have been collecting data and new information and systematically documenting them in my personal blog since 2007. Today, the blog is a repository of information of over a thousand articles about butterflies, ranging from taxonomy to photography and butterfly breeding, to the best butterfly-watching locations in Singapore.

Besides the blog and social media groups, I had the personal satisfaction of writing two editions of *A Field Guide to the Butterflies of Singapore* in 2010 and 2015, and co-authoring another book,

Caterpillars of Singapore's Butterflies, as my contribution to the growing knowledge of butterflies in Singapore.

Along my butterfly conservation journey, I was joined by like-minded individuals who provided valuable insights, without which my knowledge of butterflies in Singapore would not be as comprehensive.

The group of butterfly enthusiasts is growing, and I am particularly encouraged by many young Singaporeans taking an interest in learning about butterflies and participating in butterfly conservation efforts.

Within the community of butterfly watchers, there is always an excited buzz when a new species that has not been previously recorded is spotted — irrespective of whether they are native or exotic. Butterflies do not respect geographical borders and political boundaries like humans do. They are free to come and go as they like. What matters most to us is that today, over 350 butterfly species have made Singapore their home — a testament to our nature-friendly island nation. This diversity is remarkable for a highly developed island of only about 720 square kilometres!

Butterflies are good indicators of the state of environment in Singapore: in particular, the health of its green habitats and the diversity of plants that support their life cycles. Over the years, as Singapore evolved from a Garden City to a City in Nature, it has witnessed the creation of habitats that are conducive to butterflies in many surprising settings — from hospitals to golf courses and park connectors to urban gardens. That it is possible for urban development to co-exist with nature, specifically butterflies, has been one of the outcomes of our research and partnership with

NParks in the judicious cultivation of butterfly nectaring and host plants in nature areas.

I founded a butterfly-specialist group called ButterflyCircle in 2004 and encouraged members of the group to share their passion with the nature community through their photographs, group outings and educational talks. Our works have appeared in exhibitions, as informative signages at parks and gardens, online articles and publications. All these have contributed to the growing body of knowledge about butterflies in the quest for their appreciation and conservation for future generations to enjoy.

As a practising architect in Singapore, I always keep a look out for chances to introduce landscaping opportunities that have the potential of supporting butterfly biodiversity in the urban built environment into my projects. These could make a difference in

A Common Tree Nymph (*Idea stolli logani*) soaring effortlessly and gliding amongst the treetops in Singapore's forested nature reserves.

furthering Singapore's vision of being a City in Nature, where all creatures big and small can live in peace and harmony with humans.

Khew Sin Khoon is the Group Chief Executive Officer of CPG Corporation, a multinational built-environment consultancy firm. His passion for butterflies started more than five decades ago, when he collected butterflies in his home garden in Malaysia. He holds Honorary Research appointments with NParks' National Biodiversity Centre and the Lee Kong Chian Natural History Museum. An architect by training, he believes that nature and development can co-exist in harmony. In 2004, he founded "ButterflyCircle", an online community of butterfly enthusiasts and photographers. He is the author of *A Field Guide to the Butterflies of Singapore, 2010 & 2015.*

Chapter 21

A Social Compact in Co-creating a City in Nature

Joseph K H Koh

I am frequently asked how we can protect the more-than-900 species of spiders in Singapore. My answer is simple: preserve and enhance the ecological resilience of their habitats. But is this proposition realistic in the second most densely populated country in the world? Given our seemingly over-riding needs such as affordable housing and an efficient transport infrastructure, will conservation pale into insignificance in the ranking of government priorities?

The Social Compact

I believe it is still possible to conserve our remaining biodiversity — provided the government and civil society converge to forge a social compact in co-creating a City in Nature. The proposed *modus vivendi* can be built upon six approaches:

1. *Recognise the intrinsic value of conserving our natural ecosystems*

We do not need to compute an economic value of the "ecological services" (e.g., carbon sequestration) that our natural habitats can offer. Our natural heritage is priceless, period. A City in Nature distinguishes Singapore as one of the most biodiverse and liveable city-states in the world. Our shared aspiration to remain connected with nature is becoming another icon of our national identity. Conserving our biodiversity for the next generation must therefore be woven into Singapore's national development matrix.

2. *Agree that the four gazetted nature reserves shall not be expropriated, even marginally, for development*

These sites should be respected as the last refugia of our indigenous flora and fauna, to be safeguarded legally in perpetuity because such integral habitats are irreplaceable. The ecological resilience of these biodiversity hotspots should continue to be bolstered with a proactive effort to add more buffers and corridors between them.

3. *Steward our remaining woodlands sensitively and scrupulously*

Ideally, the government should halt further clearing of newly regenerated forests on fallowed land. These places provide new homes for wildlife, even if the new occupants may be common or alien species. However, given Singapore's acute physical constraints, there will be pressures to develop some forested areas outside our nature reserves. Even so, these areas should still remain off-limits to development if they are the only sanctuaries of critically endangered species, such as our endemic freshwater crabs, which may not survive any attempt to relocate them. All other development proposals must still be scrutinised rigorously, with a science-based approach in assessing the ecological values of the sites, and after an engagement process with the nature community.

4. *Engage constructively, in the spirit of mutual respect*

Past experience has taught us that it will be self-defeating if a government agency invokes "national needs" and turns to the nature groups only to rubber-stamp what is already a *fait accompli*. It will also be counter-productive if the nature activists approach the engagement with a single-minded determination to oppose development plans of *any* forested area. If we are driven by a belligerent "all-or-nothing" mindset, it can only blind us to viable options to conserve the more threatened species.

The successful lobbying by nature advocates to protect Sungei Buloh and Chek Jawa underlines a paradoxical lesson: We can maximise our conservation outcomes if we minimise our self-righteous outrage. Paradoxically too, we can enlarge our political space to preserve our natural capital if we narrow our focus to a constructive dialogue, with in-depth technical discussion exploring multiple options, each with its own set of comprehensive measures to pre-empt or alleviate the potential ecological damage under the respective scenario — as nature group representatives have done during their 2013–2019 engagement with the government over the Cross Island Line (CRL).

5. *Communicate early and transparently*

Transparency means we should make Environmental Impact Assessments (EIA) mandatory for all development projects in sites within or near wooded areas; we should also make public access to EIA less onerous, but with redacting to accommodate security concerns if necessary.

Timely communication is essential, for it is only human to overreact to surprises, with mutually destructive outcomes. In hindsight, I wonder if the backlash against Lornie Highway over Bukit Brown could have been dampened if the conservation advocates were told much earlier that the cheapest way to ease congestion along the old Lornie Road was to widen it with the more unpalatable outcome of encroaching into a relatively more pristine forest fringing MacRitchie Reservoir.

Consultation takes time, and it is therefore useful to provide a longer runway to clarify issues and do the necessary groundwork (e.g., biodiversity baseline surveys). More importantly, early consultation, even during the periodic reviews of the Master Plan, often leads to more fruitful and strategic measures to safeguard our wilderness, thus rendering "retrofit" mitigation measures unnecessary.

6. *Invest in longer-term habitat conservation for future generations*

It is understandable that government agencies will want to conserve taxpayer money by opting for the cheapest tender with the shortest delivery time. However, we must rethink the cost-benefit paradigm to safeguard our natural assets, and invest more time and resources so that future generations will not be irreversibly deprived of their connections with nature.

Reasons for Optimism

I am optimistic that we can achieve such a social compact because the mindsets among policy makers and nature lovers have become increasingly aligned, mediated by evidence-based assessments with the aid of new scientific tools.

Mindset of policy makers

We can see a growing political resolve within the government to retain, restore, and enhance our biodiversity and ecosystems. Even in the early days when the government was less preoccupied with conservation, it vetoed a PUB proposal to build a golf course at Lower Peirce Reservoir (1991). Since then, many ecologically sensitive sites that were initially designated for development have been protected. They include Chek Jawa, Sungei Buloh, Khatib Bongsu, the Mandai mudflat, and woodlands around Dairy Farm, Rifle Range, and Upper Thomson Road.

The government has diverted sizeable sums from the public coffers to invest in the research and development of nature-based solutions, restore lost habitats (mangroves at Semakau), reconnect biodiversity cores (Eco-Link@BKE), and avert the destruction of natural creeks (elevated Lornie Highway). In response to concerns voiced by nature advocates over the "unknown unknowns" in our nightmare scenarios *vis-à-vis* the CRL, the government agreed to excavate a more costly but deeper tunnel through granite bedrock 70 metres below the MacRitchie forest; it also agreed to relocate worksites away from areas (already outside the nature reserves) frequented by the Raffles' banded langurs.

We have also seen repeated instances of flexibility and creativity in how government officers have responded to our concerns. For instance, addressing our apprehensions about soil investigation during phase 1 of the CRL EIA project, potentially the gravest threat to the MacRitchie forest, officials came out independently with an ecologically more acceptable solution which circumvented the horrifying need for dragging heavy machinery through the forest to drill 72 bore holes for soil samples.

Mindset of the nature community

Most local conservation advocates prefer to work hand-in-hand with government agencies to shape outcomes that will best preserve our natural heritage. Our common ground is rooted in science and a sense of proportion, e.g., accepting that an eagle with a nest on an *Albizia* tree can still roost elsewhere if unavoidably the tree has to be felled for development.

Our nature activists in Singapore are not out to politicise nature. We should not doubt the benign intentions of those who might have resorted to pressure group tactics out of sheer exasperation. Neither should we prejudge the integrity of our government interlocutors. Our experience in engagement sessions so far has demonstrated that agreeing to disagree can still end up safeguarding our threatened species and widening the safety net for other wildlife.

New scientific tools and a strengthened EIA framework

The discourse on nature conservation in Singapore is increasingly underpinned by sound evidence and new scientific know-how, such as ecological profiling and modelling tools to identify wildlife corridors. Habitat protection is intimately factored into Singapore's holistic Species Recovery Programmes. With ongoing efforts to strengthen the EIA framework, all parties can now examine deforestation issues more objectively, with a more robust and less arbitrary matrix of impact magnitude and significance.

Conclusion

A social compact as proposed here will allow us to secure our biodiversity cores, and facilitate a constructive dialogue if forested areas outside the cores are planned for development. Compromises do not mean capitulation, but escape routes from stark choices, with new add-ons to minimise potential ecological damage. Where a land use issue cannot be settled through such engagement, the

A relatively rare Eight-spotted Crab Spider (*Platythomisus octomaculatus*, female) photographed at Sungei Buloh Wetland Reserve in Singapore.

political leadership will ultimately have to decide based on their calculations for the greater good of Singapore, and be held accountable by the people, including future generations. However, civil society can help to finesse their decisions with calibrated recommendations crystallised from the engagement process. We can credibly assert the rationale behind our preferred option, but if the political leadership decides to strike a different balance based on other technical or socio-economic considerations (e.g., backlash against land acquisition), the full suite of mitigation measures embedded in our fall-back positions can still kick in to cushion the environmental repercussion of their final decision.

Joseph K H Koh is a retired ambassador, an amateur spider scientist, and a passionate conservationist. He was President of the Asian Society of Arachnology (2015–2017), and Chairman of WWF

Singapore (2017–2020). He has been Chairman of the Friends of Bukit Timah Forest (FOBTF) since 2016. Joseph received the prestigious President's Award for the Environment in 2021. Joseph was intimately involved in the dialogue between nature groups and the Land Transport Authority (LTA) over the Cross Island Line (2013–2019). The views expressed in this essay do not necessarily represent those of the FOBTF and WWF Singapore.

Chapter 22

The Importance of Environmental Law

Koh Kheng Lian

We need to make peace with nature. Without nature's help, we cannot thrive or even survive on this planet Earth. It's time to re-evaluate and reset our relationship with nature.

UN Secretary-General António Guterres
27 March 2021
Earth Hour (Climate and Environment)

Introduction

Friedensreich Hundertwasser (1928–1999), Austria's *avant-garde* visual artist and architect, and an environmentalist, is well-known for his love for nature which he fused into his art.

The importance of environmental law within the framework of "Peace with Nature" cannot be gainsaid and is embedded in sustainable development. Mankind and nature should co-exist in harmony. The *New Oxford Dictionary* describes nature as "the phenomena of the physical world collectively, including plants, animals, the landscape, and other features and products of the earth, as opposed to humans or human creations."

Environmental lawyers, legislators, managers and other stakeholders should take inspiration from Hundertwasser's passion not only in the development but also the implementation of environmental law. While there are many international, regional and national laws on nature, there is a great disconnect in their implementation. What is lacking maybe is the emotional appreciation of nature. So, despite voices telling us that we need to live in Peace with Nature, in reality, particularly in an industrial or newly-emerging industrial society, economic development often takes precedence over greenery. The philosophy seems to be that until one's stomach is full, nature can wait. It has been over 50 years since the development of modern environmental law, from the 1972 Stockholm Declaration on Environment and Development (Stockholm) to the 2022 UN Secretary-General António Guterres' speech, prompted by climate change and our relationship with nature. His call that "it is time to re-evaluate and reset our relationship with nature" can trigger effective implementation.

In considering the importance of environmental law it cannot be confined to Singapore as the environment is borderless and the question of Peace with Nature is universal. Moreover, the approach to environmental issues is: think globally, act locally — it makes for a cohesive system which might otherwise be fragmented.

Importance of Environmental Law Relating to Peace with Nature

The role of law is to order the conduct of society by providing rules and solutions.

The importance of environmental law has never been clearer as it not only conserves, protects and safeguards nature to avert environmental emergencies but also has transformative power in providing "nature-based solutions" and much else besides. Since Stockholm, there has been an implosion of hard and soft laws, i.e., legally-binding multilateral environmental agreements (MEAs) including court decisions, and non-legally binding laws such as declarations, guidelines, resolutions, and agenda which are equally important as they set standards and may progressively evolve into hard laws.

The tension between environment and development calls for resolution. This was contained in the concept of sustainable development in the Brundtland Report of the World Commission on Environment and Development, 1987: "Development that meets the needs of the present without compromising the ability of future generations to meet their own needs."

Among the numerous MEAs, court decisions and soft laws, there are those that deal directly with nature, and others which though not directly are intrinsically linked, such as climate change and pollution.

A brief survey is given on the main hard and soft laws on nature conservation and protection emanating from the United Nations, the International Union for the Conservation of Nature and Natural Resources (IUCN), the Association of Southeast Asian Nations (ASEAN) and Singapore.

The first modern nature conservation instrument is the 1982 World Charter for Nature in UN GA Resolution A/RES/37/7 which recognised that the maintenance of peace depends on living in harmony with nature upon which the survival of humankind depends for its natural resources, if not its intrinsic aesthetic value. The Charter sets out five principles to guide every citizen on the conservation of nature.

Equally important is the 1995 Draft International Covenant on Environment and Development (5th edition 2017) — response to the call from IUCN in cooperation with the International Council of Environmental Law (ICEL) and support of the 1992 United Nations Environment Programme (UNEP). It serves as an authoritative checklist on sustainable development including monitoring of species and ecosystems and targets at protecting and restoring nature.

Other instruments include the 1992 Convention on Biological Diversity (CBD) together with its update, the Kunming-Montreal Global Biodiversity Framework, 2022. The CBD aims, *inter alia,* at reducing biodiversity loss, and the Framework has four overarching global goals to be achieved by 2030. On 4 March 2023 the gap left by UNCLOS (United Nations Convention on the Law of the Sea, 1982) was filled by a new agreement on the Marine Biological Diversity of Areas Beyond National Jurisdiction (BBNJ) which deals with the conservation and sustainable use of marine biodiversity.

Other biodiversity instruments include the Convention on Migratory Species (Bonn Convention) which protects migratory global species of wild animals and birds and their range habitats; the Ramsar Convention on Wetlands of International Importance Especially on Water Fowl Habitats covers a range of ecosystem services that contribute to the well-being of flora and fauna; the Convention on the International Trade in Endangered Species of Wild Fauna and Flora (CITES) regulates trade in endangered species.

Among the "soft laws" are the 1992 Agenda 21 updated to 2030 which is a blueprint for action identifying elements for implementation of environmental law. It is linked to the 2015 Sustainable Development Goals (SDGs), a shared vision for peace and prosperity; the Earth Charter 2000 which lays down the foundation for a peaceful global sustainable development; and the 2000 UN Forest Forum which addresses issues of forest management.

Singapore has ratified the CBD, CITES, and adopted Agenda 21 and the Earth Charter as reflected in, for example, the Singapore National Biodiversity Strategy Action Plan 2019, and the Endangered Species (Import and Export) Act. Other complementary laws include the Wildlife Act (formerly called the Wild Animals and Birds Act) which protects, preserves, and manages wildlife.

Singapore has played an important role in the formulation of numerous ASEAN environmental instruments such as the ASEAN Agreement on the Conservation of Nature and Natural Resources; ASEAN Declaration on Heritage Parks and Reserves (the ASEAN Heritage Parks include Singapore's Bukit Timah Nature Reserve and Sungei Buloh Wetlands Reserve); ASEAN Regional Action Plan for Heritage Parks and Protected Areas; ASEAN Statement on CITES; ASEAN Regional Plan on Trade in Wild Fauna and Flora, 2005–2010; and the ASEAN Statement on Launching of the ASEAN Wildlife Law Enforcement Network (ASEAN-WEN) in 2005.

Implementation of Environmental Laws

Without implementation, laws are dead. When effectively implemented they can be powerful tools for regulation and transformation.

Capacity-building

Environmental education is key to understanding the values of nature and its sustainable use and management of natural resources.

Agenda 21 recognised this and called upon academic and other institutions to build capacity in environmental law.

Pursuant to this, the Asia-Pacific Centre for Environmental Law (APCEL) was launched in 1996 by the Faculty of Law of the National University of Singapore, IUCN Commission on Environmental Law (IUCN-CEL) and in collaboration with UNEP. One of its objectives is to serve as a training centre in environmental law. Other such centres in the region are in China, India, Indonesia, Pakistan, and the Philippines.

ICEL Music and Culture for the Environment (IMCE)

The role of culture (including music) has in recent years been recognised by the United Nations as an enabler of sustainable development to achieve SDGs. The UNESCO Universal Declaration on Cultural Diversity, 2001 defines "culture" as "the set of distinctive, spiritual, material, intellectual and emotional features of society… and encompass ways of living together...including value systems."

In its cross-cutting trajectory, it can promote the implementation of environmental law and in particular, living in peace with nature. With this aim in view, IMCE was established in 2021. At the *International Symposium on Peace with Nature: Laws for Ecological Resilience,* held from 2–3 September 2021 in Marseille, the "World Premiere Performance — Music Caring for the Earth" was launched. It was moderated by Prof N.A. Robinson, ICEL Executive Governor with Prof Koh Kheng Lian, a member of ICEL Board of Governors, as narrator of "Voice of the Sea" — on whales and whaling, composed and played by Maestro Amos Chiya, the ICEL Representative of IMCE, a conductor, composer and pianist. His other pieces are "Monochrome Burning" on deforestation, and "Lost

Launch of Music Caring for the Earth. (Photo credit: Koh Kheng Lian and Amos Chiya)

Migration" on degraded habitats of migratory birds. Pursuant to UNGA Resolution A/RES/74/224, an "Interactive Dialogue on Harmony with Nature" was held on 22 April 2020, commemorating International Mother Earth Day — evidently, there is great potential for culture and music to bind communities and contribute to environmental sustainability.

Conclusion

The laws under review proceed on nature as a commodity — focussed on its natural resources or other crucial roles for the survival of mankind, rather than its intrinsic value, though occasionally the latter has been recognised on religious or cultural grounds. Examples are the sacred Ganges River in India and Bolivia's Universal Declaration on Rights of Mother Earth. Prof Tarini Mehta, in "Reframing the law to recognize nature's values" (newshub.360info.org, 6 January, 2023) states this "eco-centric approach" carries the "Rights of Nature in achieving sustainable development." Whether the frontiers of law should be pushed to conserve its intrinsic value is the subject for further research.

Law plays a crucial role across many aspects of nature which stands at a crossroads with humanity and helps to safeguard and protect biodiversity and ecosystems. It is a cog in a multidisciplinary wheel that can transform the world to achieve the aims of Agenda 2030 and sustainable development. Mankind must rekindle its intrinsic relationship with nature so as to achieve Peace with Nature.

Postscript

Interactive Dialogue of the United Nations Assembly to Commemorate International Mother Earth Day, 24 April 2023: Concept Note

The *Concept Note* reiterates that humanity is embedded in Nature. Hence, the importance of living in harmony and peace with nature — a constant recent theme of UNGA to achieve sustainable development through economic, social and environmental balance. The *Concept Note* also aligns with the "Kunming-Montreal Framework" which, *inter alia*, recognises the rights of Nature and

Mother Earth. A peep into the future to the poser in the "Conclusion" of my essay, above: whither the future development of the "Rights of Nature" in contradistinction to the "commodification" of Nature. The *Concept Note* endorses and strengthens the "Kunming-Montreal Framework" which supports value systems of countries that recognise the "rights of Nature and rights of Mother Earth, as being an integral part of successful implementation…and Mother Earth-centered actions, and non-commodification of her environmental functions."

Dr Koh Kheng Lian, Emeritus Prof. Faculty of Law, NUS, was formerly Director of APCEL, and IUCN-CEL Regional Vice-Chair for South and East Asia. Other appointments include — Consultant, ADB/IUCN-CEL/NUS *Capacity Building in Environmental Legal Education*; and Director, Ministry of Foreign Affairs *Capacity Building on Urban Environment*. She served as a legal officer in the Secretariat of UNCITRAL, 1980–1986, Vienna. An awardee of the Elizabeth Haub Prize in Environmental Law 2013, the Singapore Women's Hall of Fame 2014, and the Environmental Lawyer of the Year (ASEAN) 2020, her publications including conference papers numbering over 200. She currently serves on the Board of Governors of ICEL.

Chapter 23

Nature-based Solutions to Climate Change

Koh Lian Pin

During his National Day Rally speech on 18 August 2019, Prime Minister Lee Hsien Loong spoke of the need to take seriously the impacts of climate change.

The PM emphasised the government's commitment to safeguard Singapore against this existential threat through strategic investments in the research, development and implementation of climate actions.

While the Prime Minister's speech and the public discussions that followed have largely focussed on human-engineered solutions, such as the construction of barrages and seawalls for flood regulation and coastal protection, there is a growing scientific consensus that Nature itself may be harnessed to help stabilise global warming.

Indeed, under the Singapore Green Plan 2030, which was announced on Budget Day 2021, there is a strong emphasis on expanding the network of green spaces in Singapore, including nature parks and park connectors, as well as skyrise greenery. These green spaces can help to provide shade, cool the environment, improve air quality, beautify our city, and of course, sequester and store carbon.

During the 27th Conference of Parties of the United Nations Framework Convention on Climate Change (UNFCCC), which was held in November 2022 in Sharm-El-Sheik, Egypt, there was a growing voice to include nature-based solutions in global society's discourse on climate policies and actions. In fact, it is critical to consider climate change and biodiversity to be intertwined in terms of being both the biggest threats to humanity and integral parts of their solutions.

Climate Change Impacts

The Paris Climate Agreement — to which all members of both the Association of Southeast Asian Nations (ASEAN) and Asia-Pacific Economic Cooperation (APEC) are signatories — commits countries to hold global warming to below 2°C above pre-industrial levels, and to pursue efforts to limit warming to 1.5°C. According to the Intergovernmental Panel on Climate Change, this 0.5°C difference in the level of global warming can significantly increase the risk of droughts, floods, extreme weather and poverty for hundreds of millions of people globally.

The direct impacts of climate change for Singapore, including temperature increases, sea-level rise and major flooding events, will likely worsen in the future if global warming continues.

Additionally, given that Singapore's economy and the well-being of its people are inextricably tied to that of the wider Asia-Pacific region, our science and policy considerations on climate change must necessarily also take on a regional perspective to anticipate any potential indirect impacts.

For example, climate change may reduce the productivity of agriculture, aquaculture and fisheries across Asia-Pacific. As a country that imports more than 90% of its food, Singapore is highly vulnerable to climate-related impacts on regional food production and supply, especially if producer countries reduce exports to ensure their own food security.

Understanding the likelihood of climate change impacts on natural and human systems in the Asia-Pacific region is of critical importance for clarifying risks and developing strategies to future-proof Singapore against environmental, social and economic shocks.

Nature as Ally

Achieving the ambitious targets of the Paris Climate Agreement requires countries to not only undergo the rapid decarbonisation of their energy sector, but also implement changes to policy and practices in agriculture, forestry and other land use activities.

In a recent study, an international group of scientists reported that Nature can provide 37% of the necessary climate mitigation between now and 2030 for a greater than 66% likelihood of achieving the 2°C target of the Paris Climate Agreement.

These so-called "nature-based climate solutions" include the conservation, restoration and improved management of forests, wetlands and agricultural lands to increase carbon sequestration, reduce CO_2 emissions, and enhance climate resilience. These land management strategies can save up to 11 billion tonnes of CO_2 per year — equivalent to the combined emissions of the United States and European Union.

Furthermore, protecting and ensuring the health of natural ecosystems also provide co-benefits that are important for conserving biodiversity, providing clean air and water, safeguarding food security and sustaining livelihoods. A recent research led by the

Centre for Nature-based Climate Solutions at the National University of Singapore (NUS) shows that within Southeast Asia, 58% of forests threatened by loss could be protected as financially viable carbon projects, which would avoid 835 million tonnes of CO_2 emissions per year from deforestation, support dietary needs for an equivalent of 323,739 people annually from pollinator-dependent agriculture, retain 78% of the volume of nitrogen pollutants in watersheds yearly and safeguard 25 million hectares of Key Biodiversity Areas.

In the same way that low-emissions technologies and improvements in energy efficiency are worthwhile investments regardless of future climates, nature-based climate solutions are "no regrets" actions that both contribute to addressing climate change impacts and provide multiple benefits to society, including clean air and water, food security and livelihood opportunities.

The idea of nature-based climate solutions is gaining traction among international stakeholders across governmental, non-governmental and business sectors, including the United Nations Environment Programme (UNEP), the International Union for Conservation of Nature (IUCN), and the World Business Council on Sustainable Development (WBCSD), all of which have recently incorporated nature-based solutions in their institutional goals, strategies or initiatives.

Knowledge Gaps

There are, however, considerable research and research-implementation gaps that need to be addressed to identify and realise the promise of nature-based climate solutions for the Asia-Pacific region.

For example, the potential and limits of nature-based climate solutions for increasing carbon sequestration and reducing CO_2 emissions at the regional level have yet to be studied. Furthermore, the value of natural ecosystems as "green infrastructure" for enhancing climate resilience through processes such as biodiversity conservation, coastal protection and flood regulation remains unclear. Quantifying the cost effectiveness and viability of nature-based climate solutions for Singapore and the Asia-Pacific region would help inform climate and land use policies for achieving climate mitigation and adaptation goals.

Indeed, the climate mitigation potential and co-benefits of nature-based climate solutions can present exciting new opportunities for the public and private sectors to meet their climate goals, invest in carbon finance, and contribute to addressing the impacts of climate change. The transacted volume of nature-based carbon credits in the voluntary carbon market grew by over 250% between 2016 and 2018, from 14 million tonnes to 51 million tonnes of carbon dioxide equivalent.

Research led by the NUS Centre for Nature-based Climate Solutions shows that at carbon market prices of approximately US$6 per tonne, the protection of tropical forests can generate investible carbon amounting to 1.7 billion tonnes of carbon dioxide equivalent per annum globally. The researchers further show that financially viable carbon projects could generate return-on-investment amounting to US$42.1 billion per annum in net present value.

Another key consideration is that nature-based climate solutions may not always align with other interests and priorities of society — climate policies favouring one set of actions can create barriers for others.

Notably, the need of some rural communities to maintain their traditional livelihoods or expand their agricultural lands may compete with climate strategies that protect or restore forests for carbon storage and sequestration. Identifying these potential opportunity costs and trade-offs would be critical for ensuring the effective, collaborative and equitable implementation of climate solutions across the Asia-Pacific region.

For example, reforestation has recently been identified as a promising nature-based climate solution. Yet, there are context-dependent biophysical, financial, land-use and operational constraints to reforestation that demand careful consideration. Research from the NUS Centre for Nature-based Climate Solutions investigated the effects of such constraints in Southeast Asia — a region noted for its significant reforestation potential. They show that 121 million hectares of presently degraded lands in Southeast Asia are biophysically suitable for reforestation, which would contribute to climate mitigation at a rate of 3.43 billion tonnes of carbon dioxide equivalent per annum through 2030. However, only a fraction of that mitigation potential may be achievable (0.3–6.4%), if additional financial, land-use and operational constraints are considered.

Southeast Asia's Strategic Role

Given Singapore and Southeast Asia's highly skilled talent pool, significant infrastructure for test-bedding innovations and entrepreneurial environment for cross-sectorial collaborations, there is great potential to contribute to the discovery and delivery of innovative climate solutions.

Innovations and partnerships in science and technology can maximise the effectiveness of nature-based climate solutions, reduce barriers for their implementation, and create new solutions and economic opportunities.

For example, through collaborative investments into the research and development of real-time terrestrial and coastal monitoring systems using satellite, civilian drone, machine learning and other novel technologies, Southeast Asian nations can keep track of the regional carbon stocks in forests and reefs, as well as enhance the timeliness and effectiveness of emergency responses during forest fires and other catastrophic events.

More importantly, given Singapore and other Southeast Asian nations' intimate knowledge of the social, cultural and geopolitical contexts of the region, we are ideally positioned to help with the implementation of climate mitigation and adaptation strategies in socially and culturally responsible ways for achieving a carbon-neutral economy and stable climate at local, regional and global levels.

In our collective fight against climate change, it is important to remind ourselves that no one succeeds until everyone succeeds.

Professor Koh Lian Pin is the Vice Dean of Research at the Faculty of Science and the Kwan Im Thong Hood Cho Temple Chair Professor of Conservation at the National University of Singapore (NUS). He is also the Director of the Centre for Nature-based Climate Solutions, and the Tropical Marine Science Institute (TMSI) at the University. Professor Koh has 20 years of international research experience in the field of sustainability and environmental science, having worked in institutions across Europe, Australia, the United States and Singapore.

Chapter 24

My Green Journey

Tommy Koh

The Singapore I grew up in was very different from the Singapore of today. My childhood Singapore was full of kampongs, vegetable farms, pig farms and fish farms. There were many forests which had not been cleared for development. The coastline in Bedok, Tanah Merah and Pasir Ris was in its original state, before land reclamation.

I think my love for nature and the great outdoors began when I was a scout, in Outram Primary School and Raffles Institution. Together with my fellow scouts, we did a lot of hiking in rural Singapore. Every year, we would go camping. The camp sites chosen were usually by the sea, along the East Coast of Singapore.

Those happy experiences had inculcated in me a love for nature and respect for trees, animals, birds and other living things.

When I became a diplomat at the United Nations (UN), I brought with me this value as well as Lee Kuan Yew's belief that developing countries should seek rapid economic growth without destroying their environment. He rejected the popular narrative that developing countries should get rich first and clean up the environment later.

In 1969, the UN General Assembly adopted a resolution, initiated by Sweden, to hold the UN Conference on the Human Environment in Stockholm, in June 1972. A Preparatory Committee was established to prepare for the conference. Singapore joined the Committee. My main contribution was to support Sweden and the Secretary-General of the conference, Maurice Strong, and to argue against a group of developing countries which were opposed to the conference. They opposed the conference because they believed that the right to development should not be compromised by environmental considerations.

Fast forward to 1990. In that year, the UN General Assembly adopted a resolution, convening the Conference on Environment and Development in Rio de Janeiro, Brazil, in June 1992. Unlike Stockholm, the Rio conference would have two focal points: environment and development. It would be held in a developing country which hosts the world's largest rainforest. The Rio conferences came to be known as the Earth Summit.

A Preparatory Committee was established to prepare for the Earth Summit. The plan was for a Swedish Ambassador to chair the committee. The plan became untenable when the UN Secretary-General appointed Maurice Strong as the Secretary-General of the conference. The developing countries demanded that the chair should come from a developing country. My good friends, Kishore Mahbubani and Chan Heng Chee, persuaded me to take on this job. I still remember Kishore telling me that, compared to chairing the Law of the Sea Conference, this would be "a piece of cake". It was not a piece of cake at all.

I encountered many difficulties in chairing the Preparatory Committee. The main difficulty was the absence of trust between the developed and the developing countries. In the absence of trust, negotiations were long and difficult. They could not even agree on the agenda of the conference. On the final day of the meeting, in New York, in the spring of 1990, I forced the delegates to meet through the night until the next morning. It was only when the delegates were exhausted that they requested me to put forward a compromise text. The compromise text of the agenda was promptly adopted.

When the Earth Summit convened in Rio, in June 1992, I had expected the Brazilian Government to nominate one of its nationals to chair the Main Committee of the Conference as it was entitled to do. Much to my surprise, Brazil requested me to chair the Committee.

In Rio, it was a race against time. The plan of action, known as Agenda 21, contained over 300 disputed texts. We had 10 days to resolve the disputes and to produce a clean text which could be adopted by consensus. To assist me in my work, I appointed eight capable colleagues, from different regions of the world, to chair eight negotiating groups. I chaired the small negotiating group to draft the Rio Declaration of Principles on Environment and Development.

On the last day of the meeting of the Main Committee, I persuaded the delegates to meet through the night until six o'clock the next morning. We managed to adopt, by consensus, Agenda 21 and the Rio Declaration. The Summit also adopted a non-binding statement of principles on the hotly contentious question of forests.

The UN Framework Convention on Climate Change and the UN Convention on Biological Diversity were opened for signature at the Earth Summit. The Earth Summit also gave birth to a new treaty to combat desertification.

Back home in Singapore, I have been working for the environment in the following ways. First, as the patron of the Nature Society (Singapore) (NSS). Second, as the co-chair of the Advisory Committee of the Asia-Pacific Centre for Environmental Law (APCEL) at the Law Faculty, National University of Singapore (NUS). Third, as the founding chairman of the Advisory Committee of the NUS multi-disciplinary master's degree in environmental management, the M.Sc. (Environmental Management) [MEM]. Fourth, as the founding chairman of the Lee Kong Chian Natural History Museum at NUS.

I believe that we, the humans, should aspire to live in harmony with nature. This aspiration has motivated me in all my work, at the UN and in Singapore. In 1996, the UN Environment Programme conferred on me the wonderful award, Champion of the Earth. I have tried to be a good champion of the earth.

Tommy Koh is an Ambassador-At-Large, at the Ministry of Foreign Affairs and an Emeritus Professor of Law of the National University of Singapore. He is the Patron of the Nature Society (Singapore) and was made a Champion of the Earth by the UN Environment Programme (UNEP) for his leadership role at the 1992 Earth Summit. He was the President of the Third UN Conference on the Law of the Sea. For this and other achievements in negotiations, he was given the Great Negotiator Award by Harvard University.

Chapter 25

The Herpetological Society and Youth Outreach

Law Ing Sind and Law Ingg Thong,
with Sankar Ananthanarayanan and Serin Subaraj

Herpetology is the study of amphibians and reptiles, an often overlooked and reviled group of animals due to preconceived notions about their poisonous, venomous or untoward appearance. Many are, however, worthy of conservation and should be treated with respect. It was with this in mind that the Herpetological Society of Singapore (HSS) was founded in 2015.

HSS is a relatively young organisation compared to the veritable likes of the Nature Society (Singapore) (NSS), National University of Singapore's Toddycats and Animal Concerns Research & Education Society (ACRES) which were established in the 1990s and early 2000s. However, many within the nature community have viewed HSS as both a bastion and refuge for youth cohorts eager to join and champion nature conservation and outreach in Singapore.

The members of HSS have contributed to many important local herpetofaunal discoveries and rediscoveries: for example, the rediscovery of a blind snake that was not seen for 172 years as well as the description of a species of frog new to science! This and other studies by HSS furthered the state of herpetological research in Singapore in recent years. Furthermore, through the efforts of HSS, much needed attention has been brought to the plight of a group of animals that often garners hatred from members of the public. Activities that further the goal of outreach and education have been the cornerstone and the main objectives of HSS since its inception. These activities include free monthly guided walks, booths and public dialogues with global herpetofauna researchers.

But what has made our small society so successful at captivating the younger generation, and how can we integrate such interest and care towards a more cohesive call to action within the larger nature ecosphere?

On Being a Good Gardener

Of gardeners

The ephemerality of plants flowered
So fleet against the flow of time
Upon a grave lowered
Or with romantic thoughts, sublime

Some sought ownership,
With cold steel, and a snip
ended the blossom's hardship

Never did the thought cross their selfish minds, that their act of owning hastened the fading of the bloom.

Like a fading heart beat in the hospital room.

While others cultivate and nurture,
To grow with, and then mature
A simple goal, aligned with nature

Never did the thought cross their giving minds, that their act of care would bring meaning to the bloom.

A balm in the overwhelming gloom.

What then does it mean to be a good gardener of people? It often means to teach without reprimand, to care for both the joys of learning and the learning outcomes. It also means to create a safe space for learning and creativity.

It is often thought that passion is an innate quality, one that can neither be given nor taken away and that passion for a given subject is all anyone needs to succeed. However, whilst it is important to be passionate about nature and conservation, raw passion alone is insufficient for systemic change. That passion needs to be tempered, cultivated and given purpose and meaning. This is often achieved through the teachings and advice of a good mentor figure who can help instil such meaning into passion. With the right mentors, budding conservationists will be able to build on their mentor's store of knowledge while adding their own experiences, thereby expanding the capacity of shared experiences; this creates a synergy where both individuals learn from each other.

Another key aspect to effective mentorship is the ability to trust that the mentee is able to eventually grow into key roles and claim the mantle of responsibility. Such opportunities need to be available for the youth to be able to grow and achieve their full potential. This also ensures the forward movement and longevity of the community as fresh ideas and new management styles prevent the community from becoming a monolith that is adverse to constructive change.

HSS has had the good fortune of having many mentors and teachers along its journey, many of whom appear within the pages of this book, but perhaps one that has had the greatest impact on us and HSS as a whole was the late Mr Subaraj Rajathurai, affectionately called Uncle Subaraj. Had it not been for Uncle Subaraj, HSS might not have been founded! He has been a guiding presence even before the inception of HSS, when he would take us out on surveys, and was the force that brought the co-founders together. He was patient enough to teach a small group of boisterous teens the importance

The Subaraj's paddy frog (*Micryletta subaraji*), a new species to science named after our mentor, Uncle Subaraj.

of a calm mind and a well-tempered tongue when approaching and navigating sometimes insurmountable obstacles in conservation. It is rather fitting then, that HSS would name a new species of frog, Subaraj's paddy frog (*Micryletta subaraji*) after our great mentor and friend, Uncle Subaraj.

On Improving Passion

Since the advent of social media, the way individuals and communities interact has changed dramatically. At present, it is extremely easy to find online communities for almost every interest or field on platforms such as Facebook, Instagram or even TikTok. Thus, a social media presence is important when trying to establish a connection with youths as they are closely connected to their digital communities. This is an important first step in staying relevant in this digital age. There are many ways one can have a social media presence, from posting small factual tidbits about native species to inspiring personal anecdotes and experiences, but an important facet is having a genuine and humbling connection to the audience, and regarding such an audience as peers rather than anomalous figures in the internet.

But we must also be wary of social media, as it can be an addictive source of unearned validation, and an unhealthy source of motivation due to the unequal importance it places on the outcome over the journey.

After that connection is established and there is some form of rapport within the community, it is important that this community be given a safe refuge to interact and communicate with each other, thereby growing their collective knowledge from shared dialogues and discussions. This can be done in the form of community get-togethers where there is levity in the atmosphere, and where people feel comfortable. In HSS this is in the form of society-exclusive events where members have the chance to mix and interact with passionate like-minded individuals while out in nature. This can create opportunities that could bolster our connection to the society, among each other and with nature.

HSS facilitates these experiences through the efforts of our dedicated Welfare Officer and the yearly events they plan. These society-exclusive events allow HSS' members to forge and maintain meaningful relationships and thrive together, both within and outside of the context of HSS.

Conclusion

In conclusion, the use of social media is an important first step in attracting youths to a cause or community, and effective mentorship is needed to nurture them. In addition, providing youths with opportunities to take up key roles and leadership positions ensures the longevity of the community.

Ultimately, lasting youth outreach requires building and maintaining a community where members feel safe to express themselves, make mistakes, learn from others, grow and socialise.

Law Ing Sind is a conservationist, co-founder of the Herpetological Society of Singapore (HSS) and a zoology graduate from the University of Reading. His keen eyes often find him interesting animals and behaviours to document in Singapore. His interest in the natural world was piqued when he was young, having his very own sighting of a snake feeding on a toad at the tender age of 10. His interests in writing and photography are intertwined and he often finds one aiding the other.

Law Ingg Thong is one of the six co-founders of HSS. A zoology graduate from the University of Reading, he has had an interest in herpetofauna since 2011 and has spent the past few years helping as an independent researcher in comprehensive biodiversity surveys and other research projects around Singapore. He also has an interest and passion for the fields of bioacoustics and ecology.

Sankar Ananthanarayanan is a co-founder of HSS and a current PhD student pursuing his doctorate in tropical ecology at the National University of Singapore. Sankar has always been passionate about herpetology, conservation biology, and communication science. As the first president of HSS, he often found himself using the skills from all three fields in tandem to efficiently run the society and further the goals of the society.

Serin Subaraj is one of the six co-founders of HSS. He has worked as a Wildlife Consultant and field biologist in environmental consultancy since 2008. He has conducted a vast array of surveys and fieldwork around many countries in Southeast Asia. He has led multiple research and consultancy teams studying terrestrial fauna. He is currently enrolled with Curtin University as a research masters student studying tiger snake populations and behaviour in Perth.

Chapter 26

From Railway Land to Rail Corridor

Leong Kwok Peng

This is a brief chronicle of my engagement journey for Singapore's Rail Corridor.

In May 2010, *The Straits Times* carried a story that Singapore and Malaysia had agreed on a land-swop deal on the KTM (Keretapi Tanah Melayu) railway land in Singapore, with a photo of PM Lee Hsien Loong and PM Najib Razak at the Istana. It immediately dawned on me to write a quick letter to *The Straits Times*' Forum, saying that the railway land would make a fabulous nature corridor. And because I raised this issue, the Nature Society (Singapore) (NSS) asked me to drive the campaign for the Green Corridor — a term we used prior to the Rail Corridor. Thus began the decade long journey of engagements with the Government agencies to do just that.

The idea of the Green Corridor, if ever the railway land was returned to Singapore, was not new. NSS had been venturing into the KTM lands for nature walks and birdwatching since the 1990s — in particular the stretch between Old Holland Road and Bukit Timah Road. A member of NSS was in fact quoted by *The Straits Times* in

1994, saying that the space would make an appropriate green corridor.

The first people I sought for support and opinion were Tay Kheng Soon, Dr Ho Hua Chew and Dr Geh Min. They were all enthusiastic and supportive. Together with Hua Chew who provided the ecological perspective, I gathered some like-minded people, particularly Jeremy Chan and Tham Wai Hon (both architects) and their architect friends and we drew up a proposal: "The Green Corridor — A Proposal to Keep the Railway Lands as a Continuous Green Corridor".

The proposal briefly spelled out the justifications, that:

- it connects many green spaces together;
- it connects many people together;
- it provides a clean and green transport route;
- it preserves history.

As to the green spaces, we stated that the railway land is a ready-made "nature park" with a myriad of habitats from Mandai mangrove forest in the north through marshland and grassland further south, skirting pass the primary forests of Bukit Timah Nature Reserve and passing alongside secondary forests, woodlands and green belts all the way to Tanjong Pagar Railway Station.

The proposal included the abandoned Old Jurong Line that runs through Clementi and Maju Forest all the way to Shipyard Road. We estimated the potential of the Green Corridor to serve directly or indirectly 1.2 million people staying along the entire stretch. We highlighted the physical historical records of the relationship between Singapore and Malaysia relating to the railway line, and notable heritage structures like the railway stations, bridges and even the railway tracks.

We sent out the proposal to all related Government agencies and Ministers in October 2010. There was much media hype on the proposal and the future plans for the railway land.

With help from Eugene Tay, we set up a website and Facebook page to propagate the idea of the Green Corridor. Walking maps were included for the public. At the same time we started organising walks for the public to garner awareness and support, even as the trains were operating. The walks included part of the old Jurong Line. There was much support from the public.

In June 2011, the Ministry of National Development (MND), the Urban Redevelopment Authority (URA) and the National Parks Board (NParks) formed the Rail Corridor Consultation Group (RCCG) chaired by the Minister of State (MOS), Tan Chuan-Jin, which included various stakeholders like NSS and the Singapore Heritage Society. I was part of the group. The name "Rail Corridor" was adopted and became a national effort to consult and capture the ideas and aspirations of the public as to the future of this strip of railway land.

The last KTM train departed from Tanjong Pagar Station on 30 June 2011 — driven by the Sultan of Johor, and Singapore officially took over the railway land on 1 July 2011. The former railway land was then opened to the public for two weeks before it was closed for the dismantling of its railway tracks.

Thousands descended on the Rail Corridor to walk, take photographs and reminisce. Families with children, students, wedding couples, hikers, runners and cyclists were all represented. It was probably the most photographed place then. MOS Tan invited the public to join him and his team to walk the entire length from south to north on July 2011 — a distance of 23 kilometres. I remember we started with about 100 participants in the early hours of the morning from Silat Estate and ended up mid-afternoon at Kranji with just a handful of us — mostly from NSS. It was ankle-breaking, walking on the railway tracks.

Prime Minister Lee in his National Day Rally speech in August 2011 said,

> "I think that is the most vivid way to convey the things which Singaporeans are getting together and doing and getting mobilised on. One of them is the KTM railway line, the land we took back on July 1st and on which we are creating a Green Corridor."

A group of us from the Green Corridor proposal team and friends formed the Friends of the Rail Corridor and organised a Rail Corridor exhibition entitled "Re-imagining the Rail Corridor" at the URA Centre in October 2011. A design workshop involving architects, landscape designers and students was also organised in conjunction with the exhibition.

Some very interesting ideas were developed.

URA subsequently organised an idea competition entitled "Journey of Possibilities" from December 2011 to March 2012, open to both local and foreign architectural/landscape companies and educational institutions. It attracted over 200 submissions both locally and from overseas. I was one of the panel judges.

The winners include:

- "The Tiger's Garden" by Oculus Landscape Architecture Urban Design from Australia — winner of the Extraordinary & Innovative Ideas for a Great Public Space category
- "The Singapore Trail" by NUS Landscape Architecture — winner for the Inclusiveness, Accessibility & Resolving Conflicts category

URA formed the Rail Corridor Partnership (RCP) to include a wider spectrum of stakeholders in May 2012 that included a website "Rail Corridor Forum" for the public to share their ideas, and also brought a traveling exhibition and conducted workshops and field trips at several communities along the Corridor. I was very much involved in all the URA initiatives. I helped form the NSS Rail Corridor Watch Group in 2013 to work with the Singapore Land Authority (SLA) to provide feedback on the condition of the corridor. It was led by a NSS member, the late Paul Wonnacott.

I assisted in the Green Corridor Run organised by Groundswell Events in January 2013 — a mass run on the Rail Corridor from Tanjong Pagar Railway Station to Bukit Timah Railway Station that attracted over 6,000 participants in the first run. NSS was the charity partner for the run. The run took place each year with increasing participants until 2016 when it became hindered by pipe laying works by the Public Utilities Board (PUB) on the Rail Corridor. PUB did the pipe laying work on the southern half of the Rail Corridor — this required a few years of closure. I was part of the nature groups consulted.

I organised a few kayaking trips to Mandai Mangroves for Ministers Tan Chuan-Jin and Desmond Lee and their government colleagues to explore this northern-most nature area of the Rail Corridor.

NParks took over leadership of the Rail Corridor development from URA in 2017 and formed the *Friends of the Rail Corridor* (FORC) to cultivate community stewardship. FORC had a shared vision which states "The Rail Corridor is a natural and continuous green passage connecting our past and present, and a lifeline for people and wildlife. We have a collective responsibility to protect its unique character and promote its heritage for our diverse communities". I am still very much part of FORC and have been actively contributing to the discussion on various development plans including trail enhancement, railway station and bridge refurbishment, planting of native trees, and road and bridge development which involved temporary closure of stretches of the Rail Corridor.

Between 2019 and 2022 I coordinated the NSS publication of three books relating to the Rail Corridor:

- *The Green Rail Corridor: A Biodiversity & Ecological Overview*
- *Pang Sua Woodland: Sanctuary Unveiled Along the Rail Corridor*
- *Alexandra Woodland: Haven Along the Rail Corridor*

The last two were done jointly with Cicada Tree Eco Place. All of the above works highlight and describe the important unprotected nature areas along the Rail Corridor.

In 2022 a few of us from NSS decided to embark on a project to re-wild stretches of the Rail Corridor, in particular the northern stretch, as part of our contribution to NParks OneMillionTrees initiative. The idea is to mobilise volunteers and sponsors to plant trees and shrubs to improve the canopy cover and biodiversity of the Rail Corridor. We plan to first plant pioneer tree species in the open areas, followed by forest species when sufficient shade has been provided by these pioneer species. By doing so we hope also to provide more shade to users and enhance the overall aesthetics.

We foresee the project to take at least five years.

Since the 1970s and 80s, I have travelled on KTM trains to Malaysia mainly for mountain and jungle trekking, and I remember the feeling of being immersed in a rural Malayan landscape once the train departed from Tanjong Pagar Railway Station. This sentiment was also shared by a number of visitors to the Corridor back in 2011. I see the Corridor as more than a strip of recreational green space. The essence of the space lies in the rather wild green areas alongside it, without which the Corridor will lose its magic.

My aspirations for the Rail Corridor would be:

- to keep the Corridor's original alignment continuous and green;
- that all the unprotected forests and woodlands along the Rail Corridor such as Clementi, Maju, Alexandra and Kranji be preserved and their biodiversity enhanced;
- to bring back a bit more of the rail heritage;

Nature Society Singapore nature walk along the KTM railway land off Bukit Timah in 2009.

- to provide an industrial heritage trail on the old Jurong Line from Ulu Pandan to Shipyard Road in Jurong;
- to extend the Rail Corridor into Johor Bahru.

Leong Kwok Peng currently chairs the Conservation Committee of Nature Society (Singapore) (NSS), serving as a "front man" for engagement with many of the government agencies. He was former Vice-President and Chair of the Marine Conservation Group. He helped publish *Singapore Waters – Unveiling Our Seas*, and also coordinated the Coral Reef Rescue from Pulau Ayer Chawan in the mid-1990s. He joined NSS in the 1980s. He is a chemical engineer, and has spent many years in the petrochemical and water treatment industry before venturing into outdoor education to run school camps and inspire children to love nature.

Chapter 27

Colugos in Singapore

Norman Lim

Since this is an essay about colugos and my journey with this amazing species, I thought I should first introduce some brief facts about this species that can be found in Singapore. The Sunda colugo (*Galeopterus variegatus*) is one of two species of colugos in the world — both of which are located within Southeast Asia. The Philippine colugo (*Cynocephalus volans*) is found within southern Philippines, while the Sunda colugo is widely distributed across eight countries. Together, these two species comprise the order Dermoptera (that is, skin-winged), making this mammalian order taxonomically unique and thus important for conservation. In order for us to better appreciate such a claim, we can compare Dermoptera to its sister order, the Primates, where there are about 500 species (e.g., monkeys, apes, and humans). In other words, if one of the colugo species goes extinct globally, this translates to a 50% loss in diversity within a mammalian order.

Previously often referred to as "flying lemurs", "colugos" is the preferred term these days because these arboreal mammals are not capable of powered flight and they do not belong to the group of lemurs, which are members of the order Primates. Colugos rarely descend to the ground, and they rely on their sharp claws to move along horizontal and vertical structures in the arboreal environment. They feed largely on leaves during the night, though there have been some observations of them consuming flowers, fruits, insects, and tree sap. When it is time to move across a longer distance with minimal energy expenditure, they leap off from a tree, fully extend their patagium (or skin membrane), and then manoeuvre through clearances in the canopy level to achieve glides that can be more than 100 metres.

While colugos are widespread in distribution and are not threatened due to exploitation or habitat disturbance, they have not received significant scientific attention, particularly in terms of field research on their behaviour and ecology. A case in point is an uncertainty in the relationship between fur colouration and sex/gender. Colugos can range from reddish-brown to grey in their fur colouration, and research papers based on museum specimens suggest that female colugos are greyish while males can be either reddish-brown or greyish. Interestingly, there have been sightings of reddish-brown colugos with young on their underside; if reddish-brown individuals are always male, this would indicate the presence of bi-parental care in colugos. However, in late 2022, there was photographic evidence of a reddish-brown female (as colugo can be confidently sexed from its external genitalia) with a young. Therefore, there is much to be discovered about the secretive lives of colugos through further field research.

Within Singapore, it was estimated that there were approximately 1,000 individuals, based on field surveys in 2006. In those days, Sunda colugos were largely found within the Bukit Timah and Central Catchment Nature Reserves. Subsequently, colugos could be found in many other parts in Singapore, including Bukit Batok Nature Park, Gallop Road, and Wessex Estate, suggesting that the population has increased since the previous survey in 2006. Even with a respectable population density in our forests, the colugo is not often encountered by regular hikers in our nature reserves and parks, most likely due to its excellent camouflage against the tree trunk and its sedentary nature during the day. When pointing out a colugo perching against the tree trunk, hikers often query if the unusual animal is a flying fox (order Chiroptera; bats) or flying squirrel (order Rodentia). Thus, it is clear that public awareness about this unique mammal is low, and much more can be done to address this (e.g., introducing this species in our school textbooks for topics like biodiversity).

Colugos appear to be thriving in Singapore, and possible reasons include the continued existence of suitable forests, a general lack of apex predators, and the presence of effective animal protection laws. However, this does not mean that all individuals live out their physiological lifespan. As colugos rarely descend to the ground, they rely on their gliding prowess to move between fragmented patches of forests. In doing so, some individuals have ended up as roadkills, were entangled in razor wires on security fences, or had their claws worn out due to constant attempts to climb up vertical surfaces (e.g., metal hoardings) when stranded in development sites.

Thankfully, various stakeholders in the local conservation scene are working closely to address threats faced by the species. For instance, biologists have made use of geographic information systems to model the impacts of road widening on habitat connectivity and to find optimal solutions for mitigation structures like glide poles. Additionally, public agencies now actively engage the nature community in productive conversations to avoid further incidents involving security fences through changes in the designs. Veterinary innovations are also attempted to reshape the worn-out claws of rescued colugos so that they can be released back into the wild subsequently. These fruitful partnerships between academia, public agencies, and private organisations will clearly help to improve outcomes for colugos in Singapore, and such a working model can serve as an inspiration for our neighbouring countries to achieve sustainable co-existence of nature and humans.

Through all these years of observing/studying the colugos, I have gained valuable life lessons, and the biggest one of them all is patience. Even though colugos are nocturnal, for over 90% of the time you see an individual during the night, the animal will just be stationary and not doing anything (if you are fortunate enough to

Female colugo with the typical greyish fur colouration and her young.

have one in plain view and not hidden amongst the vegetation). It demonstrates to me that one does not have to be actively moving all the time, and it can be beneficial to be observant and only respond to situations when needed. Additionally, having to look up to observe the arboreal creature really strengthens one's neck muscles (to put in a nice way) and builds one's patience. More importantly, my journey of researching on the species was only possible due to the mentorship and friendship from other nature lovers in Singapore and abroad. The positive influence of the community on my perseverance to continue when things got tough cannot be overstated. To the aspiring field ecologists out there, actively seek out mentors and buddies to encourage and support you in this meaningful career choice, and you will find the journey to be most rewarding and enjoyable.

Dr Norman Lim is a lecturer at the National Institute of Education, Nanyang Technological University (NTU). Norman teaches a variety of undergraduate and postgraduate courses, ranging from animal diversity, biostatistics, to ecology and conservation. Having an interest in understudied vertebrates, he focusses on the ecology and conservation of terrestrial vertebrates, and recent research projects include investigating the ecological impacts of free-roaming dogs, habitat connectivity of colugos, and habitat selection of small mammals. He has been a member of the IUCN Pangolin Specialist Group since 2012, and serves as an Associate Editor for *The Raffles Bulletin of Zoology* since 2013.

Chapter 28

Cities and Climate Change

Jolene Lin

The United Nations projects that, by 2030, the world will have 41 megacities with a population of at least 10 million inhabitants each. By 2050, eight out of 10 people in the world will be living in cities. It is therefore the case that cities are where the climate change battle will be won or lost. Cities around the world are critical drivers of global changes. They face significant issues such as climate change and environmental degradation, rising inequalities and insecurity. Cities generate 70% of global greenhouse emissions. Eighty percent of cities globally face severe impacts from climate change such as extreme heat, drought, flood and heavy rainfall. About a quarter of cities expect the hazards to become more intense and more frequent by 2025 while one in three cities are facing such severe climate threats that they will impact at least 70% of their populations. Research by Zurich Insurance has identified 570 coastal cities with a total population of over 800 million people that are threatened by flooding if climate change causes a sea level rise of just 50 centimetres by 2050. These cities include Miami, Bangkok, Shanghai, New York City and Mumbai.

While cities are at the front line of climate change impacts, they can also be at the heart of climate action. Cities are taking steps to adapt to climate change and these actions also lead to other environmental benefits such as improving air quality and enhancing biodiversity. Cities are also fighting climate change by reducing their energy consumption and overall carbon emissions.

Singapore is a global leader in living roof design. Our "City in a Garden" has residential housing, hotels and pedestrian walkways covered with living roofs. Made of green vegetation, these living roofs mitigate urban heat. As plants reflect sunlight and release moisture, the surface temperatures of living rooms can be up to 5°C lower during the day compared to traditional roofs. This reduces the need for indoor air-conditioning and helps reduce the oppressive heat on a warm tropical day.

Universal Studios in Sentosa has the largest living roof in Asia. It measures almost 35,000 square metres! Parkroyal on Pickering stands out in Singapore's Downtown Core. The hotel features several sky gardens, reflecting pools, waterfalls and green walls. It has an impressive green plot ratio of 240%! The architects behind this beautiful green hotel, WOHA, have won several awards for their contributions towards inspiring, aesthetic and environmentally beneficial architecture.

As the largest developer of housing in Singapore, our Housing and Development Board (HDB) has developed a Sustainable Development Framework to address climate change as well as create a more livable environment for Singaporeans. From 2016, all new HDB developments have to meet a minimum Green Plot Ratio of 4.5, which means the total leaf area will have to be at least 4.5 times the site area. HDB has also adopted a 45–60% estimated green cover provision in housing projects. This measures green cover as seen from the sky. As a result, residents can enjoy abundant greenery right at their doorsteps.

HDB also has a Biophilic Town Framework to enhance residents' connection with the natural world. This is important. People will not feel the need to protect nature if they do not feel a sense of connection with it. Punggol Northshore is HDB's first biophilic district. Its biophilic features include Green Corridors, which feature dragonfly ponds, bird sanctuaries, and butterfly gardens.

Singapore has always played an active role in the international climate change negotiations. Pursuant to the Paris Agreement under the United Nations Framework Convention on Climate Change (UNFCCC), Singapore's Nationally Determined Contribution (NDC) is "an economy-wide absolute GHG (greenhouse gas) emissions limitation target to reduce its GHG emissions to around 60 MtCO2e in 2030 after peaking emissions earlier." Singapore has developed a comprehensive suite of mitigation measures to achieve its NDC and strongly believes in the importance of a "whole-of-nation" effort to address climate change. This means that the government seeks to engage stakeholders — including businesses, civil society, youths and the research community — to co-create and deliver solutions. The measures are outlined in the Singapore Green Plan 2030. The Green Plan 2030 is "a national sustainability movement which seeks to rally bold and collective action to tackle climate change". Its measures and targets include: peaking public sector carbon emissions around 2025 (ahead of the national target); at least 20% of schools to be carbon neutral by 2030; an energy reset that involves greener buildings, electric public and private vehicles, and increasing solar energy to 1.5 gigawatt-peak by 2025.

The Green Plan 2030 also expresses Singapore's ambition to be an Asian hub for carbon services and green finance. Singapore can provide a range of financial and legal services related to companies' efforts to decarbonise. Singapore can also facilitate the procurement of carbon credits for the aviation and shipping sectors as well as for domestic compliance with the Carbon Pricing Act. Carbon markets, which are largely voluntary at the moment, are experiencing a surge in growth. There is a role that carbon markets can play, but it is important both for the climate and for the economy that the development of carbon markets is facilitated by robust governance. Monitoring and verification to ensure that carbon credits truly represent cuts in greenhouse gas emissions is critical. Bogus "hot air" credits and double counting (where the same carbon credit is issued more than once by multiple registries) will destroy our efforts to tackle climate change. In this regard, the Climate Action Data Trust (CAD Trust) — a joint initiative among the International Emissions Trading Association (IETA), World Bank and Singapore Government — launched in December 2022 is an important development. CAD Trust creates a decentralised record of data from major carbon credit registries globally.

Cities have formed global networks to support each other, share knowledge and exchange innovative ideas to tackle climate change. Singapore is an active member of these global networks including the International Council for Local Environmental Initiatives (ICLEI) (Local Governments for Sustainability) and C40, a network of nearly 100 cities collaborating to help resolve the challenges of the climate crisis. A C40 member since 2012, Singapore is involved in several initiatives within the C40 network. These include the Public Transit Network which aims to invest in and support public transportation, the Food Systems Network which focusses on food policies that reduce greenhouse gas emissions and increase resilience, and the Connecting Delta Cities Network in which cities collaborate to address sea-level rise, coastal flooding and water management.

Singapore is a leading port city. It aims to play a leading role in global efforts to tackle climate change in the shipping industry. In November 2022, the Maritime and Port Authority of Singapore (MPA), Port of Los Angeles, Port of Long Beach and C40 announced that they were in discussions to establish a green and digital shipping corridor between Singapore and the San Pedro Bay port complex. The project will focus on low- and zero-carbon fuels for bunkering. It will also explore the use of digital tools to support the deployment of low- and zero-carbon ships. This project supports the Green Shipping Challenge launched during the 27th United Nations Climate Change Conference (COP27) in Sharm el-Sheikh, Egypt. Convened by the United States and Norway, the Green Shipping Challenge encourages governments, ports, cargo owners and others in the shipping value chain to commit to concrete steps to decarbonise the shipping industry.

Singapore is a wealthy nation that has attained significant social and economic progress within a few decades. It is a remarkable feat that attests to our country's ability to come together to tackle big challenges. As a city-state, Singapore is uniquely placed to work at the city level as well as the international level simultaneously. Singapore should continue to offer warm support to its neighbours within ASEAN and beyond to decarbonise and adapt to the impacts of climate change.

This essay has sought to offer a positive story about what cities are doing in the battle against climate change. In particular, Singapore has in recent years taken bold steps to galvanise action to tackle climate change, update its Paris Agreement NDC and integrate sustainability in most, if not all, aspects of life. However, many Singaporeans remain nonchalant about the climate emergency and the need to change our carbon-intensive lifestyles to leave our future generations a liveable planet. Such a mindset is sadly not unique to Singaporeans. As our lives become more urban, it becomes easier to forget our relationship with nature. It is my hope that urban efforts to fight climate change will go some way towards healing the relationship with nature. Only then will laws, policies and other governance tools succeed in driving governments, companies and individuals to earnestly decarbonise and thread more lightly on Earth.

Jolene Lin is Associate Professor of Law at the National University of Singapore (NUS). She is also Director of the Asia-Pacific Centre of Environmental Law (APCEL). Jolene's research focusses on climate change law and transnational environmental law. Her recent publications include *Governing Climate Change: Global Cities and Transnational Lawmaking* (Cambridge University Press, 2018) and *Climate Change Litigation in the Asia Pacific* (Cambridge University Press, 2020). She is currently co-writing a book on climate change litigation in the Global South (Oxford University Press, 2024). Jolene enjoys travelling, hiking and exploring Singapore's amazing public playgrounds with her two children.

Chapter 29

Nature Society (Singapore)

Shawn Lum

The Nature Society (Singapore) (NSS) is a natural history and nature conservation group that is one of Singapore's oldest and largest civil society groups. It was established in 1954 as the Singapore Branch of the Malayan Nature Society (MNS). In its 70-year history, the Nature Society has witnessed the island's transformation, and its activities and member profiles reflect profound changes in Singapore's physical and social landscapes.

Nature conservation and the protection of wild spaces in Singapore was once viewed by some as a threat to economic development, but today it has been mainstreamed into government policy. "City in Nature" is now a national objective, not a slogan for the non-governmental organisation (NGO) community. This welcome scenario, unfathomable to pioneers of local nature conservation, begs the question, however, of the future role of civil society in biodiversity protection in Singapore.

This essay is not a definitive account of the NSS. It is, rather, my attempt at making sense of the dynamics of nature conservation, nature areas, and nature groups in Singapore over seven decades. What might have contributed to these changes? What could the role of civil society be in the future to increase the odds that future generations might experience the majesty and wonder of wild nature?

Early Days and a Knowledge of Nature

The story of the Nature Society is of its interaction with the natural world, and changes to that natural world.

The Singapore Branch of the Malayan Nature Society (MNS) held its first general meeting on 17 November 1954 at the Department of Zoology, University of Malaya. The inaugural Committee is a Who's-Who of Singapore natural history. Michael Tweedie, noted zoologist and Director of the Raffles Museum (the forerunner of both the National Museum of Singapore and the Lee Kong Chian Natural History Museum), was Chairman. The first Secretary of the MNS Singapore Branch was Ivan Enoch of the Botany Department, University of Malaya. There were three Committee Members: prominent entrepreneur, noted naturalist and nature photographer Loke Wan Tho; mollusc specialist at the University of Malaya, Professor Dennis Purchon; and Dr J. W. Purseglove, Director of the Singapore Botanic Gardens.

A few things stand out about the early days of the Nature Society in Singapore. Loke Wan Tho was the only Committee Member born in Malaya, while the others were British expatriates. This of course is not surprising. Very few people in Singapore in the 1950s would have been acquainted with nature study, at least in a western sense. Few would have had studied botany or zoology, owned a pair of binoculars, or trained in taking natural history notes.

Changing Landscapes

In the British colonial era, Loke Wan Tho was among the handful of locally born people with the training to document and study nature. Such skills are more prevalent today, but there is a slight irony to this. An intuitive knowledge of nature can result from any number of ways. It can be passed down from elders to children. It can ultimately be driven by practical needs, such as allowing a forager to know what is edible from what is not, or from knowing how to keep the local fish population viable. It can result from spending lots of time in wild places. It can come from a mixture of curiosity, opportunity, and inspiring mentorship, as was the case with Loke. What these different ways of learning deeply about nature have in common is unstructured time, discovery, and guidance.

Deep local knowledge of or at least familiarity with nature, borne of experience and not from formal education declined after the 1960s and 1970s, as modernisation and development accelerated. Singapore would soon experience rapid industrialisation and urbanisation, and higher living standards. In the region, large extractive activities such as mining or logging led to great landscape changes. The expansion of oil palm production, particularly in Malaysia and Indonesia, resulted in extensive forest conversion. A generation born in Peninsular Malaysia, Borneo or Sumatra before World War II might think of primary rainforests as part of the countryside, while for their grandchildren, an oil palm plantation might evoke a sense of home.

In 1960s Singapore, villages, fishing communities, and rural lifestyles would still have been a common sight, as would mangrove-lined estuaries and rivers, and long stretches of sandy and rocky shores. After the 1980s, Singapore children would no longer grow up in a rural setting. Mangrove coverage declined dramatically, as estuaries of the Jurong, Kranji, Seletar, and other waterways were converted to reservoirs. For the post-independence generation of Singaporeans, exposure to nature would come not from being surrounded by it at home, but from a purposeful visit to see nature areas.

There is another interesting twist to the story of conservation advocacy in Singapore. Most of Singapore's original forests were cleared by the mid-1800s for plantation agriculture, beginning with crops such as gambir and black pepper, and culminating in the 1900s with rubber plantations. Villages sprung up around plantations and quarries, and wherever villages occurred, so too did orchards. In the 1970s to the early 1990s, as quarries were closed and villagers relocated to housing estates, these lands were acquired for future development. The natural ecological process of succession began, quietly and imperceptibly, to transform large parts of the landscape back to forest. Fast-growing, readily dispersed tree species, what ecologists call "pioneer species", began colonising open, unmanaged areas such as abandoned fields and orchards, former village settlements, disused quarries, and in the case of the Bukit Brown Cemetery or the former Bidadari Muslim Cemetery, resting places of the departed. Nature's greening effort led to the development of large stretches of secondary forest on abandoned land across Singapore, such as at Tengah, Clementi Forest, Bidadari, Pasir Ris, and many other areas; sites that would be the focus of nature conservation efforts from 2010 onward.

Another feature of the early Nature Society is that many of its members were academics and civil servants. Of its first Committee, Loke Wan Tho was the only one who was not from the civil service

(Tweedie, Purseglove) or university staff (Purchon, Enoch). When I joined the Nature Society in 1989, many prominent members in the larger MNS Branches of Selangor, Singapore and Penang were still botany or zoology professors. In fact, the mailing address of MNS (Singapore Branch) for years was the Botany Department of the National University of Singapore. Such a close association between an advocacy group and a university department would be unlikely today, but in 1954 the Nature Society was not a nature advocacy group, but was principally dedicated to the study and observation of plants and wildlife.

There are many civil servants who are Nature Society members, but they cannot serve in leadership positions due to possible conflicts of interests between the views and position of the Nature Society and their day jobs. Contrast this with 1954, when leaders of the Nature Society included the Director of the Singapore Botanic Gardens and the Director of the Raffles Museum — the equivalent today might be to have the CEOs of the National Parks Board and the National Heritage Board helping to make key decisions for the Nature Society.

Nature conservation a hundred years ago focussed on specific issues. For example, the Audubon Society and the RSPB (the UK-based Royal Society for the Protection of Birds) were established in the 1880s to combat the fashion industry's pervasive use of bird feathers — in hats, for example — that led to the deaths of millions of birds, threatening some egret and other species with extinction. In 1900, worldwide, there was not quite two billion people, and there were still great swathes of untouched wilderness, particularly in the tropics. Today we are over eight billion people, and in just a few decades we have managed to clear most of the lowland forests of the Sunda and West Africa, and convert vast areas of South

American rainforests and savannahs for agriculture and other uses. We have a problem.

How does a small Singapore-based conservation group such as the Nature Society help humanity avoid the cataclysmic loss of biodiversity and the degradation of our earth system?

Transformation

The Nature Society was not formed to protect biodiversity but to study it. Few would have imagined the transformation of Singapore and Malaysia, and the rapid depletion of rainforests and peatswamps in the Sunda region. In response to the loss of local nature sites, the Nature Society found itself with little choice but to add advocacy to its activities. A Conservation Committee which was born out of the Nature Society's Bird Group went to work. In a whirlwind decade straddling the 1980s and 1990s their efforts included landmark conservation successes: a proposal for the protection of Sungei Buloh, the successful effort to prevent the excision of nature reserves in the Lower Peirce Reservoir area to create a golf course, and proposals to save the Mandai Mangroves and one of Singapore's last uncanalised waterways, the Sungei (Sg) Khatib Bongsu. The first two were key conservation wins for Singapore at a time when mangrove areas might have lost out on an economic cost-benefit analysis and when golfing was still an activity on an upward trajectory. Mandai Mangroves and the Sg Khatib Bongsu were announced as Nature Parks about 30 years after their protection was proposed.

The 1990's trailblazing *Master Plan for the Conservation of Nature in Singapore*, spearheaded by Clive Briffett and Ho Hua Chew was the first effort to list and highlight the conservation value of nature sites in Singapore, and it became the template for future conservation efforts. Not all sites mentioned in the Master Plan exist as nature areas today. Senoko is as industrialised as it gets in Singapore, but as recently as the early 1990s it included a mosaic of coastal habitats, mangroves and secondary forests that was refuge to an incredible variety of wildlife, notably birds. Nature Society members gathered over 20,000 signatures in support of the conservation of Senoko, but the effort was not successful. Neither was a proposal to incorporate spontaneously formed wetlands and secondary vegetation in the reclaimed Marina South area into green areas mandated for the future district. The latter effort even drew a public rebuke from the then-Minister for National Development, and some considered preserving a nature spot in an area that was reclaimed at great expense to be ludicrous. The ponds that attracted uncommon waterfowl and the surrounding secondary vegetation of Marina South were eventually cleared. Interestingly, that area today is not a finance complex but the Gardens by the Bay.

How does one judge failure or success in nature conservation? From a strict biodiversity or ecological perspective, any loss or degradation of habitat, decline in population size, reduction in genetic variation, or the extinction of a species, is a failure. Viewed through that lens, some see local conservation successes as partial victories because a protected area could have been larger, a habitat corridor wider, the footprint of a nearby commercial or residential development smaller, a carriageway with fewer lanes, and so on. But that might miss the point about where these efforts ultimately lead.

Consider the Nature Society's achievements over the past 20 years. They may not be as dramatic as averting a major golf course project, but they led to broad public discussion and to changes in conservation and planning processes themselves. A few include the management of the Kranji Marshes beginning in 2008, the first time a government agency (Public Utilities Board) has allowed an NGO to manage a nature area. Kranji Marshes are today protected and managed by the National Parks Board. The Nature Society was a key partner in the collective that worked with the Urban Redevelopment Authority to keep construction off the former railway line that ran from Woodlands to Tanjong Pagar. Today, the Rail Corridor is a popular spot for people and a key north-south habitat link for nature. The Cross-Island Line, which will cross through a Nature Reserve, will do so underground, through the granite bedrock far under the forest — an outcome helped by engagement with nature groups. Plans for public housing have been altered to include more forested areas (e.g., Bidadari, Dover Forest, Yishun/Miltonia), and planning for such major projects now includes the feedback from nature groups earlier in the planning process.

Biodiversity is now mainstreamed into the development of Singapore. Nature is a key component of the Singapore Green Plan 2030. More people than ever benefit from and contribute to the greening of Singapore. We plant trees, monitor wildlife, go on nature walks. Bird photographers congregate in large flocks everywhere. Indicators of a nature-oriented society seem to be in place.

But I think we are only just starting on a journey that started in 1954. Despite the increase in general knowledge about nature, I feel we are a long way from the easy familiarity with nature that many had in the 1950s. The challenge is to cultivate both so that knowledge and values combine with action to form a virtuous cycle that will steer us away from the terrible biodiversity crisis we are in. Singapore has tremendous capacity — in finance, business research, education, communications, policy, and legal expertise — to affect changes needed to help nature. Much of this will come from policy and diplomacy, or from the finance and business sector. And maybe a nature group can help make this happen.

A prominent businessman was among the founders of the Nature Society, but I do not think it was because of his ties to industry. He was a talented and committed naturalist. I dream that one day we all will be naturalists, that we will all feel a powerful connection with nature, and that we will harness our talents and networks towards the conservation and restoration of nature. Maybe one day, even back to what it was in 1954.

Shawn Lum is a botanist and forest ecologist. He taught at the National Institute of Education for over 20 years before moving to the Nanyang Technological University Asian School of the Environment in 2015. His work has largely focussed on the dynamics and capacity for regeneration of isolated pockets of tropical rainforest. Shawn is a member of the Nature Society (Singapore) and served as its President from 2015 to 2023. He was born on a large island (Honshu), raised on a much smaller one (Oahu), and has made his life on an even smaller one (Singapore).

Chapter 30

The Legal Protection of Nature in Singapore

Lye Lin Heng

Laws to protect Singapore's wildlife were passed over a hundred years ago with the Wild Birds Protection Ordinance (1884). Today, almost all wild animals and birds are protected in Singapore under the Wildlife Act (1965), and some wildlife are given additional protection. There are also laws protecting trees and plants. The extent of protection depends on their precise location, as different laws and regulations apply.

Singapore is party to many international laws that protect nature, including the Convention on International Trade in Endangered Species of Wild Fauna and Flora (CITES) and the Convention on Biological Diversity (CBD), and has passed laws to implement these.

This paper will provide a quick overview of the laws that protect nature in Singapore, excluding the marine environment.

General Protection of Wild Animals and Birds

The Wild Animals and Birds Act (WABA) was passed in 1965 and renamed in 2020 as the Wildlife Act (WA), 1965, commencing

31 December 2021. It is administered by the National Parks Board (NParks) and its Director-General, Wildlife Management.

The WA prohibits the "intentional" feeding and release of wildlife — maximum fine $5,000; $10,000 for a subsequent offence (s. 5A; s. 5B). It is also an offence to kill, trap, take or keep any wildlife — maximum fine $10,000 or imprisonment up to six months or both fine and imprisonment (s. 5C). These penalties are enhanced if the person is in an "animal-related business" (defined in the Act) — fine $20,000 or imprisonment up to a year or both. Greater protection is given to certain wildlife species under the new Wildlife (Protected Species) Rules — 11 mammals, 6 birds, 9 reptiles, 3 fishes, and 8 invertebrates (fine $50,000 or imprisonment of up to two years or both). However, some wildlife species are not protected. These are listed in the Wildlife (Exemption) Order — 4 mammals (rats and mice), 4 birds, 5 lizards, and all invertebrates other than those specially protected.

Other offences include: the setting up of spring guns, snares or other traps or devices without permission (s. 7 — fine $20,000 or imprisonment up to 12 months or both); the sale or export of wildlife (s. 8 — same penalties as above); and the import of wildlife (s. 9 — fine $10,000 or imprisonment up to 12 months or both). Section 6 allows an "occupier or person in charge of any land" to "kill, trap or take any wildlife found damaging or destroying the crops or any other property on the land" — the onus of proof falls on this person.

There are wide powers of seizure and search (s. 11A, 11B) and power to arrest without warrant (s. 12). The court also has power to order forfeiture of a conveyance seized in the commission of the offence (s. 12C–E), and authorise repayment of expenses incurred in storage, housing, maintenance, transport, repatriation or disposal of any seized item (s. 12F). The court may also direct that any fine or part thereof be paid to the informer as a reward (s. 13).

Protection of Animals and Plants Under the Parks and Trees Act

The Parks and Trees Act (PTA) and its Regulations protect Singapore's nature reserves, national parks and public parks, and regulate its recreational and educational use by the public. It is implemented by NParks and its officers.

Singapore has four nature reserves — the Bukit Timah Nature Reserve, the Central Catchment Nature Reserve, the Labrador Nature Reserve and the Sungei Buloh Wetland Reserve; two national parks — the Singapore Botanic Gardens and Fort Canning Park; and one marine park — the Sisters' Island Marine Park. A "public park" is defined under the Parks and Trees Act (s. 2) to mean "any State land, any land belonging to the National Parks Board (NParks) or any other land, which is:

(a) utilised as a public park, marine park, recreation ground, playground, garden, public open space, walk, park connector or green verge; and
(b) managed or maintained by the Board."

The terms "animal" and "plant" are given wide definitions in section 2. "Animal" includes bird, reptile, amphibian, fish (including shellfish), insect or any other living creature, vertebrate or invertebrate, and their eggs or young. "Plant" includes algae, lichen or fungus.

Offences in relation to trees and plants include the cutting, collecting or displacing of any tree or plant or the clearing or cultivation of any land. In relation to animals, it is an offence to capture, displace or feed any animal; disturb or take its nest; collect, remove or wilfully displace any other organism; use any device to trap or capture any animal; carry or possess any explosive, net, trap or hunting device. It is also an offence to carry out any activity which may cause injury or death to any animal or other organism; or to release any animal or allow any domestic animal to stray into a nature reserve.

If committed in a nature reserve or national park, the penalty is a maximum fine of S$50,000 or imprisonment of up to six months or both; and, in the case of a continuing offence, a daily fine of S$500 if it continues after conviction (s. 8 and 9). If committed in a public park, the maximum fine is S$5,000 (reg.23(b)). The bringing of animals (other than a pet or guide dog) or abandonment of any animals in a public park is also prohibited (maximum fine of S$2,000).

It is also an offence to destroy, damage or deface "any object of zoological, botanical, geological, ethnological, scientific or aesthetic interest" in a nature reserve or national park (s.10) — incurring a maximum fine of S$20,000.

The Regulations prohibit smoking in national parks, nature reserves and public parks (a fine of S$2,000).

Protection of Flora and Fauna in Other Parks in Singapore

Specific laws protect flora and fauna in the parks managed by JTC, Sentosa Development Corporation (SDC), and the Public Utilities Board (PUB). The penalties differ — the maximum fine is S$500 under the JTC (Parks) Regulations; S$2,000 under the Sentosa

Development Corporation Regulations and S$3,000 under the Public Utilities (Reservoirs, Catchment Area and Waterway) Regulations.

Tree Conservation Areas

There are two tree conservation areas in Singapore, established by the Parks and Trees (Preservation of Trees) Order. These are: (1) The area bounded by Dunearn Road, Whitley Road, Mount Pleasant Road, Thomson Road, Lornie Road, Pan Island Expressway, Clementi Road, Pasir Panjang Road, Telok Blangah Road, Lower Delta Road, Ayer Rajah Expressway, Alexandra Road, River Valley Road, Fort Canning Road and Selegie Road; (2) The area bounded by Netheravon Road, Cranwell Road, Loyang Avenue, Loyang Way, Upper Changi Road North and Changi Village Road.

Trees with a girth of more than one metre measured a half-metre from the ground, growing on tree conservation areas or growing on vacant land (whether within or outside a tree conservation area) cannot be cut down without the permission of the Commissioner of Parks and Trees (maximum fine of $50,000 — S.13–15 PTA). The Commissioner may protect a large tree or group of large trees (girth of at least one metre) in a tree conservation area or growing on vacant land by serving a Tree Conservation Notice (s.15, PTA). This Notice can be revoked at any time.

Heritage Road Green Buffers

Roadside greenery along the verges of roads with mature trees and greenery can be specially protected by designating these verges as Heritage Road Green Buffers (s. 16 PTA). Five roads have been so gazetted — Mount Pleasant Road, South Buona Vista Road, Lim Chu Kang Road, Arcadia Road, and Mandai Road. It is the duty of NParks to manage and maintain these areas (s. 17). No tree or plant within these buffers can be cut or damaged without permission (s. 18 — maximum fine of S$50,000).

Heritage Trees

NParks has established a Heritage Trees Scheme "to identify, recognise and conserve majestic individual trees in our landscape." Only trees endorsed by the Heritage Trees Panel would be accepted as Heritage Trees. The criteria for endorsement include (dependent on species) a girth size of at least five metres, rarity of species, aesthetics and growth form, historical significance, cultural reasons, social and educational value. Members of the public are invited to nominate these heritage trees via an online form. However, it does not appear that trees designated as "Heritage Trees" have legal protection *per se*. To date, there are some 262 trees, located all over the island, each specifically mentioned in "Singapore's Heritage Trees Register", kept by NParks. All of these are of native, indigenous species.

Trade in Endangered Species — CITES

Singapore ratified CITES in 1986, and passed the Endangered Species (Import and Export) Act (ESA) in implementation. This was repealed and replaced with a new ESA in 2006 and this again was substantially amended in 2022, with effect from 1 November 2022. Each amendment increased penalties and tightened loopholes. It is enforced by NParks and its Director, Wildlife Trade Control.

The ESA prohibits trade in endangered animals, plants and their by-products, unless with a permit from NParks. Its subsidiary laws prohibit the sale of parts and derivatives of tigers, rhinoceros (horns) and elephants (tusks and teeth). Artificially propagated plants with proper permits may be brought into Singapore. As from 1 November 2022, ivory is prohibited from display except for educational or religious purposes.

Under the ESA, the penalty for trade in CITES Appendix I species (animals and plants on the verge of extinction) is a maximum fine of S$100,000 (up from S$50,000 previously) for each specimen (but not to exceed S$500,000 or the market value of all the specimens of that species at the time of the offence, whichever is higher) or imprisonment for up to six years or both. For specimens in Appendices II or III, the maximum fine is S$50,000 for each specimen (but not exceeding S$500,000 for all specimens, or the market value at the time of the offence, whichever is higher) or imprisonment up to four years or both fine and imprisonment. The new law makes it clear that the ESA applies to specimens on transit — proper permits must be issued by the country of export at least 14 days before its arrival in Singapore, and by the country of import or the final destination. The same penalties for breach apply.

In the case of an offence by a corporation, unincorporated association or partnership, the fines are doubled — for Appendix I species, a maximum fine of S$200,000 for each specimen (but not exceeding S$1,000,000 or the market value of all the specimens of that species at the time of the offence, whichever is higher), or imprisonment up to eight years or both; and for Appendices II and III specimens, the maximum fine is S$100,000 for each specimen of that scheduled species (but not to exceed S$1,000,000 or the market value at the time of the offence, whichever is higher) or to imprisonment for a term not exceeding six years or both.

Officers from NParks have wide powers of enforcement including powers to investigate and powers of entry, search and seizure. Persons may be arrested without a warrant, and items used in connection with the offence including any conveyance such as vehicles, aircraft or ships or may be seized and forfeited, with some exceptions.

Protection of Biological Diversity

Singapore has signed and ratified the Convention on Biological Diversity (CBD). Under Article 15 (Access to Genetic Resources), States have sovereign rights over their natural resources; and access to genetic resources is to be determined by national laws. Some steps have been taken towards implementing this. Surveys have been done of the biodiversity resources in Singapore. NParks has devised an application form which requires all persons conducting Taxonomic/Ecological Research to seek prior written permission from the Board. The Research Permit devised by NParks contains various conditions.

Conclusion

As with other cities, one of the biggest challenges for Singapore is allowing for development while conserving its natural environment. Singapore's laws do not mandate environmental impact assessments (EIAs). NParks has initiated Biodiversity Impact Assessment Guidelines to serve as a guide on the biodiversity component of the

EIA. In practice, EIAs are accessible to the public, and non-governmental organisations including the Nature Society (Singapore) work at achieving a good partnership with the authorities. At the international level, Singapore has initiated the Cities Biodiversity Index as a self-assessment tool for cities to evaluate and monitor their biodiversity conservation efforts against their own individual baselines.

Lye Lin Heng, PBM, is Hon. Fellow, Law Faculty, National University of Singapore, where she taught Environmental Law and Property Law for many years. She is Hon. Advisor and former Director, Asia-Pacific Centre for Environmental Law (APCEL). She was Vice-Dean (Graduate Programs), and initiated the NUS multi-disciplinary M.Sc. (Environmental Management) [MEM] programme, chairing the programme from its inception in 2001 till her retirement in 2019. Her publications include journal articles and books on Singapore's Environmental Laws. She is Hon. Advisor to the Nature Society (Singapore) and WWF Singapore. She was a member of the Board of Governors, IUCN Academy of Environmental Law and its co-Chair, Teaching and Capacity-Building Committee.

Chapter 31

When We Nurture Nature, Nature Nurtures Us

Kirtida Mekani

The evolution of Singapore's green journey is a fascinating case study. From "Garden City" to "City in a Garden" to our present-day "City in Nature", this nation is a small city-state that has nurtured the environment for decades — and in return, has embraced the benefits of being nurtured by nature.

In essence, our island is a beautiful illustration of how nature works — an ecosystem of inter-connections and inter-dependence. The groundwork has been laid by those before us, but more needs to be done — especially with our efforts in nurturing our own pipeline of talented environmentalists, climate change experts and other environment-related specialists in Singapore.

To achieve this, we must raise the level of engagement that our communities have with nature, and make environmentalism and sustainability second nature for every Singaporean.

How Nature Has Nurtured Me

I have often been asked, "What are the roots of your love for nature, and your insatiable drive for inspiring this care in others?" It can all be traced to a compost pit on my family's farm, back when I was a child. Nature was my first teacher, and that compost pit was my first textbook and toy, rolled into one.

As I played with the soil in that compost pit, I observed how every element in nature exists in harmony — sunlight and water would nurture a seed into a tree, which would offer food, shelter and oxygen to people, animals and insects, which would then fertilise the tree. And this interdependent cycle of nurturing and being nurtured, has been destined to continue forever.

Through that compost pit, I developed a love, admiration and respect for nature. And through my work as an environmentalist, I hope that I can create similarly special moments for others — whether they are everyday Singaporeans who enjoy gardening, students who are discovering the wonders of nature through school, or corporate leaders looking to create positive change by supporting green initiatives.

Navigating Towards a Sustainable Future

Presently, our nation is home to excellent environmental initiatives. These include the Singapore Green Plan 2030, our net-zero emissions target for 2050, our efforts to enhance biodiversity across the island, as well as ground level aspirations to use less plastic, recycle more, and others.

But the key to long-term success in this area is not solely a top-down approach to driving nationwide programmes — it is transforming "environmental initiatives" into "everyday habits".

One of these "everyday habits" that we need to instil in ourselves is an appreciation for a better quality of life, rather than obsessing over simply having "more". Presently, materialism is causing us to buy more, use more, and waste more — but it does not have to be this way. When we learn to value quality over quantity, we can start reducing waste and enjoying a higher quality of life.

Additionally, it is only when we have made replenishing what we use, planting trees, and learning from nature has become a part of our everyday lives, that sustaining our environment will become second nature — making our efforts feel easy and natural.

To drive us towards a future that is truly green and sustainable, we will need to nurture our own stream of environmentally-focussed talents — talents who will inspire their fellow Singaporeans, and be our green ambassadors to the world. While we will continue to bring in talents from overseas, our pipeline of local talents will be essential to the success of our long-term environmental ambitions.

This is my hope for Singapore, and my vision for our future generations.

Making Nature Second Nature

Over the years, we have cultivated many outstanding nature-focussed programmes, such as the Plant-A-Tree programme, community garden groups, and many others. Importantly, these initiatives are not simply government-instituted activities conducted in isolation — they engage various communities across Singapore, from individuals to corporations, and instil an appreciation for nature in both young and old.

I am especially happy with how the Plant-A-Tree programme has brought Singaporeans from all walks of life closer to nature. To date, the programme, which I conceptualised in 2007, has connected

100,000 people with nature and seen over 65,000 trees planted across the island. Importantly, the programme was rolled out with the National Parks Board (NParks) as a national movement and now strongly supports our nation's ambitious OneMillionTrees initiative that is at the heart of Singapore's journey towards becoming a City in Nature.

Meanwhile, our over 1,800 community gardens are beautifying our community spaces, instilling a love for gardening in everyday people, and connecting hearts through a common admiration for plants and nature. Additionally, NParks has also been creating community nurseries to bridge the gap between Singaporeans and nature. At these community nurseries, volunteers get to grow native plants from seeds collected from nearby parks and forests.

Our schools are headed in a "green direction" too, with more pre-schools incorporating "discovery through nature" types of lessons into a holistic curriculum that extends beyond traditional academic subjects. Although these immersive, nature-oriented lessons are not yet commonplace in most classes here, some institutions are taking the lead.

For instance, the United World College of South East Asia (UWCSEA) is educating and nurturing the next generation of eco-changemakers with its Rainforest Nursery Project, which gives students "hands on" time in specialised nurseries with over 650 seedlings of vulnerable and critically endangered rainforest species of plants. Commonwealth Secondary School has also instilled their own "eco culture" by setting up several eco-habitats within the school — giving students a fascinating opportunity to observe real eco-systems and appreciate the wonders of nature. At Meridian Secondary

School, they have an engaging green programme with a therapy garden for kids to relax in, while appreciating nature.

I firmly believe that the mother of all learning is in the "doing", and that's what makes these initiatives special. They allow Singaporeans to be directly involved with nature, to "get our hands dirty" and learn by doing — and to make nature, second nature.

Lessons from Nature

Nature can be our greatest teacher, and this is perhaps best illustrated in our study of biomimicry. By studying nature, humans have progressed in our design thinking capabilities — crafting ingenuous solutions to everyday issues and insurmountable obstacles alike.

After all, nature has already solved most of the problems we are seeing today — it is our responsibility to seek out these answers in nature, and use them to overcome present-day challenges. And in many ways, we already have.

Before humans took flight, birds opened our eyes to the possibility of doing so. Mangroves shared their secrets to stopping floods. And when the automotive industry needed glass that would not shatter in an accident, potentially causing serious injury to drivers and passengers, we took inspiration from nacre (mother of pearl) to create glass that bends instead of breaking — thus saving lives. Velcro, turbines, wetsuits, adhesives, and so many other innovations have been the (direct and indirect) results of the lessons that nature has taught us, and this is just the beginning.

In Singapore, rapid urbanisation has led to a significant increase in our electricity use — especially for air-conditioning in buildings.

While engineering more energy-efficient air-conditioning systems is one solution, we can also look to nature for answers. For instance, if we can design buildings that are able to regulate their temperature the same way that our skin (or the skin of animals) does, we could see big energy savings in this area. The good news is that we are already doing so, with local scientists and designers presently developing a biomimicry design toolkit for tropical building skins.

Beyond buildings, thought leaders are also studying how ant behaviour could help us to improve traffic flow on congested roads, how understanding termite nests may enhance building designs, and much more.

Despite still being in its infancy, biomimicry has already taken us to exciting places and solved many of our biggest challenges. As we continue to understand nature more intimately, the possibilities will continue to expand, and that's exciting to think about.

By studying nature, nature is nurturing our minds.

The Essence of Charity, Contribution and Paying It Forward

Of course, all these incredibly impactful initiatives are not run on love alone — funding is instrumental to the success of any movement, and this is true for environmental efforts as well.

It is heartening to see that here in Singapore, we have systems in place to raise funds for our nationwide greening and community building initiatives. Some of the most prominent organisations that are making this happen are the Singapore Environment Council (SEC), a non-profit organisation that influences thinking on sustainability issues and environmental efforts in the region; and the Garden City Fund (GCF), a charity that supports Singapore's greening efforts, urban biodiversity conservation model, and community engagement activities.

Other active non-governmental organisations (NGOs) include the Nature Society (Singapore) and the Worldwide Fund for Nature (WWF) Singapore. The Nature Society has served as a conscience for greening Singapore since our early days, and has positively influenced greening efforts across — and beyond — our island. For example, proposing the protection of the Sungei Buloh Wetland Reserve as a natural conservation area for migratory shorebirds and other indigenous wildlife.

Meanwhile, WWF Singapore — through its innovative Eco-Schools programme — has helped more than 20,000 students in 126 primary and secondary schools in Singapore to become sustainable changemakers in their school communities with action-based learning.

This constructive dialogue between NGOs and the government is the catalyst we need for more positive environmental initiatives. This collaborative approach will give Singapore more innovative solutions for overcoming the issues we encounter, and give every Singaporean a more personal stake in our nation's environmental ideals and sustainability practices.

Planting the Seeds of Our Future

Over the years, I have had the honour of serving as the former Executive Director of the Singapore Environment Council (SEC), volunteering with NGOs like the Nature Society (Singapore), being on the management committee of the Garden City Fund, co-founding Biomimicry Network Singapore, and contributing on the boards of the Botanic Gardens Conservation International, WWF Singapore, Biomimicry Network Singapore, Garden City Fund, and other institutions that are focussed on promoting environmental causes.

Through these organisations, I have been able to create initiatives that have spread further — and to more people, schools and businesses — than I otherwise could have, as an individual.

I believe that leveraging this "multiplier effect" is essential for ensuring the success of any environmental initiatives. For instance, when I was a part of the SEC, I initiated a programme that contributed to the publication of "Greening our Young Minds", which is a handbook for teachers to use when creating their own unique nature-focussed programmes and lesson plans for students. And to share my personal thoughts on approaching life through the lessons that nature has taught me, I penned and distributed my book, titled *Compassion for Life Through Nature: The Essence of Jeevdaya.*

My motivation for doing all this is simple. I want to acknowledge the blessings and joy that nature has given me, all throughout my life — and pay it forward.

My message to you is simple, too. Consider how nature has blessed our lives in this City in Nature. We live in an urban environment that is filled with beautiful, lush greenery. The air we breathe is fresh and life-giving, thanks to the oxygen offered by the trees around us. Our delicate ecosystem is in balance and singing in harmony, because we have nurtured nature, and nature is nurturing us.

Consider playing your part in this balance. There are so many opportunities to do so, from planting a tree to cleaning the beach, or even making a small effort to recycle your trash. When each of us takes a few small steps towards sustainability, we collectively make giant strides towards our larger green goals.

As a nation, we are on the right track. But there is still work to be done.

We need to build our pipeline of environmental innovators and talents, accelerate our efforts in creating a circular economy that is restorative by design, and create even more opportunities for Singaporeans to be

Planting a *Campnosperma auriculatum* (Terentang) tree at Spottiswoode Park.

involved with nature — making environmentalism "second nature" to citizens.

When we can achieve all this, we truly will be on track to blooming our City in Nature. Let us continue to nurture nature, and allow nature to nurture us.

Kirtida Mekani is a multi-faceted individual who dedicates her efforts to the four key pillars in her life — the environment, education, arts, and business. As a business leader, Kirtida has proven expertise in fundraising, institutional advancement, and capacity building. In education, she has spearheaded forward-thinking initiatives in schools across the nation. In 2015, Kirtida was bestowed the prestigious President's Award for the Environment. She was also nominated for the Singapore Women Award in 2014, and recognised as a 2012 Community in Bloom (CIB) ambassador. Kirtida is also an accomplished artist and author of her book, *Compassion for Life Through Nature: The Essence of Jeevdaya.*

Chapter 32

Here be Dragonflies: An Ode to Singapore's Flying Dragons

Marcus Ng and Robin Ngiam

Medieval maps, at least those commonly depicted in movies and other fantastical tales, often mark an uncharted quarter of the world with the phrase, "Here be dragons". Singapore is more often associated with another mythical beast — the apocryphal lion of Sri Tri Buana — but a contemporary map of Singapore's island would not be wrong if it came with the quip, "Here be dragonflies."

Those who grew up in a rather different Singapore, one replete with piggeries, poultry farms and fish ponds, may well agree. For dragonflies once filled the air above such settlements and darted around the pools that dotted Singapore's rural landscapes. They must have been a dazzle of colours to youngsters then: a flutter of wings and lithe bodies in reds, blues and yellows that danced against the wind to herald the hottest hours of the tropical day.

Today, members of the pioneer generation may bemoan the loss of such bucolic scenes. Ponds have been filled, farmsteads levelled and villages bulldozed for new towns with dragons as fountains and playgrounds. Some also lament that as a result, dragonflies have become scarce and seldom seen, for the regular swarms and nocturnal incursions they once encountered have faded from view.

It is true that parts of the island were, and remain, no place for dragonflies — too dense, too bare, too disturbed and too brutal for any but the least demanding of odonates. That said, such inimical environments may well have been more prevalent in the decades when industrial estates took precedence over nature parks and the garden city was still a work in progress, more akin to a concrete jungle than today's community in nature.

Dragonflies in the City

Dragons, real or re-created, may have faded from our collective memories, but as Singapore grew, greened and grappled with aspirations that saw beyond the bare necessities of nation-building, dragonflies wormed their way back into reservoirs, canals, ditches, lilyponds and lakeside gardens. They may not be as readily apparent as when kampongs were more real than spirit, but the dragonflies are still here, even if no maps mark them, if we can learn to pause a little more, look down, peer up and see beyond the veneers of modernity that shroud the city's natural layers.

Look around your neighbourhood, your walk to the Mass Rapid Transit (MRT), your nearest park connector or nature way. Wherever there are pockets of vegetation — an unmown field, a butterfly garden, the fringe of a still-unshaven hill, even the secret gardens atop multi-storey car parks — there are likely to be dragonflies. For young adults often wander far from their breeding grounds to fuel up in open green spaces before they return to their birth-sites or seek out fresh territories. Not all will survive this foray into suburban domains; many are caught by birds, lizards and spiders, while others succumb to more human hazards: pesticides that care not whether you are a bloodsucker or feed on them; wheels that crush low-flying dragonflies on streets and sidewalks; fumes and fierier emissions from smokestacks and other industrial installations.

Countless dragonflies, especially species active at twilight such as duskdarters and duskhawks, also end up in habitats for humanity, lured by artificial light onto landings, balconies and stairwells. Some may pass the night on walls, but many meet their end in cobwebs or expire after smashing their bodies into dead ends and dry corners. Even delicate flyers such as sprites and wisps may find their way into high-rise rooms and hallways, as immature individuals undertake nocturnal dispersals that result in a fatal side quest.

Dragonflies Around Our Homes

Marcus: Moribund damselflies are commonly seen at my home in Yishun, even along higher corridors, where they vie with mayflies and moths for nooks to perch or perish in peace. Not a few squeeze their way into laundry yards and living halls, where they probably float unnoticed before dying in a dustball of domestic debris. Dragonflies such as Dancing Dropwings and Common Scarlets also show up fairly frequently, drawing the attention of children and cicaks (geckos) alike as they crash through the void deck and enmesh themselves into municipal fixtures.

Such cases of mortality are (hopefully) anomalies in a neighbourhood where I have counted nearly 20 species from just my block and its immediate vicinity, and up to 26 species if nearby parks are included. My block's roof garden, despite having no waterbodies, plays host to Coastal Gliders that cling to the highest twigs of starfruit trees,

Yellow-barred Flutterers that hunt from pandan thickets, and Blue Perchers that hug the unruly turf.

Just across the road, a vacant field turns into an ephemeral marsh during wet spells that allow sedges and bladderworts to out-compete plainer grasses. Black-Tipped Perchers and Common Bluetails dart about shallow pools after micro-moths and leafhoppers, while Saddlebag Gliders and Wandering Gliders patrol the higher echelons in the hostile company of swifts and swallows. Dancing Dropwings and Coastal Gliders also turn up when the normally shorn vegetation erupts in between mowings.

A 10-minute walk away, a small pond in Yishun Park comes alive around midday as Sultans, Grenadiers and Spine-tufted Skimmers take turns to patrol its perimeters. Later in the afternoon, Blue Sprites and Emperors risk the maws of American Bullfrogs as they insert their eggs into purple waterlilies. The understorey of this forested knoll also harbours duskhawks and duskhawkers, which emerge at sundown to feast on a cloud of flies; some are drawn to the lights of a nearby hospital, where they may hawk over an artificial canopy or explore the passageways of a planted basement, from which they may never re-emerge.

Robin: I reside in Ang Mo Kio, where dragonflies abound in the parks scattered across this neighbourhood. But these parks also offer a lesson in how precarious life can be for species that are more sensitive to changes in the urban environment. Sandwiched between two housing estates, Bishan-Ang Mo Kio Park has become a landmark green space with its meandering waterway that swells into a floodplain during heavy storms. This river charts a leisurely course through lush banks with pockets of riparian vegetation, which furnish breeding and roosting spots for many common dragonflies and the occasional rarity.

Small ponds in the adjacent parkland act as refuges for odonates that prefer stiller waters. Some years ago, one of these pools hosted a colony of Fiery Coraltails, a lovely damselfly with deep red males. These damselflies were easily spotted as they formed heart-shaped mating wheels before landing on a floating leaf to insert their eggs into submerged plants. Many generations persisted until a row of trees next to the water were removed. Shorn of the shelter provided by the boughs, the population dwindled and vanished. A decade later, these shade-loving damselflies are still missing, even though the pond still teems with other odonates that can withstand the full fury of the tropical sun.

Even tolerant species will not survive, however, if an entire habitat is lost. In another corner of Ang Mo Kio, work on a new expressway has consumed part of a town garden, including a pond where Variable Wisps and Trumpet Tails once hunted alongside rarer species such as the Blue Adjutant and Bronze Flutterer. Only time will tell if these odonates, hardy or otherwise, will return when the dust has settled and the garden regains a waterbody.

Dragonflies in Our Forests

Further afield, there are other dragonflies that occupy the wilder corners of the city, having endured two centuries of change that transformed an island of primeval woods into a colonial hub. The British saw Singapore's forests and swamps as uninhabitable realms that cried out to be tapped and tamed — hard timber for cold cash, tigers for trophies, and malarial wetlands to be drained for crops and cantonments. Only a few oddballs such as Alfred Russel Wallace ventured under the canopy in search of zoological treasures. Their nets yielded, among other insects, several dragonflies new to science and yet still largely unknown to many who call Singapore home.

Today, nearly 170 years after Wallace first surveyed Bukit Timah, some of the dragonflies that he collected still haunt his former hunting ground. Compared to the rest of the island, this hill has suffered little from loggers. Hence, it harbours trees that are large enough to form breeding habitats for specialised, forest-dependent dragonflies such as the Bombardier. One of Wallace's discoveries from Singapore in 1854, this rare dragonfly has a penchant for high-rise nurseries such as rain-filled tree holes and buttress pans, where its nymphs can forage for other larvae in a fish-free environment.

With its reddish hues and shiny face, the Bombardier is hard to miss along Wallace Trail, where adults may come down to bask during sunny spells. This path, which transforms into a creek at parts after heavy downpours, also offers another dragonfly that Wallace first netted at Bukit Timah, but one that is much harder to spot, for it seldom strays from the darker nooks of shady brooks. Despite this, the Malayan Grisette is still a welcome sight, for like the Bombardier, this silvery damselfly persists only in hilly streams that have suffered little disturbance by modern man.

Wallace was also the first to collect a jewel of a damselfly during his time in Singapore, which was spent mainly around Bukit Timah. Sadly, this species, the Fiery Gem, can no longer be found there. The cool, well-shaded streams it inhabited have been lost or denuded of aquatic vegetation, and the gems never returned, even after the foothills gained a secondary lease of life as a forest reserve. Today, the Fiery Gem inhabits a singular refugium, Nee Soon Swamp Forest, a wetland formed by the headwaters of Sungei Seletar that is home to many plants and animals that exist nowhere else on the island.

It is no surprise that the native dragonflies now confined to Nee Soon Swamp Forest — such as the Interrupted Threadtail, Arthur's

Clubtail and Pot-bellied Elf — are all highly threatened with local extinction. Their habitat is reasonably secure, but introduced predators, such as African catfish and South American cichlids, that have established themselves in the surrounding catchment pose an existential risk to dragonfly larvae as well as other native aquatic fauna should they invade the Nee Soon basin. In the longer term, the swamp faces the peril of climate change that is expected to cause longer and more intense periods of drought, from which entire populations of stream life may never recover.

Nee Soon Swamp Forest is off-limits to the public due to its ecological sensitivity. But its winged denizens not infrequently show up at the forest edges of the abutting Upper Seletar Reservoir Park, and may also grace the future Nee Soon Nature Park off Upper Thomson Road. Elsewhere on the island, many of Singapore's 127 extant dragonfly species continue to haunt the wetter stretches of its reserves and parks, as well as more wooded corridors and gardens between the coasts and by the bays. At times, urban swarms may gather above roads and lawns, floating out of reach but well within view. But for the most part, all it takes for one to detect Singapore's dragonflies is a willingness to slow down just enough to make out gossamer wings from tangled banks.

An Island of "Dragons"

The Lion City is also a land of "dragons". They may not spew fire or inspire fear, but Singapore's dragonflies still command a strength that spans the country and provokes a response that wavers between wonder and resignation. For these insects, which blend beauty and beast in one miniature mould, share our spaces but not Singapore's plans. They may submit, for a moment, to observation or a gentle

A Fiery Gem (*Libellago aurantiaca*), a damselfly that survives locally only in Nee Soon Swamp Forest.

touch, but can never be tamed or taught to play by the rules. And the sheer sight of their bodies in motion, alert at watch or aflight against the wind, offers a glimpse of life intense and untrammelled, creatures in control of what little they have in a world that is on the brink of tumbling into a fate of its own unmaking.

Marcus Ng is an independent writer and researcher. His interests include the natural histories of Singapore and Malaysia; insects of Southeast Asia (in particular dragonflies and moths); and the natural and human histories of Singapore's coasts and islands. He was the curator of *Balik Pulau*, a special exhibition on Singapore's islands at the National Museum of Singapore, and two thematic galleries featuring the William Farquhar Collection of Natural History Drawings: *Danger and Desire* and *Magic and Menace*.

Robin Ngiam is a biodiversity consultant who has worked on dragonflies since 2005, spanning taxonomy, ecological surveys, conservation policies, environmental impact assessments (EIAs), training courses, outreach and guided tours. He has extensive publications on dragonflies from Singapore and Borneo (Sarawak). Sharing a passion for dragonflies, Robin and Marcus wrote *A Photographic Guide to the Dragonflies and Damselflies of Singapore*, which was published in 2022.

Chapter 33

Hard Truths from a Flawed Naturalist

Peter K. L. Ng

Of all the distinguished names in this tome, I would arguably be the least qualified to write a piece on *Peace with Nature*. As my critics so maintain — I am a "killer by nature" — tainted and morally unqualified. There is so much blood on my hands, I have no right to call myself a "conservationist" or even a sentient "natural historian". The blood has washed away any credentials I may have or have had. And I agree — to a point. Killer I am by necessity, hunter I am by profession. I am unapologetic. I am at peace with this paradox. Let me now share some nuggets of "wisdom" I have learnt from spending a lifetime hunting crabs and animals...trying to do the right thing; and how I live with the killing.

I have had a love-affair with crabs since 1978 — for 45 years now. I have no idea how my life got entwined with crabs — it just happened one day when I undertook a project for my old alma mater. And as the old saying goes, the rest is history. I like crabs. I have a passion — some say an inordinate obsession, for them. I like catching them, studying them and understanding what they do, and trying to find out what species are out there. And I have become good at this. This endeavour has sent me all over the world looking for them, from chasing down old specimens collected 250 years ago to hunting down strange new ones in God-forsaken lands. To go where few or none have gone before. To find what no one has known before. Finding a new species or a rare species is wonderful feeling, to know that you hold in your hands an animal that has not been named before. Or finding something that has not been seen for hundreds of years. Discovering new species is not just a hunt, although I must admit it is fun. There is also the long and tedious process of scientific sleuthing to be sure of what it is — it is detective work at its best. One must be a linguist, historian and Sherlock Holmes all rolled into one. While there is the thrill and exhilaration of the "hunt", there is actually a lot of long, hard, boring work as well! Rarely is there beauty without pain — one sometimes has to suffer for the science. I am glad to report that after 45 years, that elation from discovering new and rare species still feels the same. That "eureka" moment is a feeling like no other.

The lengths we will go to search for rare things often bring comparisons with the "daring dos" of Indiana Jones, but it is a patently inappropriate comparison. Biologists like me are not searching for man-made objects, important as they may be. We are hunting for the products of millions of years of random mutation and ruthless selection — outcomes not yet known to us, maybe unknowable by mortals — and seeing where they fit into the fabric of life as we perceive it. Or as my religious friends sometimes exclaim — "God's creations". This foundational knowledge is one of the pillars for conservation. We cannot conserve what we do not know.

I hunt both the dead and the living. And for the living, I have to kill them. It is not possible to determine what species they are from a sighting or a photograph. That would not be science — it would be mere "birdwatching". To be a science, for the finding to be objective, testable and examined by others, there must be some dead bodies on which the finding is based. Dead bodies that others can check and maybe find new ways to test out a thesis that a species is new. This need to kill has gotten me into all sorts of scrapes and debates on the morality of such exercises. As if killing an animal is a crime and a sin no conservationist should partake in — rubbish. The sheerest hypocrisy are from people who lecture me on killing the animals I study and yet love a roast chicken on their plate, ignoring the obvious fact that someone had to slaughter the bird for the table. That the blood is not on their hands does not in any way obviate their complicity! Conservation *is* a battle. A forever war that we must undertake to keep as much of our biodiversity intact. Anyone who thinks otherwise, that battles won are permanent victories, is naïve. Or stupid. The few deaths engendered by research activities form the basis for which countless more lives and species may be saved. *This* is the truth of all conflict — that some must die so that others may live. Oscar Wilde was right to remark: "Ideals are dangerous things. Realities are better. They wound, but they're better". In conservation (and war), we must dream ideals but live realities — even when we do not like those realities.

We are being ring-fenced into a world that likes black and white. This preference is a lie in itself and an exercise in hypocrisy. Rarely is conservation about good and bad — we live more often than not in degrees, in shades of grey that defy categorisation. Sometimes, our choices may well be between unpleasant and terrible. And this is not the worst thing that can happen — it is wise to remember Henry Kissinger's caution: "The great tragedies of history occur not when right confronts wrong but when two rights confront each other"! Even Nature itself is overflowing with blood and gore.

So what is good or bad? As humans, we can be judgemental — anthropogenically and unfairly so. A sentence I picked up once from *The Custer Wolf* by Roger Caras (1979), one of my favourite books in my youth, echoes in my brain: "Wolves may not love in the sense men love, but they love in their own way, and no one has yet shown that it is not as good".

Of the hundreds of species I have discovered all around the region, perhaps those from home give me the most angst. People often ask me what is your "favourite species discovered"? Are those from Singapore the best or most important? Do they give you the most satisfaction and pleasure? I hate these questions. But because some of the crabs I named were from Singapore, it is understandable people believe that "home is where the heart is". In all honesty, believe it or not, I actually do not feel that much for the species I discovered. The sense of discovery at the time of the event is a "feel-good" moment for sure. But it passes and I move on to pursuing other challenges and the next unknown. Discovery is a journey — not an end in itself. It is not an accomplishment to be crowed or mulled over, or even deserving of honours. In many ways, it is an endeavour without a soul or a conscience. It is what a good soldier does. Do the job at hand, solve the problem on the table, and then move on to other battles. And there are so many.

I remember a poignant conversation I once had with a very senior government officer in charge of conservation in Singapore, who, luckily, is also a good friend. He was chastising me for taking a nonchalant stand on the new species of freshwater crabs I discovered from Singapore over 30 years ago. "It's your species we are trying hard to conserve! Don't you feel anything at all and want to do more to save it?" he justifiably growled at me. My reply was simple — "It's not MY crab. It has never been MY crab. I just happened to discover and name it. Whether a country wants to conserve it for whatever reason, it's their call. Not mine. I have done my job. The next part of the challenge is yours and the rest of the community. If they want to — conserve it. If they rather it becomes extinct — that is also their call." *Que sera, sera.* To conserve something, anything, the people must want to. It is *not* the job of the discoverer to sound the battle clarion for conservation. I can (and perhaps I should) but I prefer to concentrate on what I am good at — chasing and discovering strange animals. It may be selfish, but the world is a big place and there are so many strange crabs yet to be discovered! And I have only one life.

The crabs are a study in themselves. To be honest, I am happy that I am the discoverer of three endemic species of freshwater crabs on Singapore's island. To be the person who did the necessary homework to ascertain that they were new to science. That the island has three species unique to the country is important and does set the stage for conservation work in land-challenged Singapore. It is good for Singapore, I suppose. The irony of all this is not lost on me. Imagine — if I had not done the work, then we would be happily going on with our lives and activities, unaware that we may be inadvertently condemning the crabs to extinction through our various activities. You cannot conserve what you do not know. Yet while the three crabs are now clearly on the government's and community's radar screen for conservation (and all the "headaches" it will bring), innumerable species are not. Imagine the crabs that were not discovered. Imagine it is only sometime in the future and that a young man or woman, who happens to be rummaging through the shelves of a museum, comes across old specimens collected in the 1980s by one long-dead Peter Ng, and then discovers that they are new to science. Then they go back to the place they were

The author handling a Coconut crab (*Birgus latro*) he found in the Philippines in the 2000s.

collected and find the crabs are no longer there, long extinct. This could have been the fate of the endemic and globally threatened Singapore Freshwater crab (which carries the rather interesting scientific name *Johora singaporensis*). That would have indeed been a very dark tragedy.

In conclusion, as dark as my take on Nature may be, it may be good to remember the powerful words of the German philosopher Friedrich Nietzsche who wrote the masterpiece *Beyond Good and Evil* — "Whoever battles monsters should see to it that in the process he does not become a monster himself. And when you look long into the abyss, the abyss also looks into you." (translated from German). In our endeavours to study, understand and conserve biodiversity, we must not commit hubris and become the monster we now battle against. And it is so easy…

Peter K. L. Ng is in the Department of Biological Sciences and an associate in the Lee Kong Chian Natural History Museum at the National University of Singapore (NUS). He has been teaching in the university since 1990, has helped establish a multitude of teaching modules, and also been involved in various administrative tasks for the university and government agencies. He has worked on a wide variety of animals and issues in Singapore and the region, focussing on aquatic animals including fish and crabs.

Chapter 34

The Re-introduction of the Oriental Pied Hornbill to Singapore

Ng Soon-Chye with Marc Cremades

My journey with Nature has been, and still is, a journey in which I (SC Ng) met so many people from all walks of life, and I have been blessed by my association with these dedicated and passionate people, many of whom have larger-than-life personalities. This written piece is but a small slice in the kaleidoscope of my humbling, yet enormous experience with nature. This story is but a small peek into the vast experiences of the people I have met. And it is a pleasure to share this particular journey with Marc Cremades, a special friend. I come from a medical background, especially in human reproduction, where I developed the first in-vitro fertilisation (IVF) programme in Singapore, and was responsible for Asia's first "test-tube" baby in 1983. Marc's background was even more exciting: he spent 10 years on conservation projects in Madagascar, as well as worked on two wildlife movie documentaries (one being the award winning "Winged Migration"). In addition to co-initiating the Hornbill Project, he has also contributed to numerous breeding and conservation programmes for the Jurong Bird Park. He is now tasked to rejuvenate two new attractions in the Mandai Parks (Bird Paradise and Rainforest).

We are now relatively familiar in Singapore with the sight of this huge black-and-white noisy bird, the Oriental Pied Hornbill, seen even in Orchard Road. This was not the case in the early to mid-1990s, when occasional sightings were probably either escapees or visitors from Peninsular Malaysia to Pulau Ubin. The Oriental Pied Hornbill was recorded for the first time in Singapore by Sir Alfred Russell Wallace in 1855. It seems to be subsequently observed but not formally recorded. It was only in 1994 when two observations were recorded of at least a pair on Pulau Ubin. The first nesting was recorded on the same island in 1997. The proximity of the southern Peninsular Malaysian forest facilitated the Oriental Pied Hornbill's return to Singapore.

This Hornbill Project story started when I had a chance meeting with Marc Cremades during a bird watching trip in Sungei Buloh Wetlands Reserve, with the first record of discussion on the project with Marc on 2 November 2003. Our first partnership was with the National Parks Board (NParks), who was very supportive of the idea. During the life of the project, we had fantastic support from various NParks officers including Wong Tuan Wah, Dr David Davison, Soon Kiong Koh, Robert Teo, James Gan, Alan Tan, and Mark Lim.

The next partnership was with Jurong Bird Park (Daisy Ling and Dr Wong Hon Man) and with a tertiary academic institution to involve their students, giving them an opportunity to be involved in conservation. As I was then an adjunct in the School of Biological Sciences in Nanyang Technological University (NTU), I managed to convince the School to be involved. We had over 50 NTU students participating over five years, and Ms Lai Huimin was particularly outstanding. Prof Kok Zuea Tang, from the National University of Singapore (NUS) Computer Studies Department, and Dr Tan Kok Kiong who was then with the Department of Electrical and Computer Engineering, were also particularly helpful. In addition to local help, we also had international help, including Professor Pilai Poonswad, the world authority on Asia Hornbills and Dr Alan Kemp, the authority on Hornbills. Funding for the project from generous benefactors included especially the late Lady Yuen Peng McNeice, and her son Terry; and Mr Philip Ng of Far East Organisation. And when the project first started in Pulau Ubin, local knowledge and help came from a host of Ubin residents, especially Mr and Mrs Sapieh, Mrs Li Hua and Yeo Chong Huat. This extensive list emphasises the need for a network of help and hands, and that success will come only when there is involvement at all levels.

Our first field studies were classical observations with binoculars and video cameras. We started to count the number of round trips to the nest cavity of the male and identify the nesting materials and the food offered to the female. We very quickly realised that our data was very random and inadequate. In order to solve the mysteries of this singular nesting strategy and re-establish a sustainable population of the Oriental Pied Hornbills in Singapore, we embarked on a more scientific approach. For the next six years, we monitored up to five pairs of Oriental Pied Hornbills in their cavity nests and their surroundings during the breeding season (from December to May). Furthermore, we made a comparison of our data with two pairs of Oriental Pied Hornbills in captivity in Jurong Bird Park. Special mention must be made of two sites: (1) the Istana; (2) the Sungei Buloh Wetland Reserve. The celebrity pair in the Istana were Sada and Lili, and the pair in the Sungei Buloh Wetland Reserve were Bobby and Serene.

Through these five to six years (with the help of Hoo Chuan Lim and Alvin Tan), we improved the cameras and the sensors every year to monitor systematically and accurately the movements of the birds, the interactions between the individuals of the group; and identified diets, competitors for the cavity, and the predators of the chicks. With our "intelligent" nests, we gathered sufficient data to create the first growth analysis of the chicks, the amount of nest material and food supplied by the male. We were also able to monitor significant changes to the weight of the parents from the incubation of the eggs to the raising of the chicks. We further investigated the concentration of carbon dioxide and oxygen exchange between the cavity and the surrounding environment of the habitat, and discovered that there were fluctuations which could be correlated with moulting and chick activities.

The full nesting timeline of an Oriental Pied Hornbill was charted for the first time with information from the very beginning: from the male identifying the nest, courting the female, mating, supplying materials for the nest, the female sealing the nest, laying up to three eggs, moulting of her feathers, incubating the eggs, raising the chicks, educating the chicks, opening of the cavity, to teaching them the first flight. Also recorded for the first time was the "infanticide-cannibalism" of the weakest chick. During the same season, we equipped the male with a Global Positioning System (GPS) to understand the territory that he covers, the altitude, speed and frequency of flight. Knowing their behaviour and needs, we had a basic understanding of what the Oriental Pied Hornbills need to survive in Singapore. We also deduced the ecological role this species has in the habitat surrounding the nest, at least for half a year.

A computed tomography (CT) scan was also conducted to understand the muscular distribution and the anatomy structure.

We also initiated a DNA survey on the Oriented Pied Hornbill in the wild and in Jurong Bird Park to make accurate assessment on the genetic diversity to avoid cross breeding and strategise potential translocation.

The project resulted in two major "academic prints": The first was a book, *Hornbills in the City*, which described the project's re-introduction efforts and the chronology of events; and the second was an oil-painting of a pair of Oriental Pied Hornbills, by the late William T. Cooper (a renowned bird artist) who studied the birds in Pulau Ubin before he painted them. The book was published by NParks in 2012; and the painting, commissioned by SC Ng to commemorate the 5th International Hornbill Symposium in Singapore, is now exhibited in an In Vitro Fertilisation (IVF) Centre in Novena. In terms of scientific publications, the first report of our observation of infanticide-cannibalism in the Oriental Pied Hornbill was in the journal *Forktail* in 2007. The majority of the scientific reports from this project were published in the *Raffles Bulletin of Zoology* in Supplement 24 (30 March 2011), which were the proceedings of the 5th International Hornbill Conference held in Singapore from 22 to 25 March 2009.

The Singapore Hornbill Project (SHP) was the Winner of the Conservation and Research Award given by the 4th International Symposium on Breeding Birds in Captivity in 2007 and the SHP was selected by the International Union for Conserving Nature (IUCN) for its Global Re-introduction Perspectives: 2016.

The success of the re-introduction has been judged by the many complaints I have heard that the Oriental Pied Hornbill is now a nuisance!

This successful re-introduction illustrates that other large species, such as the Rhinoceros Hornbill and the Cream-Coloured Giant Squirrel, can be re-introduced provided the environment can be adjusted to enable survival of these re-introduced species. Such habitat "priming" will include successfully nurtured secondary forests. These large species are at the top of their respective food chains, and are usually used as an index for the health of the forests. They are usually elevated to icon status for the said forests. There are also other iconic species here in Singapore, such as the Smooth-coated Otter, the Leopard Cat and the Sunda Pangolin.

The Singapore Hornbill Project's success can be highlighted as an ideal example of successful wildlife integration into a developed urban environment, and of successful shared living spaces with wildlife. This success is primarily due to a trilogy of good government policies, NPark's involvement in consultation with relevant

Oriental Pied Hornbill in flight. (Photo credit: David Tan Siah Hin)

non-governmental organisations (NGOs), and a positive public. Special mention must be made of Mandai's integrative approach to educate the public with their exhibits, as well as behind-the-scenes work on outreach and research. The current interest in our wildlife bodes well for Singapore's future.

Ng Soon-Chye is a gynaecologist by profession, with sub-speciality in infertility. He was responsible for the first in-vitro fertilisation ("test-tube") baby in Asia, delivered in 1983 in Singapore. He pioneered the technique of SUZI which is the precursor of the current micro-injection (ICSI) technique, with the world's first delivery in 1989. He still practises at Novena Specialist Centre. He has a passion for nature, especially bird-watching, and since his younger days, has been involved with the Malayan Nature Society (Singapore branch) and now, the Nature Society (Singapore) (NSS). He did bird-ringing in the 1970s with David Wells, when the forests of Malaya were still pristine.

Marc Cremades is the Vice President and Team Lead for Attractions Development at the Mandai Wildlife Group. He is the founding member of the team, and is leading the conceptualisation and implementation of a new generation of wildlife parks in Singapore: Bird Paradise and Rainforest Park. He has over 30 years of experience in the study and management of conservation and breeding programmes for animals in Singapore, and across five continents. Many of these have been recognised with awards, and published in books, films and TV documentaries. Other notable projects include the creation of a Protected Natural Park in Madagascar and an Oscar nominee movie.

Chapter 35

How Much for the Environment?

Euston Quah

Public decision-making and policies should ideally reflect an understanding of the public's values. This is true of public projects and programmes, and even more so when they involve non-market goods of which the environment occupies a large component. Because society's values about the environment are not generally expressed in the marketplace, non-market goods valuation has, over time, become an important input into government decision-making. That the price of such environmental goods and services are not readily revealed by way of the market does not mean that these goods have little or no value. It requires, however, an indirect approach to imputing values. Increasing concerns over environmental degradation have amplified the role of environmental economics and the necessity of valuing non-pecuniary environmental resources as tools of analysis to facilitate the optimal design of policies.

Why the Need to Value the Environment?

Economists do not initiate with the assertion that all pollution and environmental degradation should be eliminated because they believe that society must strike a balance between economic growth, development and environmental quality. This often involves trade-offs between environmental goals and economic production of goods and services, which necessitates putting monetary values on nature and the environment. This is also central to the ideas behind sustainable development. By taking the environment for granted, equivalent to non-pricing in the use of environmental assets, the danger will be that the carrying capacity of the natural environment will be ignored to the extent of satisfying excess demand. For example, there is no incentive to protect the air quality since there has never been any price charged for the use of this resource — similarly for the usage of water from rivers and lakes. Concern for valuing the environment and expressing the need to put dollar values on the services yielded by environmental assets have been treated by some environmentalists as offensive. Here, it is important to emphasise that environmental economists are merely attempting to gauge how much people are willing to pay to conserve or to improve the environment. Alternatively, for environmental degradation, people might be asked to reveal the compensation sum required to accept their welfare losses. How these money sums are elicited from the responses of people is another question separate from the need to put a monetary value on the environment.

The monetisation of environmental assets provides a means to measure the intensity and degree of concern for the environment. If, in place of monetary values, the political system of "one person one vote" will be applied in decision-making involving some environmental improvement or degradation, then a measure of the intensity of preferences for alternative proposals would be lost. Consequently, if decisions on projects in which some improvement on the project are made on the basis of a number game, then the value for the environmental improvement would have been mismeasured, and the wrong decision made. For a long time, public policy makers have held the view that it was difficult, if not seemingly impossible, to value empirically and monetarily environmental goods or bads, including scenic views, quietude, recreation, biodiversity, water and air pollution. These goods were often classified as "intangibles". Over the decades, however, much new literature has developed in the areas of resource and environmental economics to the extent that such terms as "intangibles" have become meaningless to economists. These so-called "intangible" environmental goods are now capable of being measured and monetarily valued.

Valuing and measuring such "intangibles" is, however, not an easy task since the lack of ownership rights to environmental assets often imply no market transactions, and hence no market prices to indicate economic values. But to ignore such valuations or to ascribe descriptive features and to list them in many project evaluations and environmental impact analyses is essentially to reduce them to a monetary value of zero, being added neither to benefits nor to costs. The result is that any policy decision tends to take these "intangibles" for granted, or worse, to appeal to a subjective element of their valuation, usually their own value judgement. At times, where environmental bads such as noise and vibration, poor air quality, destruction of landscapes and aesthetics are encountered in public projects, ignoring a money value that corresponds to the damages sustained will greatly under-estimate the cost of the project. Placing a monetary value on environmental goods and bads is thus warranted in any social cost-benefit analysis.

The elicitation of monetary values to the environment, in essence, provides an efficient resource allocation. It does this by comparing one resource use with another. Take, for example, a proposed commercial or housing development, and that of keeping a pristine forestland. On one hand, we have a development proposal which can be estimated to be worth S$300 million. Contrast this to the pristine forestland which has flora and fauna, biodiversity, forest animals and trees, hills and natural landscapes. Unless we know the value of the latter in monetary terms, it will be futile to decide which resource allocation is efficient for the needs of society. What economics is trying to do here is to derive a common denominator: in this case, using money as a measuring rod to assess the worth of different types of goods. Both development and housing goods, and environmental forestlands are important, but we need to put both types of goods on an even footing for comparison.

Valuation Methods

Most of the valuation methods used to price the environment revolve around deriving a demand curve for the good in question, and this can be summarised in two approaches. Revealed preference approaches solicit monetary values from careful observations of people's actions in the market. One form of the revealed preferences method is the hedonic pricing method, which uses price differentials in existing markets as proxies of prices with certain attributes. As in real estate values, for two properties with similar attributes, where one has an abundance of nature in its neighbourhood and the other has none, the market price will often be higher for the property which has surrounding nature compared to the one without. Similarly, in place of nature, properties can differ in quietude, clean air, scenic landscapes, etc. Such attributes often command a premium price in the marketplace.

Let us assume we want to compute the value of a reduction in ambient noise levels. An overly simplified illustration of the principle of hedonic pricing may be to compare the prices of two properties, which are similar in every way except for the ambient noise level. Suppose property A is worth S$2 million and has an average ambient noise level of 20 decibels (dB) while property B is worth S$1 million and has an average ambient noise level of 35 dB. What we can infer then, is that the "price" of a reduction of noise by 15 dB is S$1 million. In actual hedonic pricing models, however, it is common to apply multiple regression techniques to find out the marginal effect of a particular attribute on price. This can then be used to find out the value of that attribute.

The contingent valuation method is, by far, the most direct and intuitive method to derive values for non-market goods such as those of the environment. Essentially, it involves eliciting the maximum amount that people are willing to pay for welfare improvements and the minimum that they are willing to accept as compensation for welfare loss, to derive a demand curve for the good in question.

To do so, one designs a survey that measures people's responses to a hypothetical change in an attribute or amenity in terms of the maximum they would be willing to pay to enjoy a benefit, or the minimum they would be willing to accept to forgo it. The amount that they are willing to pay or accept would logically be the monetary sum that leaves them at the level of welfare as before. The process may involve simply asking respondents to state a single value or more sophisticated methods like bidding, where respondents are asked whether they would be willing to pay (or accept) successively higher (or lower) amounts to derive the maximum (or minimum) willingness-to-pay (or acceptance). The willingness-to-pay or willingness-to-accept of the survey sample is then extrapolated for the whole population and adjusted where necessary. The values are totalled to provide an estimate of the area under the demand curve for the hypothetical change in that variable, which may be interpreted as the value of the good.

There are many other approaches to the valuation of the environment including the travel cost method which is useful for placing values on such things as heritage, recreational and leisure sites by estimating the cost of travel incurred to get to the site. By using travel cost as a proxy for price, demand curves can be derived to establish values.

Concluding Remarks

The critical issue with monetising the environment is not really philosophical or ethical as we often hear but rather centres on the need to do it, and to do it in a practical, defensible way. Policy makers encounter such issues and challenges when comparing one resource use with another — in such cases, it would really help decision makers to be able to assess competing options by a monetary valuation of resources. The use of money is only a convenient metric for valuation. As society continues to understand and appreciate the world's ecosystems and the contributions of nature and the environment to our livelihoods and quality of life, it is important to derive such economic values and to make them explicit and salient in the policy arena so that they cannot be ignored in decision-making, for what are generally regarded as "intangibles" are, really, "tangibles".

Euston Quah is Albert Winsemius Chair Professor of Economics at the Nanyang Technological University, with research interests in Cost-Benefit Analysis and Environmental Economics. He has published over 100 papers in journals, and lead opinion articles in media. Widely cited, his internationally known book on Cost-Benefit Analysis with E. J. Mishan published by Routledge, UK is now in its 6th edition, 2021. The Asian edition of his *Principles of Economics* with Gregory Mankiw is now a 3rd edition Cengage published book, 2021. Professor Quah is also the only person who headed both the economics departments at the National University of Singapore, and at the Nanyang Technological University.

Chapter 36

A Crazy Fondness for Stick-insects

Francis Seow-Choen

I have always liked animals. My earliest memories were of catching grasshoppers and mantids in my garden in the 1960s. After I enrolled in St Andrew's School, and learned to read, every trip to town had to have a visit to the bookshop to look for books in the "Animals" section. The best weekend trips with the family were to the Botanic Gardens or Johor Zoo to see animals, or to the beach to catch some fishes or other beach life.

In my childhood, I always lived next to rural kampongs. As such, many of the kids in the neighbourhood taught me a lot about the local animal life. Time out of school was spent largely in fields, ponds, marshes and shrub-land areas, catching, playing and breeding these animals. It seems like everywhere was green, and wildlife could be found almost anywhere, especially since home was just next to the Kallang River. In those days, the river banks were natural mud and very well vegetated, full of fishes and other creatures that thrive in such environments. Those were halcyon times. Unfortunately, Kallang River, next to where one of my old houses was, has now been given cement banks, which of course does not promote wildlife, in the same way as the muddy and vegetated ones did.

Real information about animals was hard to find in those days. The best way of getting in-depth information of the animals we were interested in was by visiting the National Library to look up books on animals. The other way was by studying the collection of stuffed animals in the National Museum. The National Museum and the National Library were two of my favourite weekly places to visit. I devoured books like *Turtles of the World* by Peter Pritchard. I collected *Animals*, a magazine edited by Armand Denis. One of the writings that influenced me greatly was, *To the Zoo in a Plastic Box*, written by John and George Newmark. Both were headmasters of schools, but catching insects and reptiles for zoos was their "ECA" (Extra-Curricular Activity). Their writings inspired me to emulate them; catch animals, breed them and start a zoo of my own. Nothing beats handling and breeding animals if one wants to understand or study animals.

Some books I borrowed for months on end were *Birds of the World*, *Reptiles and Amphibians of the World, Mammals of the World*, etc., by Hans Hvass. Learning from neighbourhood kids was a good starting point for a young kid. But real knowledge must be acquired from books written by experts. Most, if not all of such authors, have dedicated their lives to understand and study the animals in their books. These books taught me not just about animals and their behaviour, but also about zoological nomenclature and systematics. I developed a deep interest to identify and classify animals. I had jotter books where I drew as many species of different genera of fishes, or birds or turtles or mammals. And I kept adding more and more jotter books on different animals. These books led to my pursuit of identifying and classifying stick-insects in Southeast Asia. And, of course, to publishing my findings in book-form.

Studying in St. Andrew's Primary School brought me into even more contact with animals. I was a school monitor in Primary Three, tasked with noting down the names of boys who came late to school. On days, during daily school assembly, I was commended highly by the discipline master as the most punctual and conscientious monitor under his charge. Unfortunately, it was the day just before I found out that Potong Pasir, just behind my school, was a vast area of farmland with waterways and ponds. I was, thereafter, never ever at my post at the gate again. A few of my classmates would come along sometimes. Fighting fish, gouramys, other local fishes, turtles and snakes were commonly caught. Some bought nets, some made nets. One particular memorable net was made from a sewn-up underwear. Many times, we would return to class and school wet and smelly, having fallen into a stream or pond in pursuit of some beautiful animal. The happiness of having caught something special continued to bring us back to Potong Pasir very often during those days at school. Learning about animals from books or television gives us "head" knowledge. Nothing however, beats "heart" knowledge, which can be obtained only by constant interaction and handling of animals. Unfortunately, Potong Pasir became a housing estate during our time in school. The farms, waterways and the animals there were soon gone forever.

My mother was the person who gave me my first stick-insect. Watching these insects hatch, and change from dull brown twigs to crazily-coloured fully-winged adults was the start of a lifetime of adventures. Interestingly, their "shit" was medicine for a whole host of illnesses, according to traditional Chinese medicine. This might sound like "bullshit" to some. However, a friend did a M.Sc. on stick-insect frass. He found these insects concentrated Vitamin E 1,000 times more in their frass compared to that of the concentration in leaves. This fact might have had something to do in my later life as a colon and rectal surgeon, having daily dealings with "shit" issues. But that is a story for another time.

In my youth, I had not realised that Singapore was smack in the middle of the biodiversity hot-spot of Southeast Asia! During a field trip to Tasik Chini, Pahang, Peninsular Malaysia, in the 1980s, I chanced upon specimens of *Phobaeticus serratipes*, the longest species of stick-insect in Peninsular Malaysia. This large species was longer than the length of a man's forearm. I later described one particular 555 millimetre specimen of this species as the longest insect in the world. It was listed in the Guinness Book of Records for several years. Fellow Malayan Nature Society members later told me that they had seen stick-insects in Singapore too. I was soon making regular trips to Singapore's forest paths. But before that, I met up with Prof Denis Murphy, the father of Singapore's entomology. I sought his advice on collecting insects in our nature reserves. He told me to "just do it". "No one else will do it, if there is any trouble refer to me!", he said. He also gave me a microfilm version of Redtenbacher and Brunner's "The insect-family of Phasmids". It was all in Latin and a little German and I had no way of understanding much of it. Nonetheless, these first steps started my lifelong study of stick-insects.

During that time, my children who were then around primary school-going ages, were old enough to walk with me at night. I wanted to help them know, understand and love nature. Initially, I brought them to a couple of guided early morning birding trips. The birds were always very far away, up in the trees, or far away on some bushes. My young boys always got bored. They would, however, be intrigued and proceeded to look for grasshoppers and other more interesting creatures on the sides of the paths we were on. Insects they could catch, handle and inspect much more closely. In truth, animals in the hand are much more appealing and interesting than tiny dots of birds, seen only through large heavy binoculars. There were, however, always folks in the bird group that would chide them for catching or handing insects. "Don't disturb the insects. Don't touch them", some of them would fiercely shout. Little children do not learn to love nature or wildlife by a "don't go near, don't touch, don't handle, don't keep" policy. Sadly, many rather well-meaning but ignorant people believe in this policy. A lack of interaction with nature is the surest way to breed disinterest in children, which results in apathy and fear towards wildlife as adults. Making entry into forest trails after dark illegal is one way of inculcating fear of the night forest.

I decided then that my sons should come along with me, during my night walks in Singapore's nature reserves. I was not against them touching anything. This was much harder than it sounded. Little kids are easily tired and getting them to sleep before a night walk is not always possible. Sometimes, this meant that although they walked in, they usually had to be physically carried out, as they would complain of being tired and sleepy whilst in the forest. Once, we were in Pulau Tioman for a family holiday. The boys played in the sea the whole day. In the evening, as was my habit, I would go into a forest trail to look for stick-insects. My eldest son came along as we took the steep forest trail from Kampung Tekek to Kampung Juara on the other side of the mountain. Just after we crossed the top of the hill, he said he was sleepy. Thereafter, it was him asleep, piggy-backed on me, while I looked for stick-insects.

Since then, they have grown up to be fine young men, who love nature and are very comfortable in the jungles of Singapore and Southeast Asia. I realised too, that spreading and inculcating love for nature and animals is possible. A positive personal demonstration is the best communication tool to get this message across, especially to friends and family.

As for the other people in the world, nothing beats communication by a well-illustrated word, especially when produced by an acknowledged expert. So I sought to be the expert on stick-insects.

Life indeed is a journey. The ancient Chinese are right; "豹死留皮人死留名" (a leopard dies leaving only its pelt as a memory of itself; a man leaves his name [what he has done] when he dies). What each of us leave when our time is up, is only our name. Each name can be one of the numerous nameless leaves that fall from the Tree of Life, or each of us can become a fruit that will impact another life. When we start our life, or when we end it, not one of us can decide. But what we do with the time we have will determine if we vanish after our time or become a name still mentioned long after we are not around. Some of my dear old friends, God bless their souls, live each day for themselves, meeting other friends, eating, drinking and making merry in retirement. They do deserve it, having worked hard all their lives. As for me, that is not my calling. Even for some friends who love nature, nature hikes are for health, photography is for personal gratification and being the first to spot a bird ("lifer") is for self-pride. There is no secondary impact on the natural world. I want to make an impact, not just on this generation but on the generations to follow. I hunted stick-insects, studied them, named them, published on them. Books educate minds, influence thinking, change behaviours and impact the world. These apply to all spheres of life. Our world, our natural world and

An adult female *Singaporoidea meneptolemus*. The then new genus *Singaporoidea* was erected by Seow-Choen in 2017, and named after Singapore. This was because the original description of this species was based on a specimen found in Singapore. This species was described by a British entomologist in 1859. Since the establishment of the genus *Singaporoidea*, species belonging to *Singaporoidea* have been found and described from Peninsular Malaysia, Sumatra, Java and elsewhere in Southeast Asia.

especially our animal world, needs more educated, thinking and influential people who will inspire the rest of us to rise up and do the necessary to ensure that mankind continues to interact deeply with the animal-kind of planet earth.

Francis Seow-Choen is a colorectal surgeon in private practice. He was previously head of the Department of Colorectal Surgery at Singapore General Hospital as well as Head of Surgical Oncology at National Cancer Centre. He has been on the editorial board of many surgical journals and has honorary fellowships in many national colorectal societies. Apart from his professional work, he is an associate researcher with the Lee Kong Chian Natural History Museum and the National Biodiversity Board in Singapore. He has published 10 books on stick-insects and has described and named more than 250 new stick-insect species from Southeast Asia.

Chapter 37

Managing Seagrass Meadows for Resilience in Highly Urbanised Coastal Cities: A Singapore Case Study

Siti Maryam Yaakub

Seagrasses are marine flowering plants that grow in soft sediments in shallow and sheltered coastal and marine environments. Seagrasses are an important marine ecosystem, providing numerous ecological functions such as nutrient cycling, nursery grounds for crustacean and fish populations, maintaining a healthy marine system and in climate mitigation by absorbing and sequestering carbon. They also provide a range of ecosystem services that support nature education, culture and economic livelihoods of coastal communities in Southeast Asia.

Globally, seagrass ecosystems are under threat from urbanisation, coastal development, deteriorating water quality, and climate change. It is estimated that the global areal extent of seagrass has been decreasing at a rate of 7% per year since the early 1990s. To ensure the long-term resilience of seagrass meadows, effective strategies for management and conservation are crucial. Historically, there are many lessons that can be learned from the loss of seagrass ecosystems worldwide, but highly urbanised coastal cities such as Singapore, provide a unique context from which lessons on managing ecosystem resilience and development can be derived. These themes are discussed below, together with some opportunities for ensuring the continued existence of seagrass ecosystems in Singapore.

Managing Water Quality

Maintaining good water quality is fundamental for seagrass growth, with two key factors being light penetration through the water column and nutrient loads. Historically, large contiguous meadows existed on the east coast of Singapore, extending from Changi in the northeast to present day Siglap in the southeast. Coastal development and land reclamation in the 1960s and 70s destroyed a large proportion of these seagrass meadows. However, the longer-term implications of coastal development and land reclamation activities reduced overall water quality by introducing fine suspended sediments to the water column through activities such as dredging and infilling. This reduces the amount of light reaching the seabed and impacts benthic photosynthetic flora and fauna, such as seagrass and corals and can result in mortality over prolonged periods. It also has a wider sphere of impact as these fine sediments can be transported over long distances before settling.

The implementation of Environmental Impact Assessments (EIAs) can help minimise direct and indirect impacts from coastal development to sensitive marine habitats including seagrass meadows. EIAs in marine environments in Singapore are robust;

most assessments are based on modelling approaches coupled with habitat specific ecological thresholds to assess the anticipated magnitude of impact from coastal development work such as dredging and land reclamation. This allows for planning and implementation of pre-emptive mitigation measures and environmental monitoring and management during construction to ensure impacts are minimised or negated.

Despite these stressors, seagrass meadows continue to thrive in Singapore waters, particularly in shallow intertidal environments where tidal exchange provides the opportunity for photosynthesis at low tide when the height of the water column is smaller, allowing light to reach the seabed. Other enabling conditions for seagrass growth and survival in Singapore include strict environmental laws that prevent discharge of pollutants and sewage into drains and waterways which are released into coastal waters.

Working with Nature: Ecological Engineering for Resilience

To date there are no large-scale seagrass restoration efforts in Singapore. This is likely due to the low rate of success in seagrass restoration efforts globally, and the high cost associated with seagrass relocation and transplantation. However, there are a few examples in Singapore of seagrass meadows recolonising and establishing in previously reclaimed coastal areas through naturally occurring processes driven by hydrodynamics. For example, seagrass meadows have colonised the reclaimed sedimentary environments along East Coast Park and at Tanah Merah. Studies have shown that these dispersal and colonisation events are made possible through a combination of coastal engineering and hydrodynamics.

Engineering coastlines to mimic sheltered bays with sedimentary environments recreate environmental conditions that are suitable for seagrass growth. Furthermore, submerged structures such as breakwaters reduce wave energy and create conducive areas for seagrass growth. These features can be oriented to harness the hydrodynamic regime (e.g., waves and currents) that transport seagrass fragments from nearby populations and built to retain them allowing seagrass to establish. However, natural recruitment and recolonisation can only happen if the newly created sites are connected to existing seagrass populations.

Connectivity between seagrass populations is a contributing factor in building ecological resilience. Meadows that have frequent genetic exchange with other populations are genetically diverse and this allows populations to recover quickly from impacts. Understanding connectivity and relatedness between seagrass populations also allows for the better management of seagrass meadows in Singapore and can help prioritise sites for conservation and protection. Prioritising seagrass meadows that are genetically diverse and are connected to other seagrass populations safeguards meadows that are important for the maintenance of seagrass in Singapore waters. Although the recolonisation of seagrass in reclaimed sedimentary environments in Singapore has been largely serendipitous, there is a clear pathway for replicating this in future coastal development and planning to incorporate nature into coastal development.

Community and Stakeholder Participation

Community and stakeholder participation is an important component in the management of seagrass meadows in Singapore. Singapore has one of the longest-running citizen science seagrass habitat monitoring programmes in the region. Run by a group of volunteers with support from the National Parks Board (NParks), TeamSeaGrass regularly monitors the health and conditions of key seagrass meadows in Singapore, including Chek Jawa on Pulau Ubin, Pulau Semakau and Cyrene Reef. The group is part of a global network for seagrass monitoring sites under the Seagrass-Watch Programme, and uses a standardised method and parameters for assessing seagrass meadow health. TeamSeaGrass currently has a database of more than 10 years of monitoring since its inception in 2007, which has helped managers understand the condition of seagrass meadows in Singapore. It has also been an integral in allowing the community to participate and to foster stewardship of seagrass ecosystems in Singapore. TeamSeaGrass also participates in national nature conservation and outreach initiatives in Singapore such as the Festival of Biodiversity, building awareness in the general public of the importance of seagrass habitats.

While public participation in nature outreach is relatively well-established, one area that could benefit our understanding of seagrass meadows in Singapore is the participation of local coastal communities. There are local communities residing in coastal areas in Singapore who have a historical connection to coastal ecosystems. These communities, often comprised of fishing communities and coastal residents, have a wealth of traditional knowledge and practices related to the marine environment, including seagrass habitats. This includes gleaning practices in seagrass meadows during low-tide, knowledge of sustainable harvesting practices and traditional and cultural knowledge of marine environments.

Involving these communities in seagrass conservation allows for the preservation and promotion of cultural values, practices, and traditions associated with seagrass ecosystems. It recognises the cultural importance of seagrass and encourages the transmission of this cultural knowledge to future generations. It is important to recognise and respect the unique perspectives, cultural values, and rights of these coastal communities when engaging them in seagrass conservation and management. Collaborative efforts that incorporate traditional ecological knowledge and community-led initiatives can contribute to more holistic and sustainable approaches to seagrass conservation in Singapore.

Ensuring Future Resilience: Include Seagrass in Climate Change Strategy

Article 6 of the Paris Agreement provides a framework for international cooperation in mitigating greenhouse gas emissions and promoting sustainable development. One aspect of Article 6 is the encouragement of voluntary cooperation between countries in implementing their Nationally Determined Contributions (NDCs). These NDCs outline the efforts each country will undertake to address climate change.

Integrating seagrass conservation into NDCs is an important step towards recognising the role of coastal ecosystems in climate change mitigation and adaptation. Seagrass meadows have the ability to sequester and store significant amounts of carbon dioxide (CO_2) from the atmosphere, making them valuable "blue carbon" ecosystems. Including seagrass conservation in NDCs acknowledges their carbon sequestration potential and emphasises their protection and restoration as a climate action strategy. Singapore, as a coastal nation, can take several implementation actions to include seagrass conservation in its NDCs. Some examples include:

- Conduct a comprehensive assessment of seagrass distribution and health in Singapore's coastal waters. This involves mapping seagrass meadows, assessing their condition, and identifying priority areas for conservation and restoration efforts.
- Initiate seagrass restoration projects to rehabilitate degraded or lost seagrass meadows.
- Develop a long-term monitoring programme to regularly assess seagrass health, distribution, and carbon sequestration potential. There are existing seagrass monitoring programmes such as TeamSeaGrass to build on.
- Develop and enforce policies that support seagrass conservation, such as integrating seagrass protection requirements into coastal development guidelines. An example could be to have requirements in EIAs to understand and assess impacts to the carbon sequestration ability of seagrass from coastal development.

By implementing these actions, Singapore can effectively include seagrass conservation in its NDCs, demonstrating its commitment to climate action, biodiversity conservation, and sustainable coastal management.

As a rapidly developing coastal city, Singapore faces numerous challenges in balancing urban growth with the conservation of its coastal habitats. Using Singapore as a case study for understanding the interactions between seagrass resilience and highly urbanised coastal environments is helpful in contextualising the challenges and opportunities facing other rapidly developing coastal cities around the world. It provides valuable insights into the complex interactions between seagrass resilience and highly urbanised coastal environments. The lessons learned from Singapore can inform and guide the development of sustainable management strategies in

A seagrass meadow of *Enhalus acoroides* (Tape Seagrass) at low tide in the man-made lagoon in between Pulau Hantu Besar and Pulau Hantu Kechil, with oil bunkers at Pulau Bukom in the background.

similar coastal urban areas, ultimately contributing to the preservation and protection of seagrass ecosystems on a global scale.

Dr Siti Maryam Yaakub is a marine ecologist working across tropical marine ecosystems. She specialises in seagrass ecosystems and applications of nature-based solutions for climate change mitigation and adaptation. Dr Siti is currently the Director of the International Blue Carbon Institute at Conservation International. The institute works with blue carbon scientists and practitioners in developing projects and policies that protect and restore coastal blue carbon ecosystems. In her spare time Dr Siti leads TeamSeaGrass, a citizen science group monitoring seagrass habitats in Singapore.

Chapter 38

The Smooth-coated Otters of Singapore

N. Sivasothi aka "Otterman"

In November 1998, electrifying news was celebrated amongst naturalists in Singapore about a long awaited outcome — a pair of smooth-coated otters had been regularly sighted at Sungei Buloh Nature Park (now Sungei Buloh Wetland Reserve). When a pup was added to the family in 1999 and 2000, the status of the smooth-coated otter was cemented — otters were resident in mainland Singapore once again after a period of more than three decades!

It had been a long wait indeed. When the British took possession of the island in the 19th century, widespread agriculture and settlements eliminated and polluted natural ecosystems. From 1965, the rapid urbanisation of independent Singapore amplified the impact and extirpated the native short-clawed and smooth-coated otters. Indeed, by the 1960s, otters were concluded to be visitors rather than a resident species. The close scrutiny of naturalists in the 1980s and 1990s were rewarded only with the rare and precious glimpses of single, transient individuals, typically along the northern coast. These "*anjing ayer*" (water dogs) of the Malays were on an exploration trip across the Straits of Johor, presumably dispersing from more intact ecosystems in southern Peninsular Malaysia.

The return of smooth-coated otters to Sungei Buloh was a validation of the establishment of a nature park at Sungei Buloh, after persuasion by Nature Society (Singapore) and a positive government response. On 6 December 1993 the park was officially opened and would welcome resident otters only five years later. This highly impacted area of former farms and prawn ponds had been conserved based on the presence of iconic latitudinal migratory birds of the East Asian–Australasian Flyway. The protected mangrove forest and mudflat ecosystems secured a refugia in that corner of the Johor Straits, which still faces impactful transformation today. With concerted management efforts and the expansion of the protected area to more than 400 hectares, the Sungei Buloh Nature Park network protects many other species and includes resident smooth-coated otter families today.

In the absence of mainstream news coverage and before social media existed, the presence of otters remained the privileged knowledge of just a few. As otters began exploring habitats across Singapore (and possibly more individuals migrated from Johor) in the 2000s, the shoreline-using public, mostly unfamiliar with otters, were reporting sightings of "seals", "seal lions" and "crocodiles" along north-eastern mainland Singapore (Sembawang, Punggol, Serangoon, Pasir Ris and Changi) and then south to Tanah Merah and East Coast Park, aided by the network of coastal and inland parks.

Sixteen years after they first returned to Singapore, the public would discover otters in their midst in 2014 when a pair of otters arrived at Marina Bay. Staff of Gardens by the Bay excitedly shared sightings of a wandering otter over WhatsApp. As the reports flooded in before Chinese New Year, the exploring male was promptly named "Ah Huat" (Mr Lucky). He led us to his mate secluded deep in the gardens, in preparation for giving birth to the Garden's first resident pups! Then-Minister of National Development, Mr Khaw Boon Wan announced the news on his Facebook page, and heralded the news as testament to the clean waters of the Bay. Now a reservoir, Marina Bay had undergone a historical transformation from a legacy of lifeless, oxygen-depleted rivers which had poured sewage, animal carcasses, and other pollutants into the sea.

The waterways of Singapore are canalised rivers, widened to mitigate urban flooding. The clean waters, an important source of drinking water for the nation, are host to over a hundred species of largely exotic species of fish. The fish-eating smooth-coated otters had discovered a veritable buffet table with very little competition, and favour feeding on cichlid fish and catfish 15–19 centimetres long (standard length). It is critical for these semi-aquatic carnivorans to dry themselves off periodically and to deposit their pheromone-enhanced faeces called "spraints" on land. Also needed were resting and sleeping spaces. All these were provided by the green spaces adjacent to the waterways, and the nooks and crannies in urban spaces. In an unusual reversal of fortune, the urban-adaptable smooth-coated otter had a found a space to prosper.

The nature-deficit Singapore public would congregate to Marina Bay, Kallang Basin, Bishan-Ang Mo Kio Park, and Singapore River fascinated by these social, amphibious mammals which squeaked, chirped, whistled, hunted and played as a family unit. And many otter families were not shy, shocking veteran naturalists as these once elusive mammals ambled just metres away from their feet!

A new breed of otter-watchers emerged to follow and document the charismatic animals regularly, posting hundreds of charming photos and videos on Facebook and YouTube (initially OtterWatch, FastSnail and OtterCity), attracting an audience in the tens of thousands by the 2010s including an international following. Documentaries by National Geographic, BBC and NHK featured Singapore's otters and in 2017, readers of *The Straits Times* chose Bishan otters to represent Singapore in her 51st year.

The proximity of the otter families would provide National University of Singapore (NUS) undergraduates an unrivalled opportunity to cut their teeth in urban wildlife ecology research, and some 20 studies were conducted since the 2010s of distribution, group size and home range variation, habitat use, activity patterns, behaviour, pup development, diet and foraging efficiency, population dynamics and human–otter conflict. They were supported by staff of relevant wildlife entities such as Animal Concerns Research & Education Society (ACRES), National Parks Board (NParks), Wildlife Reserves Singapore and the Public Utilities Board (PUB) in addition to otter-watchers, all of whom had been collaborating for over a decade, and who would officially form the Otter Working Group in 2016.

Over two decades, otters had dispersed and grown to 17 families occupying waterways, reservoirs, mangroves and beaches throughout Singapore. Each was named after the location they first raised pups at, and reflected the current total number of the group, e.g., Bishan 17, Marina 7, SBG 4, Zouk 14 during the 2017 population census. That number would vary as new pups were born, adults dispersed or died, or were killed in battle or on roads. Families averaged 10 individuals but some romps reached a size of more than

20 individuals. Linear homes ranged from 5 to 15 kilometres with larger families occupying larger territories composed of several foraging grounds and resting spaces.

The prized living space was Marina Bay and its source rivers of the Central Watershed and thus this became a battle ground. An entire family would be involved in territorial altercations, with adults, sub-adults and juveniles fighting in close formation. Mainstream news and social media captured these ongoing feuds spanning multiple battles in waterways over the years. A harrowing private video of a pup sinking into the water with a puncture wound to its head was a reflection of the harsh truth of the ecological limits of the environment, its carrying capacity, something the public would come to learn were part of the rules of nature which apply to all wildlife.

In 2020, this competition for space would take a visible turn of events during the pandemic when the Zouk 7 family was spotted in several locations such as Bukit Timah Road, Newton, Kampong Java, Serangoon Road, the Istana, Alexandra and Pasir Panjang. Viewed on a map, it made sense — they had ventured out from Singapore Botanic Gardens after raising pups, and lost battles to the resident families of the Singapore and Kallang Rivers. Doomed to a nomadic existence in the urban matrix of the catchment of the Central Watershed, they have energetically used drainage networks leading to small drains in estates, and crossed busy roads (famously crossing Orchard Road outside the Istana) to seek out urban ponds to eke out an existence and they were not expected to prosper. Despite the odds, Zouk 7 has prospered to the present size of Zouk 17 and they may retake a waterway once again.

The Otter Working Group first came together to reunite lost pups with their families, rescue and treat badly injured otters, track roadkills and actively educate the public. Gradually, we found ourselves having to also work with estate managers and private property owners to suggest exclusion and prevention measures to keep otters out of their koi ponds. Non-dominant otter families forced out of waterways by rivals now seek refuge in residential properties and utilise areas of high human use. This poses a new challenge, mainly due to the heightened defensiveness of otter adults over their pups particularly in the first two months of their lives. With an ever-changing landscape in Singapore, new (human) neighbours emerge in what were once dormant spaces, requiring intervention to achieve human–wildlife coexistence. The combined efforts of the Otter Working Group are being actively applied to address the novel situations which emerge in a crowded landscape. Once again, the solutions with our uniquely Singapore signature will serve other cities in future.

The nature community celebrates the lofty goals of the vision of a "City in Nature". Given due relevance as the first pillar in the Singapore Green Plan 2030, this vision will require the evolution of knowledge and empathy by urban citizens, long isolated from a meaningful relationship with nature. And they in turn will require a knowledgeable and empathetic approach by the nature community to help them achieve a Peace with Nature.

To find out more about otters in Singapore, see https://otter.nus.edu.sg/

Thanks to the individuals and institutions in the Otter Working Group and all otter-watchers for their tireless devotion to the smooth-coated otters of Singapore. Thanks to Jeffrey Teo for the photo and Adrian Loo for the review.

Bishan 5 in 2015, comprising the iconic Bishan mum (RIP 2022), Bishan dad (RIP 2018) and their first litter of three pups at the canal next to Bishan-AMK Park. (Photo credit: Jeffrey Teo)

N. Sivasothi, aka "Otterman" has been immersed in mangroves and wildlife for research, education and conservation at the National University of Singapore since the late 1980s. He also actively promotes youth development, public education and environmental stewardship. He is coordinator for NUS Toddycats, the International Coastal Cleanup Singapore, OtterWatch, and (in partnership with NParks) The Biodiversity Roundtable and The Biodiversity Friends Forum. He is an active contributor to numerous wildlife working groups, ground-up partnerships and closed-door engagements to mitigate development impact. He is now an active advocate for habitat enhancement and community participation in the OneMillionTrees movement.

Chapter 39

Birds of Singapore

Morten Strange and Bee Choo Strange

Since we started birdwatching here in Singapore in the late 1980s, the interest has exploded, especially so in recent years. By some estimates, today there are more than 3,000 active "birders" in the country, capable of recognising all wild bird species by sight and sound, up from perhaps less than 100 three decades ago. This number does not include the thousands of other casual observers who simply just enjoy looking at and/or photographing the common birds around them, while working gradually to improve their identification skills and understandings of avian taxonomy and behaviour.

Of all the life forms, birds are the class of animals that most people can enjoy. While Singapore has capable naturalists and scientists studying frogs and moths and tidal mudflat creatures, those animals are difficult for the general public to name and appreciate. Birds however, are everywhere. They are varied, vocal, and most are active by day; some species are adaptable and can tolerate and even thrive in a disturbed urban environment. Although many others cannot, we will get back to that shortly.

How are birds different from all other animals? No, they are not unique because they fly; first of all, not all birds fly and secondly, many insects and even some mammals (bats) do as well. The feathers set birds apart; all birds have them and no other animals living today do. Birds spend a lot of their time preening and keeping their feathers in good condition; they moult all their feathers regularly, migratory birds usually have markedly different plumages during breeding and non-breeding seasons. Of course, it is also the feathers that we birdwatchers primarily use to identify the various species in the field. Many birds have distinctly different male and female plumages; they all start with a juvenile/immature plumage and later moult into full adult trait; for some larger birds like raptors and gulls, this can take a number of years. While most feathers get their colour from pigmentation, the sunbirds, and especially the males, have iridescent feathers that reflect the sunlight in dazzling clarity, a feature that comes in handy for them during courtship displays.

Another largely unique feature among birds is their toothless beak. The exact size and shape of the beak, or bill, varies enormously between bird families and species and reflects the lifestyle of the group. Insect-eaters have sharp little bills to grab small invertebrates, fruit- and seed-eaters have stronger bills to crush food, shorebirds have long bills to probe in the mud and raptors have sharp curved bills to tear larger prey apart. In the field, plumage, bill shape, and structure as well as vocalisation all help us identify the species. In fact, experienced birders quickly recognise a bird, even during a brief glimpse at a distance by its "gizz" or "giss", referring to its "general impression of size and shape", borrowed from air force plane identification slang.

To be a good birdwatcher, you really only need one thing. No, it is not a pair of binoculars — you can very well watch birds without optical enhancement, although binoculars obviously do help. What you really need most of all is a guidebook that can help you identify all the species that you can potentially see in your country. In Singapore, for a long time our main tool for this was *A Field Guide to the Birds of South-east Asia* by Ben King, Martin Woodcock and E. C. Dickinson (1975), combined with *The Birds of the Malay Peninsula, Singapore and Penang* by A.G. Glenister (paperback edition, 1971). Then finally in 1997 came Lim Kim Seng and Dana Gardner's *Birds: An Illustrated Field Guide to the Birds of Singapore*; shortly after that, in 1999, A. Jeyarajasingam's *A Field Guide to the Birds of West Malaysia and Singapore* and finally, Craig Robson's *A Field Guide to the Birds of South-east Asia* (2000). They say that bird books are a bit like busses: You wait and wait, and then finally two or three come along at once. Since then, in this century, we have been spoiled for choice regarding accurate bird documentation for Singapore: Several new excellent modern books on Lynx Edicions as well as Princeton University Press are available today, plus of course numerous online websites and apps.

Once you have your illustrated field guide, you do not have to go far to enjoy birdwatching. In fact, you do not have to go anywhere. We stay on the fourth floor in an apartment building, and outside of our windows to the south is a large African Tulip Tree; the tree flowers at various intensities practically all year and every day we have the enjoyment of observing multiple birds at eye level, right outside our windows. Over the years, we have seen 45 different species in that tree, including six parrots, four woodpeckers, four pigeons/doves and four starlings; this is not counting birds flying through the airspace or landing nearby — only birds actually using the tree to feed or rest count!

So, you do not really have to keep birds in cages. Just look around you, and there are plenty of birds to take pleasure in. As you move away from the urban park environment, into another habitat such as the rainforest, freshwater swamp or tidal wetlands, the mix of bird species will change and that is the whole benefit and excitement of birdwatching — the constant change of variety. In another chapter in this book, Yong Ding Li covers how the avifauna changes with the time of year, thanks to annual migration, and Vina Dharmarajah mentions the sheer aesthetical and therapeutic benefits of birdwatching to humanity.

But let us point out that since we started birdwatching in the 1980s, the hobby of keeping birds in captivity has diminished in importance compared to the number of people now flocking into Singapore's green spaces. Yes, many mainly go there to exercise and take in the fresh air, but more and more also admire and study the biodiversity of natural areas. As a consequence, poaching has become less rampant; species like the Oriental Magpie-Robin and Spotted as well as Zebra Dove that were previously uncommon and desperately shy can now be observed commonly at close range. In fact, from a conservationist's point of view, Singapore has some of the best wildlife laws of any country we can think of. Unlike in most other developed countries, there is no hunting season and as such no hunting culture; all vertebrate animals are protected all year against killing and capture (barring a few, mainly introduced species, which are considered pests). Some might say that enforcement is lacking on occasions, but in general, excellent legislation and public attitude offer good protection for local birds and wildlife.

The Oriental Magpie-Robin is not the only Singapore bird that has come back from the brink of local extinction. When the National Parks Board did a preliminary study of the birds in Singapore during 2022, in preparation for the third upcoming edition of *The Singapore Red Data Book*, published in collaboration with Nature Society Singapore (NSS) and others, 24 species were assessed to be "bouncing back" as reported in the press at the time. They included charismatic birds such as the Blue-crowned Hanging Parrot, Grey-headed Fish Eagle, Blue-eared Kingfisher and Buffy Fish Owl. From anecdotal observations, we can confirm that these and indeed a number of other birds appear to be more numerous today than previously.

As a case in point, urbanised Singapore has become an unlikely stronghold for one of the greatest songbirds of the region, the globally critically endangered Straw-headed Bulbul which has been virtually extirpated from much of its range in the Sunda subregion and practically disappeared from Indonesia — exactly because of its powerful, bubbling call that has made it a prized catch among captive bird collectors. In this regard, none other than the *Wall Street Journal* featured Singapore as a role model for nature conservation in a January 2023 article. The Straw-headed Bulbul — together with another great passerine songster ruthlessly trapped throughout much of its range, the White-rumped Shama — was successfully uplisted to Appendix 1 during the 19th meeting of the Conference of the Parties to the Convention on International Trade in Endangered Species of Wild Fauna and Flora (CITES COP19) meeting in 2022, partly due to lobbying by Singapore non-governmental organisation representatives and scientists.

However, all that does not necessarily mean that all is well in the Singapore world of birds. When the first complete checklist to Singapore birds was published by the then-Malayan Nature Society (MNS) in 1986, the Singapore Branch listed 284 species then. The authors were almost exclusively expatriate scientists and volunteers. After many years of expanding annotations and updating records and taxonomy, the NSS Bird List in 2022 had 421 species. An alternative list, managed by a team of capable young scientists and their supporters keep an amazing record of all birds in Singapore available on the Singapore Birds Project website; with a slightly different taxonomy and record keeping criteria — their list of species numbered 427 in 2022.

In other words, on average, three to four new bird species turn up in Singapore every year. Which is great, right? Not so fast. There are many reasons for the expanded checklist, apart from Singapore's nature conservation efforts, important and partly successful as they may be. Taxonomic splits over the years have simply increased the number of bird species worldwide. Some forest birds have been displaced by forest clearance in nearby Malaysia and turn up here in single numbers as environmental refugees. But most importantly: More skilled observers out there in the field see so much more. Most of the birds added to our local list are rare vagrants; they may be common further north in Asia but were rarely seen here until now. With digital photography catching on, difficult-to-identify birds can now be separated and confirmed after-the-fact by studying photographs of them later.

But while the checklist of birds has expanded on paper, many resident birds are in fact not doing well. They are still here, but they are squeezed by habitat clearance and invasive species taking their place. The Baya Weaver has been replaced by the Golden-backed, Long-tailed Parakeet; replaced by Red-breasted, Red-crowned Barbet; replaced by Lineated…the list goes on. When we started birding in Singapore, we did not see the Pink-necked Green Pigeon and Javan Myna in the water catchment forest. Today the forest has thinned out and it is full of these and other garden birds, while forest specialists like the Malaysian Eared Nightjar, White-bellied Woodpecker, Black-headed Bulbul, Chestnut-winged Babbler and Lesser Green Leafbird that used to be regular are rarely seen now.

When our son Mark was in primary school, he used his compact digital camera and took this excellent photo out of our bedroom window of a Common Flameback male sitting in the tree outside, we did not even know it had white dots in the primaries! Morten sold off his photographic equipment that year: If you cannot compete with a school kid, you might as well give up bird photography.

There is much to do for Singapore birdwatchers, going forward. We need to organise a nation-wide Atlas survey of resident birds and translate this into better protection, restoration and re-wilding of the green spaces we have left — not just for birds, but also for the environment in general and for the thousands of people who enjoy going out there to watch them every day of the year.

Morten Strange is a retired petroleum engineer, retired nature photographer and retired publisher. He lived in Singapore from 1980 to 1993 and again continuously since 1999. He has been a member of Nature Society (Singapore) since 1984, and is now a life member and active on and off. In 2014, Morten qualified as a financial analyst. When he is not studying capital allocation or writing about economic and environmental issues, he enjoys long walks in the woods looking at the critters, as well as spending time with his family. Check mortenstrange.com for more.

Bee Choo Strange is a former mechanical engineer and Managing Director of Nature's Niche Pte Ltd. Post-retirement from business, she helps out as the International Coordinator of the Hornbill Research Foundation (since 1992) and Program Manager of the IUCN SSC Hornbill Specialist Group (since 2017). She has been organising conferences, workshops and liaising with the international community working on hornbill research and conservation. She is also a life member of Nature Society (Singapore) and has been a member since 1987.

Chapter 40

The Power of a Story

Audrey Tan

I never was a nature buff growing up.

My younger self would not have expected to be making a living extolling the virtues of nature, calling attention to the problems confronting the planet, and communicating the solutions being developed to counter the twin planetary crises of climate change and biodiversity loss.

But this is the path I have been on since entering the workforce some 10 years ago in 2013 — first as an environment journalist at *The Straits Times*, Singapore's national broadsheet, and now as the lead for a budding science communications team at the National University of Singapore (NUS)'s Centre for Nature-based Climate Solutions (CNCS), and Tropical Marine Science Institute (TMSI).

So how did a city girl oblivious to the signs of nature in peril grow to develop an appreciation for wildlife in Singapore?

My personal journey into the environmental space is why I believe strongly in the importance of communication — about the wonders of nature, threats to its existence, and possible solutions — in sowing seeds of awareness that could eventually blossom into action for a healthier planet.

It has been a meandering journey, one I am still on, with every story I collect — each interview I do, every account relayed to me — helping me gain awareness of the green and blue oases found in the country, an appreciation for the inhabitants of these wild spaces, and a better understanding of how environmental communication should evolve in the years ahead.

Making It Personal

The first story that got me interested in the non-human species was the story of Snuffles, my toy poodle who turned 13 in May 2023.

I had purchased him from a puppy mill in 2010, and he came home riddled with diseases and parasites. As he recovered from his afflictions, I read about puppy mills and the horrible conditions they subjected breeding animals to — how they were confined in cramped conditions that allowed diseases to spread easily, how female dogs were made to produce litter after litter of puppies with little rest, and so on. I was horrified.

It was the personal connection, seeing something dear to me — Snuffles — suffer the consequences of puppy mills that prompted me to start speaking up on how society could help to safeguard the welfare of companion animals. I started volunteering at an animal shelter and, after I joined *The Straits Times*, wrote many stories about the animal welfare scene in Singapore (I even had a nickname in the newsroom — "the dog and cat reporter").

I credit Snuffles' story as being the turning point in my life that got me interested in environmental issues. My journey started with an interest in animal welfare, which slowly expanded into conservation and climate change matters. The experience made me realise the power that stories can have in making things personal for the audience.

For example, it is one thing to read about the rich biodiversity in the Amazon, but something else completely to know that similarly weird and wonderful creatures can be found in our own urban backyard. Amazonia may have toucans and armadillos, but here in Singapore, we have hornbills and pangolins.

Someone once left a comment on a story I wrote on marine life in Singapore that left an impression on me. "Wow, I never knew we had corals in Singapore," she said. As the popular saying goes: In the end, we will conserve only what we love; we will love only what we understand and we will understand only what we are taught.

Making stories personal for the audience can help people see their reality in a new light and help them recognise that they do have some things in their wild spaces worth fighting for.

Sparking a Fire

How can a spark grow into a fire? How can an individual's awareness of the other Singaporeans living in Singapore's forests, coral reefs and seagrass meadows fire up a national movement that recognises the importance of nature?

For me, it was the presence of role models, all of whom had such infectious passion for nature, that helped to broaden my interest in the environment beyond animal welfare, by fanning the flames of my curiosity of wildlife and how they can be better protected.

The fire of Mr Louis Ng, when he was chief executive of wildlife rescue group ACRES (Animal Concerns Research and Education

Society), in raising awareness of the illegal wildlife trade led me to probe the involvement of Singapore entities in the global trade in endangered species; the perseverance of primatologist Dr Andie Ang in her pursuit of learning more about the critically endangered Raffles' banded langur opened my eyes to the importance of field work (and animal poop) in learning more about the natural world, while the quiet charisma of botany expert and Nature Society (Singapore) (NSS) president Dr Shawn Lum, drew me into the fascinating world of plants and their web of underground networks.

When people with knowledge about native wildlife and their ecology share their expertise — especially on little known or neglected species or issues — with others, they can spark a chain of excitement, like a flame that creates warmth for all those gathering around it.

I recall trudging through the Clementi Forest one morning in 2021 with Mr Lim Liang Jim, who was at that time the Group Director of Conservation at the National Parks Board. He introduced me to "forest kombucha" — a reference to the oily sheen clinging to the surface of a puddle in the forest. Microbes in the water break down organic matter such as dead leaves, making these nutrients available once again to the rest of the forest. The oil on the surface was a by-product of these processes.

I was fascinated. That encounter deepened my understanding of the interconnectedness of nature — protecting a forest was more than just about leaving trees standing, I realised, but also about ensuring that the entire ecosystem, down to the microbes on the forest floor, had a fighting chance of survival. I never forgot the lesson, and it informed many other stories that I later wrote.

In Singapore, many new conservation groups are joining stalwarts such as the NSS in calling attention to other interesting species in our forests and seas, like what the Herpetological Society Singapore is doing for reptiles and amphibians, or what Our Singapore Reefs is doing for marine life.

These are the little fires helping to kindle local interest and awareness in native biodiversity; sparking conversations about how these creatures can be conserved in the face of development.

Constructive Dialogue

Fires have the power to destroy, or be a force for good.

In land-strapped Singapore, the tussle between development and conservation can be emotionally charged. For constructive dialogue over the fate of Singapore's nature areas, there needs to be greater efforts to promote understanding of how land use decisions are made and the trade-offs involved.

The Singapore Government seems to be making greater efforts at consulting stakeholders in charting the Republic's green journey now compared to 10 years ago, seeking public feedback on environmental impact assessments (EIAs), climate change targets, and many other issues.

There have, for example, been a number of highly controversial EIAs in Singapore in recent years, including those done for the Mandai hub of wildlife parks and the Cross Island MRT line. The problem is that many of these assessment reports are technical in nature, spanning thousands of pages long and full of jargon. Similarly, many other environmental publications, whether reports on the state of the climate, or studies on wildlife populations in Singapore, cater mainly to the scientific community.

Stakeholder consultation can only go so far if there is little understanding of the contents of such reports.

Tensions over how Singapore's limited land area should be used — whether they should be set aside for conservation or used for housing or other infrastructural developments crucial for the country — will only continue to mount going forward.

There are also other issues to consider, such as how the country's City in Nature ambitions to weave more greenery into the city will bring humans and wildlife into closer proximity to each other — heralding potential conflict.

Singapore is also party to a number of international agreements, such as the United Nations Framework Convention on Climate Change (UNFCCC)'s Paris Agreement to tackle climate change and the Convention on Biological Diversity (CBD)'s Global Biodiversity Framework to halt the decline of nature, which will have implications on how the country manages its biodiversity too.

The environmental communication scene has changed a lot since I first started working in this space 10 years ago, with social media and global developments helping to raise the profile of nature and all the benefits it provides to humanity.

But even as awareness of nature grows, and even as champions of biodiversity continue to emerge, the road to biodiversity conservation in Singapore will still be fraught with challenges.

Singapore will, as it has always done, rise to the challenge; using scientific studies on wildlife populations, EIAs and other modes of inquiries to help it strike a balance between all its competing needs.

The next frontier, then, is to see if the results of these studies can be communicated in a way that can constructively inform public debate.

Audrey Tan is the science communication and outreach lead at the National University of Singapore's Centre for Nature-based Climate Solutions and Tropical Marine Science Institute. She was previously an award-winning environment journalist at *The Straits Times*, Singapore's national broadsheet, where she covered a variety of environmental issues such as biodiversity conservation and climate change for 10 years. Audrey holds a master's degree in climate science and policy from the Scripps Institution of Oceanography at the University of California San Diego, and is also an advisory committee member of the Pulitzer Center's Rainforest Journalism Fund for Southeast Asia.

Chapter 41

The Greening of NUS Campus: From Iconic Ambience of Bukit Timah Campus (BTC) to Global Sustainability Leader

Tan Eng Chye

In any discussion on the history and development of the greening of the campuses of the National University of Singapore (NUS), the iconic campus of Bukit Timah, now known as the Bukit Timah Campus (BTC), would feature as the cardinal starting point.

There are several factors that combine to make the BTC such an indelible part of the NUS story. It was the first institution dedicated and designed for higher learning in Singapore. Then there are the distinctive buildings and layout, with its unique British-era colonial architecture of arch corridors, covered walkways, and red-pitched roofs. There is the extensive historical association, from the many luminaries who once spent time on campus, as well as historic events such as the robust and passionate quadrangle debates, such as when the People's Action Party (PAP), then led by Mr Lee Kuan Yew, sought to persuade students over the future direction of our fledgling nation. These events have bestowed upon the grounds a special air of dignity, significance and gravitas.

And then there is the landscaping, which has been described by Professor Maurice Baker as “wonderfully wooded and bucolic”. Originally a lowland forested area, the land was cleared for the establishment of Raffles College in 1929. Over time, a diverse and heterogenous range of trees, ranging from native species such as Tembusu and Angsana, to exotic varieties from India, Africa and even Brazil, gave the BTC a special character and ambience. Many of the BTC’s alumni from Singapore’s early post-independence era have spoken of their cherished memories gathering under the shade of these great trees: reading, studying, reflecting, and on occasion, even engaging in the pursuits of romance.

It should also be noted that economic imperatives, as well as opportunities for research, greatly factored into the evolution of the natural landscape at the BTC. The land was originally acquired in 1879 as part of the Singapore Botanic Garden’s attempts to establish an Economic Garden — to experiment with crop species such as rubber, coffee, etc. Later on, the NUS Botany Department would play a major contributing role in transforming the BTC into a kind of living arboretum, with a diverse range of tree species.

Over the span of its history, different institutions have called the BTC home for a period, including the National Institute of Education (NIE), government agencies and the Singapore Management University (SMU). The news in 2005 that the BTC would be handed back to NUS was met with great joy and celebration by the NUS community. A critical piece of NUS heritage was returning to the fold.

After taking over the campus, NUS embarked on an extensive process of preservation, upgrading and refurbishment. We were greatly pleased when in 2009, the six buildings that made up the former Raffles College — Oei Tiong Ham Building, Manasseh Meyer Building, Federal Building, Eu Tong Sen Building, Li Ka Shing Building and CJ Koh Law Library, plus the two quadrangles — were gazetted as national monuments. Today, the BTC is a thriving centre of learning and new ideas, anchored by the Faculty of Law and the Lee Kuan Yew School of Public Policy, as well as affiliated institutes. The lush, leafy environs of the BTC continue to be a trademark feature and experience of the campus.

NUS' evolution and development over the course of its time on the BTC reflect three distinct strands which have become central to NUS' way of planning and operating. The first is that NUS has shown itself to be a deeply responsible steward of heritage and nature. Infrastructure and nature need not be in conflict, but rather can be developed in a manner that is harmonious, effective and pleasing. The second is that NUS fosters a diverse and thriving natural ecosystem which allows for continuous opportunities to learn more about Singapore's natural environment and gain new capabilities and skills in the skillful and thoughtful management of natural resources. The third is that NUS is always anticipating and adapting to changes, and making the most of existing and emerging opportunities.

With changing times, new demands, aspirations and challenges arise. By 1969, the BTC housed some 4,350 students, a capacity for which it was never intended. A new campus was needed, and Kent Ridge was the site chosen, with an original intended capacity of

8,000–10,000 students. It is noteworthy that in a 1976 press release announcing building works on the new campus, emphasis was made on preserving the natural beauty of the site, and complementing the contours of the topography.

More than 40 years after the first move into Kent Ridge, and after several building phases, NUS now spans three campuses (Kent Ridge and University Town, BTC, and Outram), totalling some 166 hectares, with Kent Ridge itself occupying some 141 hectares. NUS has itself transformed into a globally-leading, comprehensive university with more than 30,000 undergraduate students, 15,000 graduate students, and more than 12,000 faculty, researchers, and staff. With 13 undergraduate schools, four graduate schools, and 30 university-level research centres, it has become a powerhouse of education, research and innovation.

And yet NUS has never forgotten its close connection to nature, and the special atmosphere created when it blends the built environment harmoniously with nature. In many buildings, great effort and care was taken to build around, or incorporate grand and distinctive trees as part of the verdant heritage and splendour of the campus. Examples include the magnificent Rain Trees located within Ridge View Residential College, the Angsana Trees at the Town Green, and the grand Tembusu Trees at the Education Resource Centre, University Town.

Every era has its defining challenges. For the BTC cohorts, it was the challenge of building a common ethos during a time when our young nation was buffeted by challenges. For NUS today, the most consequential challenge of its time may be that of climate change and sustainability. One sobering fact is that one-third of Singapore lies less than five metres above sea level, and in danger of submersion from projected rising sea levels.

Fortunately, the institution now has the combination of talent, resources and capabilities to make substantive contributions towards making Singapore and the world safer, more secure, and more innovatively sustainable.

NUS has taken successive, progressive steps to place sustainability among the core pillars of an integrated university framework. It established the Sustainability and Climate Action Council in 2021, which includes senior members of the NUS community, and which is chaired by the NUS President, to oversee and coordinate activities across education, research, innovation and enterprise, campus operations and administration, as well as community engagement across the NUS community. Uniquely, the ambit also covers equipping graduates with future-ready skills and fostering sustainability awareness and mindsets. Senior Vice President (Sustainability and Resilience) Prof Low Teck Seng oversees implementation of the many initiatives, driven by the Council.

In the same year, NUS released its Sustainability Statement, which commits the University to ongoing efforts to promote inter-disciplinary sustainability research to mitigating climate change, fostering a culture of sustainable development in its campus and in its students, and leveraging on the campus as a collaborative testbed for the testing of green ideas and solutions. Sustainability accomplishments and benchmarks have also been highlighted in NUS' inaugural Impact Report (2016–2020), which documents NUS' value creation efforts over several key dimensions.

NUS' sustainability efforts have several key thrusts, but I would like to highlight three particularly salient aspects here.

The first is that its efforts incorporate a global and regional dimension. No single party can hope to reverse climate change alone; international collaboration and partnership is essential. NUS has been accredited by the United Nations Framework Convention on Climate Change (UNFCCC) as an observer organisation since 2014, and it has attended the annual Conference of the Parties (COP) summits since COP20 as official observers. This keeps it up to date on the latest issues and developments, and provides a platform to build strong networks of global partnerships.

In addition, NUS has also been working closely with partners across the region, especially in Southeast Asia, on projects and initiatives that have a regional impact or application. There are many examples, but one recent highlight would be the five-year, S$15 million research project known as the Carbon Market Integrity Research and Development Programme Singapore, or Carbon Integrity SG, to support the establishment and monitoring of high-quality nature-based carbon projects across the region. This project can be potentially important, as an estimated 58% of forests in the region are under threat and could currently be protected as economically viable forest carbon projects, generating a return of US$25 billion per year.

The second is NUS' recognition that in dealing with climate change, both the challenges and solutions are likely to be complex, interlinked, and involve diverse stakeholders. As such, it believes that research and education approaches should closely synergise and reinforce each other, and should adopt a multi-disciplinary and collaborative framework. It has formed eight integrative research clusters, with the most relevant being the Sustainability and Urban Solutions cluster, which pursues ideas and solutions optimised for tropical, urban and Asian settings. Areas under research include sea-level rise mitigation, sea-water desalination and sustainable urban transport systems. But NUS also sees a converging future where diverse research domains will drive breakthroughs by leveraging on synergy and collaboration. Examples include artificial intelligence (AI) and data analytics, for environmental monitoring, and new energy alternatives, such as an anticipated hydrogen-based economy.

In education, NUS has introduced sustainability principles and concepts into a diverse range of academic subjects, such as Architecture and Building, the Humanities, Law, and Engineering, etc. It also offers specific sustainability-themed undergraduate degree programmes, many of which adopt a multi-disciplinary approach. In line with its focus on lifelong learning, NUS also offers postgraduate programmes in sustainability, be it a master's degree, offering deep dives in technical or scientific approaches, or specially curated, modular programmes from diverse disciplines, for busy learners seeking to gain exposure in emerging areas. Sustainability topics have also been introduced into its common curriculum and general education programmes to instill the critical thinking and sense-making competencies needed in this complex era.

In general, NUS' objective is to foster high sustainability awareness in its students, and a mindset that appreciates the many factors involved, and trade-offs needed to balance environmental, social and economic concerns.

And finally, we see NUS as being able to play a pivotal role as thought and practice leader by transforming its campus into a living lab for sustainability technologies and solutions. Its goals for a carbon neutral campus by 2030 include zero-waste precincts with recycling rates of 80–90%, a climate resilient cool campus, and electrifying the campus fleet hopefully by 2025, etc. It is also exploring the purchase of quality carbon offsets for remaining unabated emissions.

NUS SDE 4 — Singapore's first new-build net-zero energy building. (Photo credit: Courtesy of NUS College of Design and Engineering and Serie Architects. Photography by Rory Gardiner)

NUS recently launched its first Greenfield and net-zero energy building, SDE 4, which features an array of intelligent environmental sensors, and an innovative hybrid cooling system which supplies 100% fresh pre-cooled air, to achieve a comfortable indoor thermal environment for users. We also launched two Brownfield projects, SDE 1 and SDE 3, which were buildings built in the 1970s, now retrofitted to meet stringent net-zero standards. In a campus where some 40% of buildings are more than 30 years old, there are tremendous opportunities ahead to spearhead innovative and thoughtful adaptive reuse of existing infrastructure.

One strongly supported portion of its 2030 programme is the Campus in a Rainforest initiative, the highlight of which is a

100,000-tree planting programme. Its present count is about 32,000 trees, and is well on track.

Through careful planning and nurturing, all of NUS' campuses are endowed with the lush, verdant landscapes that are a distinctive trademark of the University. Starting with the BTC, NUS has demonstrated a commitment and sensitivity to the preservation and conservation of its natural and built environment, a cherished legacy to be passed down to future generations. At the same time, it has remained firmly focussed on meeting the challenges and opportunities of the future through innovation, bold re-imagination and adaptation. As sustainable development emerges as a central issue of our time, NUS is well poised to contribute with great impact, enhancing Singapore's common security, prosperity and heritage.

Professor Tan Eng Chye was appointed President of the National University of Singapore (NUS) on 1 January 2018. He is the University's 5th president, and the 23rd leader to head Singapore's oldest higher education institution. Professor Tan is a passionate and award-winning educator. He was a pioneer architect of the current academic system in NUS, and has seeded many initiatives such as the Special Programme in Science, University Scholars Programme, University Town Residential College Programme, Grade-free Year, and Technology-enhanced Education. He was recognised with the University Teaching Award for Innovative Teaching in 1998, and other teaching awards.

Chapter 42

Gardens by the Bay

Kiat W. Tan

Greenery has always been central to Singapore's identity. Since the 1960s, Singapore has cultivated an international reputation as a Garden City. The challenge moving forward was for it to take its greening efforts to the next level so that greenery remained pervasive even in the midst of urban growth. Hence the shift from "Garden City" to "City in a Garden", and now "City in Nature".

Gardens by the Bay brings to life the vision of Singapore as a City in Nature. Located in the heart of the Marina Bay central business district, it comprises three waterfront gardens — Bay South Garden, Bay East Garden, and Bay Central Garden — spanning an area of 101 hectares. Few countries have dedicated such a large expanse of prime land for public use. That a most desirable part of Singapore has been set aside for its people speaks of the Government's commitment towards ensuring that greenery continues to be accessible to all.

The idea for Gardens by the Bay was first presented to the Singapore Cabinet in 2004. In-principle approval to develop the concept was given the following year. There were three policy drivers behind Gardens by the Bay:

- Reinvent Singapore as a global city of distinction;
- Ease the pressure of overwhelming visitor numbers to Singapore's first national garden, Singapore Botanic Gardens;
- Develop the horticulture industry in Singapore.

With these policy drivers, the concept of Gardens by the Bay began to take form. It was necessary for the value propositions for the Gardens to evolve from the policy drivers and become aligned to Singapore's economic and social imperatives. These value propositions offered by the Gardens were as follows:

- A Distinctive Global City — Gardens by the Bay will contribute towards making Singapore an attractive place to live, work and play, like iconic parks in the heart of cosmopolitan cities, such as Central Park in New York and Hyde Park in London.
- A Source of National Pride to Singaporeans — Gardens by the Bay will be a national garden for all Singaporeans to enjoy.
- A Premier Leisure Destination — Gardens by the Bay will be a world-class horticulture-themed attraction. It will offer a compelling leisure experience and enhance Singapore's attractiveness as a tourism destination.

A study trip was arranged to visit the major gardens of the world for inspiration and to gather information for staging an international master-plan design competition to develop a new, horticulture-themed garden for the city of Singapore.

A competition was staged in 2006 to secure the participation of leading international architects, planners, and landscape designers in creating a world-class garden. It drew more than 70 entries by 170 companies from 24 countries and was judged by an international jury. An exhibition of the master-plan designs drew an overwhelming 85% approval rating by the public surveyed.

Gardens by the Bay broke ground in 2007, marking the commencement of development. To build a garden of this nature and scale in five years was an ambitious undertaking. The project was unprecedented and ahead of its time, going beyond horticulture and landscape design to encompass a multitude of disciplines from architecture to structural and environmental engineering. Adding to that, the development team had the mammoth task of transforming a barren reclamation site, bereft of roads, drains and electricity, into a luxuriant garden attraction.

Every aspect of Gardens by the Bay was carefully considered — from the aesthetics and functionality of the landscape design, the diversity of the plant material deployed, and the sustainability of the systems, to the social value that the Gardens would acquire in time to come.

While the actual physical construction of the Gardens and its structures was taking place, a global plant sourcing expedition set out to acquire the vegetation for landscaping the external gardens as well as for planting in the cooled conservatories. The palette of plant material selected, including rare species of orchids, mosses and ferns, exotic hybrid ornamental greenery, and unique specimen trees and shrubs, was intended to set the Gardens apart from other gardens in the world.

Movement of the huge specimen plants and landscape material was a major logistical operation that required much coordination whether on land, air or sea. The plants for the cooled conservatories came from nurseries from all corners of the world, some taking as long as 60 days by sea to arrive in Singapore. The transportation of giant trees from the cargo port to the Gardens had to be carried out in the dead of night so as not to disrupt traffic.

Prior to the actual installation on site of the landscape material, the Benjamin Sheares Bridge provided shelter and storage beneath for some of the huge trees. Singapore's dedicated horticulturists spent many an exhausting day and sleepless night to ensure the successful transference of the foreign vegetation and landscape material to the Gardens. Today, looking at the plants thriving in Gardens by the Bay, it is easy to forget the aches and pains it took to achieve the desired result.

Present-day visitors are drawn to the horticultural displays and calendar of events planned all year round. As living classrooms, the flora and fauna habitats that comprise the Gardens' landscapes also serve to raise awareness of the precocity of biodiversity among school children and the public.

The two cooled conservatories, namely the Flower Dome and the Cloud Forest, have become iconic landmarks in Singapore. Within each glasshouse is an environment equable for the display of flowering plants from targeted regions around the world.

In the evening, the Supertree Grove undergoes a remarkable transformation. Festooned with coloured lights, the Supertrees glow in synchrony to a rhapsody of popular melodies that issue from speakers camouflaged among the epiphytic plants that envelop each vertical garden. The Supertree Grove, like the rest of the outdoor gardens, is free for the public to access. While a modest admission charge is levied by the two conservatories, individuals who are financially challenged are admitted *gratis* under Gardens by the Bay's community outreach programme, Gift of Gardens, which provides free admission to local charities and Singapore residents who may not have the resources to visit or are individuals with disabilities. This policy is commensurate with the primary mission of managing Gardens by the Bay to serve as a People's Garden for all residents of the nation.

A centrally sited circular green lawn, The Meadow, serves as a venue for concerts staged in the open air. Here, the skyscrapers of the Marina Bay downtown form a dramatic backdrop in the skyline. Some of the top international performers from the entertainment industry have graced the stage for such performances.

Large bodies of water throughout the grounds of the Gardens attract birds and animals as well as nature lovers armed with camera equipment, binoculars, and telescopes. Bird watchers spot native species as well as rare avian arrivals from the temperate regions of the world. The avian travellers stop by during their annual migrations to feed among the mangroves and aquatic plants at Kingfisher Wetlands in the Gardens.

Since the day it opened its gates on 29 June 2012, Gardens by the Bay has become the destination of choice for visitors from home and abroad. The value of the Gardens was underscored during the COVID-19 pandemic when many local residents sought the outdoors and came to Gardens by the Bay to reconnect with nature. It not only illuminates the power of nature to soothe the mind and spirit but also reinforces the important role that a national garden can come to play in the lives of the populace.

Today, Gardens by the Bay is a prime recreation centre for the nation. For foreign visitors to Singapore, the Gardens has become a leading attraction for young and old alike. Increasingly, in order to find respite from the stress of suburban life, humans have begun to seek havens like Gardens by the Bay.

Waterfront view of Gardens by the Bay. (Photo credit: Gardens by the Bay)

A pioneer in the transformation of Singapore's landscape, **Dr Kiat W. Tan** has built his career around the stewardship of nature. He served over 30 years in the public service and held many senior appointments, including founding CEO of National Parks Board in 1990. When he stepped down from the role in 2006, he continued to lend his professional expertise to steer the development of Gardens by the Bay, becoming the Gardens' founding CEO until his retirement in 2018. Dr Tan continues to devote his energies to Singapore's City in Nature vision as Advisor to National Parks Board and Corporate Advisor to Gardens by the Bay.

Chapter 43

Resurrecting a National Heritage — The Lee Kong Chian Natural History Museum

Leo Tan Wee Hin

We are constantly reminded of the existential threat of climate change, environmental degradation, loss of ecological habitats and corresponding reduction in biodiversity. These impact all life on earth. Governments, Non-Governmental groups, Corporates, Communities and Individuals are all addressing this issue in numerous ways but when it comes to nature and the environment, most tend to focus on the living flora and fauna, often ignoring the preserved animals and plants residing in science museums.

Appreciating and learning from preserved biological specimens are equally important if we want to be good stewards of the planet. Natural History museums have a critical role in researching, teaching and reaching out to the general populace. Singapore's natural heritage not only documents the past but also helps us to understand the present and to plan for the future. As an illustration, the sperm whale that died on Singapore's shores in 2015 and its skeleton displayed in the Lee Kong Chian Natural History Museum, is not just a relic to be gawked at because of its size or that it may have been killed by pollutants (viz plastics) in its gut. Significantly as a species, it accumulates a massive amount of carbon in its fat and protein-rich body (estimated about 35 tonnes of carbon dioxide (CO_2) at death) and sinks to the seabed. The carbon stays on the bottom as the carcass is eaten by bottom-dwelling species and is not released to the surface. Furthermore, during their long life, an estimated number of 300,000 sperm whales remove close to 200,000 tonnes of CO_2 a year, which might make them a valuable carbon sink. Wherever they swim, their enormous body excrements help fertilise the oceans with iron and nitrogen, thus permitting the rapid growth of photosynthetic phytoplankton which absorb CO_2 and give off oxygen (O_2). It is estimated that whales play a vital role in the health of the oceans where they enable phytoplankton to provide up to 50% of the oxygen found in the atmosphere and capture about 40% of all the carbon dioxide produced.

Just think, if the great whales' (e.g., baleen and sperm whales) dwindling populations can be protected and allowed to multiply, we will have a nature-based solution to strengthen the push against global warming and climate change.

Museum exhibits can help a visitor to visualise what it was like in the past when sperm whales numbered over a million and are now less than a third mainly owing to overfishing. Even as efforts are being made to reduce whale hunting at present, the current dangers of biodiversity loss, pollution and global warming offer opportunities for visitors to think of practical solutions to protect these ocean giants and other endangered species to help maintain dynamic equilibrium in the environment.

Singapore had a natural history museum which was completed in 1887. Once an icon of the region for over a century, the Raffles Museum housed Southeast Asia's mainly zoological collection for research and exhibition. Conceived by Sir Stamford Raffles in 1823 as the Singapore Institution, it materialised as Raffles Institution (the school) and housed the fledgling Raffles Library and Museum, the latter getting a new home on Stamford Road in 1887.

With a focus on Southeast Asian zoological research and educational displays, the reputation of the museum grew with its rigorous curation and collection of insects (including an almost complete collection of Malaya/Singapore butterflies), molluscs, fish, birds, reptiles, mammals and other miscellaneous species. The *pièce de résistance* was a 12.8 metre baleen or blue whale skeleton which was hung in the rotunda of the museum and towered over everyone. Another remarkable specimen was the leathery turtle which was found dead on Siglap Beach in 1883. There has not been another sighted on our shores since then.

Generations of Singaporeans and residents visited the museum and I am sure it had an influence on their lives, one way or another. For one, the museum made an impact on my inclination towards Zoology and I became a marine biologist. What stood out for me were the extinct animals on display, particularly the fossilised marine shells and corals. Why did they disappear from our shores? Museum displays provoke questions even if they do not readily provide answers.

In 1960, the museum was repurposed and renamed the National Museum to emphasise more the history and contributions of the many races, in the making of modern Singapore. It was to be remodeled for nation building and gravitated towards history, culture and anthropology.

Despite great efforts to set up a new natural science museum, a science and technology centre, the Singapore Science Centre (SSC), was mooted in 1970 with the intention to house not only the zoological collection of the National Museum but to have hands-on exhibitions to showcase the applications of scientific principles in everyday life. The animal collection was renamed the Zoological Reference Collection (ZRC) and would be moved to the new science centre building in Jurong when completed. Unfortunately, the SSC had no use for the massive number of specimens and would only accept the mounted ones for exhibition. Ultimately, the remaining reference collection which made up the bulk of the collection was transferred to the then-University of Singapore (SU) in the Bukit Timah campus.

Owing to a complicated chain of events, the ZRC led a precarious nomadic life and miraculously survived three major moves — from National Museum to SU and from the zinc-roofed Romney Huts at Ayer Rajah (now National University Hospital) (1972) to Nanyang University's vacated Library (1980), and penultimately to three floors of the new National University of Singapore (NUS)'s Science Library where the zoological collection remained from 1987 to 2014. The University recognised the value of the collection for both teaching and research. It was renamed the Raffles Museum of Biodiversity Research (RMBR) in 1998 to emphasise the critical importance of biodiversity to humankind.

During this sojourn, research studies and field expeditions by NUS biologists and international collaborators continued unabated and led to the discovery of new species and the publication of the results, in books and international scientific journals. The museum collections grew to twice its original size and so did the museum's reputation. The RMBR had an equally important role in education and outreach and opened a small public exhibition gallery in 2001. Owing to its location, the public had difficulty accessing it until one fateful day in May 2009, on International Museum Day, when some 3,000 visitors thronged the cramped RMBR to view both the gallery and the research collections.

What followed was an outpouring of public and media interest in Singapore's natural heritage. Letters and press articles querying the absence of a natural history museum in Singapore created a buzz and thus began a transformative journey to restore or resurrect a forgotten treasure to its rightful place in society as a national heritage.

Prophetically, the then-Chairman of the National Heritage Board Professor Tommy Koh, had the visionary foresight to send Professor Peter Ng (Director of RMBR) to the United States in 2005, to find out why some museums were so successful and to plan for a new museum in Singapore. However, the stars were not in alignment and so the idea stayed that way until 2009.

Soon after a *Sunday Times* article entitled "Let's Have a Natural Museum for Singapore" (Tan Dawn Wei, 14 June 2009) was published, an anonymous donor challenged the RMBR to go ahead and build it with a promise of S$10 million if the project materialised. That was what triggered two foolhardy scientists (Peter Ng and I) to accept the challenge of fundraising for a new museum.

In keeping with the theme of this book, I shall not dwell on the frenzied race to build the Lee Kong Chian Natural History Museum (LKCNHM) as it is well documented in the book *Of Whales and*

Dinosaurs by Kevin Y. L. Tan, (Prologue by Peter K. L. Ng) published by NUS Press (2015). Suffice to say, if it were not for the tremendous outpouring of support (financial, moral and in-kind) from all walks of the community, we would not have restored this national treasure.

We were challenged to rebuild the Raffles Collection into a world-class natural history museum by our major benefactor Dr Lee Seng Tee of the Lee Foundation. Thus, the LKCNHM was conceived to reach out, not only to museum and nature buffs but to diverse audiences, in particular, to the future adults — Singapore's student populations.

The public galleries were designed to pivot away from static displays to create an inviting ambience, blending the sophistication of an art gallery, the hands-on approach of a science centre and the factual persuasion of a science museum.

More importantly, every exhibit has a story to tell, from simple graphics to mounted displays. For example, the illuminated photograph of a kingfisher reflects the beauty of nature but the aerodynamics of its beak inspired a Japanese engineer to redesign the original bullet train such that it did not create a sonic boom each time it emerged from tunnels. This is biomimicry at work and reminds us that if we learn from nature, we stand to improve our lives.

Three majestically mounted 150-million-year-old fossilised dinosaur skeletons provoke much food for thought. Dinosaurs lived for almost 170 million years as the pinnacle animals of their time. Can *Homo sapiens*, the new apex species which has been around for just 300,000 years, survive that long? How did dinosaurs adapt to their environment as they were found in almost all parts of the globe?

Can we understand why or how they could adapt to exceedingly warm 40°C and greater than 400 parts per million CO_2 environments? The past holds clues to answers for our present and future challenges.

Every exhibit in the LKCNHM galleries has its natural history story presented aesthetically and sets visitors thinking about why some species went extinct, why others are barely surviving and how the existential threat of climate change and global warming will impact all life on earth.

It may be filled with stuffed and preserved animals, but our Noah's Ark of the Dead is a "living legacy" for humankind to ponder its fate. If animal and plant species (i.e., our biodiversity) vanish from the planet, what will happen to us?

What price our natural heritage? (Photo credit: Lee Kong Chian Natural History Museum)

We have to be one with nature if *Homo sapiens* are to survive even a tenth of the reign of the dinosaurs. I believe that our future well-being begins with inspiring and educating the young.

Leo Tan Wee Hin is a marine biologist and conservationist, with research interests in mangrove regeneration and science education. He is an Advisor to the Lee Kong Chian Natural History Museum at the National University of Singapore (NUS). He chairs National Parks Board's Garden City Fund; is a Board Director of Temasek Foundation Ltd and Temasek Foundation IPC Ltd; Singapore Governor of the Asia Europe Foundation; Board Director of Mandai Park Holdings; Governing Member of the Singapore Environmental Council; Board Director of Conservation International Asia-Pacific and Fellow of the Singapore National Academy of Science. He has also served as Chairman of NParks Board, CEO of the Singapore Science Centre and Dean of Science and Director, National Institute of Education, Nanyang Technological University (NTU).

Chapter 44

Chek Jawa

Tan Yong Soon

Singapore is a small island city-state. Even with a Government policy of active land reclamation, which has added to its total land area by more than 20% from the 1960s, Singapore remains land scarce. Hence there is a need for long-term integrated planning to cater for economic growth and a good quality of life, maintain a clean and green environment, and make the best use of its land resources.

The Urban Redevelopment Authority (URA) is the government agency entrusted with the long-term integrated planning. The URA does this through the Concept Plan (now called the Long-Term Plan) and the Master Plan. The Concept Plan is reviewed every 10 years or so. The Concept Plan rethinks what Singapore can look like in the next 50 years and beyond. The Master Plan is reviewed every five years and translates the broad strategies of the Concept Plan into detailed plans to guide the development of land and property. It is the statutory land use plan that shows the permissible land use and density for developments in Singapore.

When I was posted to the URA as its CEO in June 2001, the work on the Concept Plan 2001 had just been completed. It had started in 1998, with the public consultation exercise commencing from

August 2000 following the formation of focus groups. A public forum was organised in December 2000. Feedback from the entire engagement exercise was incorporated into the draft Concept Plan that was exhibited from 28 April to 11 May 2001. A final public dialogue was held on 11 May 2001 to gather feedback on the draft plan before the release of the final plan in July 2001. My focus was to review the proposals in the Concept Plan and to subsequently incorporate them into the Master Plan 2003.

The presence of marine life in the Chek Jawa inter-tidal zone was first raised during the final public forum on 11 May 2001 by Joseph Lai, who had stumbled upon it recently. A newspaper feature article was published on 8 July 2001. It carried comments by Chua Sek Chuan and Shawn Lum, chairman of the Marine Conservation group and the Plant group respectively, of the Nature Society, on the beauty and the significance of the new discovery. The public started to visit the place and letters, including one from Geh Min, President of the Nature Society, were published in *The Straits Times* Forum Page to urge the preservation of Chek Jawa.

Reclamation of Chek Jawa had been decided as early as 1992 and mentioned in the Master Plan 1998. Detailed preparations were already underway. A study commissioned by the Housing and Development Board (HDB), the agency that was in charge of the reclamation works, had found that the reclamation would not have significant impact on the dugong population (an endangered mammal that mainly subsists on seagrass), because the seagrass in Chek Jawa was found to be patchy; moreover, there did not appear to be a resident dugong population there. The National Parks Board (NParks) had surveyed the area around Chek Jawa and found it did not have established coral reefs or reef communities; it would transplant the affected plants to other parts of the island. The URA thus put out a public reply in July 2001 to explain the need for the reclaimed land, the actions taken and that the reclamation would proceed as planned in December 2001.

The inter-tidal marine life was missed by government agencies and the Nature Society (Singapore), experts and laymen, until it was stumbled upon in December 2000. Would the new discovery at this late stage merit a re-thinking of the planned reclamation? As a public servant, my job is to improve the quality of living of Singaporeans and their future generations. I strongly believe in the importance and priorities of security and economic development, having spent much of my career in the Ministries of Defence and Finance. But both security and economic development are means to an end. The end is a better quality of living and sustainable development for Singapore and Singaporeans. Decision-making must be evidence-based. Intellectual humility, the willingness to be open to learn from others, to listen, and to seek clarity is important. And should significant facts change, there must be courage to change the decision.

Behind closed doors and away from public eyes, I signalled to my staff a willingness to review the matter. The URA staff was to carefully study the evidence received from experts, members of the public and the Nature Society (Singapore), which sent in files with photographs of what they had found in 2001. The URA would then study the merits of keeping the place and the implications of proceeding with or calling off the planned reclamation.

New studies of the marine life in the Chek Jawa inter-tidal zone made available to the URA did reveal the rich and unique biodiversity value of the area. URA planners studied many options, including different reclamation profiles and their implications on land use and environmental impacts. Could the reclamation be modified so that we could preserve the marine life and also have land for our use? URA officers involved include my deputy and Chief Planner Koh Wen Gin, key people in the Physical Planning division such as Michael Koh, Lim Eng Hwee and Hwang Yu-ning, as well as younger planners such as Lim Swee Keng and Mieko Otsuki. They were conscientious, curious, and creative. They weighed the implications and worked at various options. The matter was urgent as the reclamation contract had already been awarded and preparatory work had begun. The URA put up papers at the Ministry of National Development (MND)'s HQ meetings, and briefing and discussion sessions were held with Minister for National Development, Mah Bow Tan.

I invited Minister Mah to visit Chek Jawa during a low tide to see the place for himself. He accepted and the date was fixed on 18 October 2001. On that day, my key planning staff and I gathered at Changi Point, together with the NParks Chairman Leo Tan and the NParks CEO Tan Wee Kiat. We were met by Loh Yan Hui from the HDB, the project director of the proposed reclamation.

While waiting for the Minister and the Permanent Secretary, we heard on radio that Parliament was to be prorogued. Despite the fact that General Elections would be held soon (it was later set for 3 November), Minister Mah turned up. Chek Jawa was clearly an important issue close to his heart. We took the boat to Pulau Ubin. On site, NParks officers briefed us on the flora and fauna and the ecosystems in Chek Jawa, while HDB officers briefed us on the impending reclamation works. We walked along the shore and saw rich marine life — anemones, sea stars, sponges, horseshoe crabs and others. We witnessed the joys and excitement of Singaporean families and friends, including young children, having fun trekking on the shores, discovering and examining various sea species. There was a sizeable crowd. The Minister spoke with a number of them and spent three hours on the ground to obtain a good appreciation of the area.

On the way back to Changi, we all felt Chek Jawa would be worth preserving. Back in the office, URA officers worked frenetically to finalise the report. Expert views from the NUS Department of Biological Sciences, Tropical Marine Science Institute and Raffles Museum of Biodiversity Research, as well as detailed reports from the Nature Society (Singapore) and other interested parties were taken into consideration. Revised land reclamation profile options, costs and implications were re-examined. The conclusion was that reclamation, if carried out, would have to be limited to a very small area so as not to harm the fragile ecosystem. However, reclaiming such a small area would not be cost-effective. Coordination was conducted with various government agencies to seek and finalise strategic viewpoints as not proceeding with the planned reclamation would have important implications.

The Government agreed to put off the land reclamation works and retain Chek Jawa in its pristine state for the continued enjoyment of all. The decision had the caveat, "for as long as the Pulau Ubin island is not needed for development". Minister Mah met with interested parties and experts before the official announcement was made on 14 January 2002. Chek Jawa, a unique natural area and one of Singapore's richest ecosystems, was thus saved for the enjoyment of Singaporeans and visitors. It was placed under the management of NParks.

Everyone — the public, nature lovers, public agencies and the Government — contributed to this good outcome. Members of the public — especially the Nature Society (Singapore)'s marine conservation section — provided new information on the area's biodiversity, information that was insightful and detailed. The feedback was reasoned and not confrontational. The Government and its agencies were open to feedback, gathered additional expert views and took a pragmatic approach. The URA's planning process was rigorous, and yet URA planners were open to look at new information and had the courage to review its long established position. The Government took the long view and endorsed sustainable development and was willing to reverse its decision.

The Chek Jawa decision is an example of clarity and courage in decision-making. It is not so much a turning point in government policy as it is a good model of public consultation at work. It was made possible because the public and government agencies had collaborated positively and responsibly.

The civil service was keen to learn from the episode and the URA collaborated with the Civil Service College to write a case on Chek Jawa for teaching purposes in its senior programmes.

Singapore will always have to balance development with nature. Not every issue can be resolved to the satisfaction of all parties. But working together, with a culture of collaboration and caringness — care for the community beyond our immediate family, care for both people and nature, and care for the long term and future generations — we will all be able to unlearn, reinvent and achieve for the good of Singapore.

Tan Yong Soon is a former senior civil servant who served as Permanent Secretary in the Ministry of the Environment and Water

Resources, and for Climate Change in the Prime Minister's Office; Chief Executive Officer of the Urban Redevelopment Authority, Deputy Secretary in the Ministry of Finance and the Ministry of Defence, and Principal Private Secretary to the Prime Minister. He is Professor in Practice at the Lee Kuan Yew School of Public Policy, National University of Singapore, where he started the LKY Senior Fellows in Public Service Programme. He coauthored the book, *Clean, Green and Blue: Singapore's Journey Towards Environmental and Water Sustainability* and edited the book, *50 Years of Environment*, as part of World Scientific series on Singapore's 50 Years of Nation-Building.

Chapter 45

International Climate Negotiations: Reflections from Singapore's Chief Negotiator for Climate Change

Joseph Teo

When I was asked to take on the role of Singapore's Chief Negotiator for Climate Change, I knew it was a big responsibility. I was unsure if I could fill the shoes of my predecessors and do Singapore proud.

Four years on, I am glad I took on this key role, which is a real privilege. It has enabled me to work on an issue that is existential to Singapore. The Singapore government has established this position as it takes the issue of climate change seriously. My key task is to represent and lead the Singapore delegation at the officials' level in the international climate negotiations, including at the year-end annual conferences on climate change, more commonly known as the COPs (or Conference of Parties). So, what does the Chief Negotiator for Climate Change do and how does the role contribute to attaining peace with nature?

First, and at the broadest level, I work with my counterparts across the globe to finalise outstanding negotiations on, and fully implement the Paris Agreement, which is the only multilaterally agreed framework for global climate action. Under the Paris Agreement, 196 countries have agreed to hold the increase in global temperatures to well below 2°C and pursue efforts to limit the temperature increase to 1.5°C.

Our current efforts admittedly fall short of this goal and we need to urgently scale up our collective actions. However, the way forward will not be easy, particularly when there are 196 different countries involved, all with different starting points, circumstances, concerns and interests. The challenge in the negotiations is to address these concerns and interests, identify the areas of convergence, and find common ground and solutions to advance global climate action. This might entail difficult compromises and trade-offs, leading to outcomes at the annual COPs that might appear weak or insufficient to address the planetary crisis.

The Paris Agreement and the United Nations Framework Convention on Climate Change (UNFCCC) process are admittedly not perfect. But we should not throw the baby out with the bath water. The alternative is a break down in the multilateral system, which is a far worse outcome than what we have today. As a small country that is disproportionately affected by the effects of climate change, Singapore depends on all parties working together to make progress on this existential issue. This is why Singapore has been a strong advocate of a multilateral, rules-based approach to addressing climate change. My role in the negotiations is to work with my counterparts, including fellow members of the Group of 77 (G77)/ China and the Association of Small Island States (AOSIS), to push for as strong an outcome as we can get at each COP, while keeping all countries committed to the multilateral process.

We made an important contribution last year. The agreed decisions at COP27 in Sharm El-Sheikh would not have included a reference to the importance of multilateralism had the Singapore delegation not intervened to make a pitch for it. At a difficult time when some countries may be tempted to take unilateral actions or impose restrictions to protect their own interests, this reference will serve as a useful reminder to all Parties even as we face new challenges, to stay united and work collaboratively to advance our shared objectives under the Paris Agreement. Climate change is a problem of global commons. To effectively address this global crisis, it requires all countries to make a contribution and work together for the common good of our planet. This is what Singapore will continue to advocate for and what I will work towards.

Second, the Chief Negotiator participates in inter-agency discussions and has an input in the formulation of climate policies, particularly with respect to Singapore's obligations under the Paris Agreement. To have a voice at the negotiating table, Singapore must be seen to walk the talk. My role is to apprise the inter-agency process of its international climate obligations, key international trends, and the risks, reputational or otherwise, to Singapore if we do not act. Like in the climate negotiations, the inter-agency discussions are not always plain sailing. Different agencies will often highlight the constraints they face and the challenges of moving faster. But this is where the usefulness of the multilateral process comes in. My role is to remind my colleagues of what is at stake and to underscore the importance of Singapore fulfilling its international obligations. It helps that our political office holders are committed to taking strong and decisive climate action and see value in seizing the opportunities of the transition to a net-zero future. After lengthy and very careful deliberation among the different agencies, Singapore has decided in 2022 to raise its ambition to achieve net zero emissions by 2050. This is a stretched target given its constraints as a small country with limited opportunities to deploy renewable energy at scale. But we have not allowed Singapore's constraints to be an excuse for inaction and are fully committed to press ahead with our net-zero transition to ensure that Singapore will continue to thrive in a carbon-constrained world. Under the 4G leadership, we have launched the Singapore Green Plan which charts out bold and concrete policies and actions to achieve our net-zero goal. I am pleased to share that Singapore is one of 29 countries to submit an updated climate pledge at COP27 in line with the Glasgow Climate Pact. This is testimony of Singapore's support for the multilateral process.

Third, a key task of mine is to lead the Singapore team and ensure that it is making a positive contribution to the process in line with Singapore's interests. It helps that I am supported by a strong, competent, and dedicated team of negotiators, with their hearts in the right place. Continuing in the tradition of my predecessors, the Singapore team under my watch knows that they need to be active participants in the negotiations. This entails knowing their brief, networking with their counterparts, and helping to advance negotiations and work, which includes putting forward practical, bridge-building proposals that can garner broad consensus in a room. Many take on key roles in key committees and bodies within the UNFCCC process. Through the years of active participation in climate negotiations, the Singapore team has earned the trust of other delegations and are known to be constructive participants. I am honoured to be leading such a dedicated team.

Personally, I am proud to make a positive contribution by co-facilitating the Glasgow Dialogue in 2022. The Glasgow dialogue was established to discuss the arrangements for the funding activities to avert, minimise and address loss and damage associated with the adverse impacts of climate change. This is an issue of concern to many developing countries, notably small island developing states. While we had faced some issues over whether the Glasgow Dialogue had the mandate to produce a report, we had a very useful and constructive exchange between the Parties and different stakeholders who are working on the ground to provide assistance to developing countries in this key area. I believe the constructive discussions at the Glasgow Dialogue at its inaugural session helped plant the seeds for the breakthrough agreement at COP27 to establish new funding arrangements, as well as a dedicated fund, for loss and damage. The fund, when established, will be a new addition to the existing architecture of support for developing countries under the Paris Agreement. I am pleased to have played a small role at its incipient stages.

Beyond my co-facilitation role, I am also pleased to support our Ministers at COPs. I am proud to share that since I took on this role in 2018, Singapore's Ministers have been consistently called upon to co-facilitate key issues at COPs.

At COP24 in Katowice in 2018, Minister Masagos Zulkifli co-facilitated ministerial consultations on mitigation with his Norwegian counterpart, which culminated with the successful adoption of the Katowice Rulebook and the establishment of the enhanced transparency framework. This new framework will raise the monitoring, reporting and verification standards under the Paris Agreement and will give all Parties the assurance that each country is playing its part to reduce their emissions in support of the Paris goals.

The following year, Minister Masagos Zulkifli successfully co-facilitated with his Spanish counterpart negotiations on the overarching decision for COP25, which was the only outcome to emerge from the Chile-Madrid COP25 in 2019. Notwithstanding the failure to conclude outstanding negotiations on other issues, notably Article 6, the overarching decision — appropriately called the COP25 Chile-Madrid "Time for Action" — served to keep all Parties committed to the multilateral process of climate action at a difficult time in the process.

At COP26 in Glasgow in 2021, Minister Grace Fu, who took over from Minister Masagos as our Head of Delegation, was given the difficult task of co-facilitating with her Norwegian counterpart, ministerial consultations on Article 6 by the UK COP26 Presidency. Past Ministerial co-facilitators had tried but failed to find consensus on this difficult issue since the Paris Agreement was adopted. Notwithstanding the difficult circumstances we were operating under, i.e., COVID-19, we managed, with the support of all Parties, to finalise a deal on Article 6, which was one of the key deliverables of the Glasgow Climate Pact. The deal on Article 6 enabled the UK COP26 Presidency to claim, as part of its legacy, that it has managed to successfully conclude all outstanding negotiations on the Paris Rulebook. More practically, the deal on Article 6 and its mechanisms would enable Parties to collaborate with each other to raise climate mitigation and adaptation ambition, while preserving high standards of environmental integrity. Yet again, I am proud that the Singapore team led by Minister Grace Fu had played a small part in putting in place the final touches of the Paris architecture, which will help raise global climate action.

As can be seen from the above, Singapore has made a positive contribution at key stages in the UNFCCC negotiations process to help build the Paris Agreement and strengthen the multilateral system of cooperation on climate change. While our collective efforts still fall short, the processes and mechanisms we have helped to build will serve to strengthen the momentum of global climate action in the years ahead. This is our small contribution to advancing peace with nature and I am indeed privileged to have played a small role in this endeavour as Singapore's Chief Negotiator for Climate Change.

While it may be tempting to conclude that climate action rests with only those who are in a position of influence to do so, I would like to remind readers of a quote by Robert Swan who wisely cautioned that: "*the greatest threat to our planet is the belief that someone else will save it*". We are all stewards of creation and have the responsibility to protect it. Every action, no matter how small, counts!

Let me therefore invite you to play your part to advance peace with nature. You can start by making a pledge to take climate action by clicking on the QR quote below.

Singapore Minister for Sustainability and the Environment Grace Fu co-facilitating Ministerial Consultations on Article 6 with Norway Minister of Climate and Environment Espen Barth Eide at COP-26 in Glasgow, UK, in 2021. Also in the picture are then-UNFCCC Executive Secretary Patricia Espinosa, and UK COP-26 President Alok Sharma. (Photo credit: Ministry of Sustainability and the Environment)

Joseph Teo was appointed Singapore's Chief Negotiator for Climate Change on 2 July 2018. Prior to this appointment, Joseph has held various positions in the Ministry of Foreign Affairs (MFA), including Singapore's Deputy Permanent Representative to the United Nations in New York. In his current role at the Ministry of Sustainability and the Environment (MSE), Joseph has been a keen advocate of sustainability and climate action. Joseph is also a member of the Caritas Care for Creation Committee, Caritas Singapore.

Chapter 46

Singapore's Blue Heart: The Sisters' Islands Marine Park

Karenne Tun

Singapore's Marine Environment

Singapore is situated at the conflux of several regional oceans and seas; its coastal waters benefit from regional hydrodynamic connectivity which, in turn, support an impressive array of marine biodiversity, including around a third of the world's hard coral and half of the world's mangrove species, and comparable seagrass diversity to the bordering countries of Malaysia and Indonesia. These keystone taxa support a wide range of other marine species from many other marine taxa. And, despite the two centuries of coastal changes that Singapore has witnessed, data indicate that its marine environment continues to support rich biodiversity.

To ensure that Singapore's marine biodiversity continues to thrive in its waters, NParks' adopts a science-based approach through the Marine Conservation Action Plan (MCAP) to strengthen the conservation of our native marine biodiversity. The MCAP is guided by the Nature Conservation Master Plan, which sets out strategies to safeguard key terrestrial and marine habitats through its four thrusts of conservation of key habitats; habitat enhancement, restoration, and species recovery; applied research in conservation biology and planning; and community stewardship and outreach in nature. To complement this, Singapore has strict laws governing the management of both land- and sea-based sources of pollution. Under the Integrated Urban Coastal Management framework initiated in 2009, it takes a Whole-of-Government approach to ensure that the marine environment is protected even within one of the world's busiest port areas. Our thriving marine biodiversity is testament to the effective management of pollution within Singapore's coastal waters.

The Sisters' Islands Marine Park

In 2014, NParks established the Sisters' Islands Marine Park (SIMP), which spans 40 hectares around the Sisters' Islands and along the western reefs of St John's Island and Pulau Tekukor. SIMP's vision is to be an exemplary marine park that conserves Singapore's thriving marine biodiversity through sound science and inspires community stewardship through outreach and education. The area was selected based on agent-based modelling studies which revealed that the coral reefs around the Sisters' Islands are potentially important source reefs that can provide larvae to other reef areas in Singapore.

It was a tremendous learning opportunity for me when NParks formed the Friends of Marine Park (FMP) network to bring together a diverse community of individuals and interest groups, of sectors ranging from academics, nature interest groups, educators, boaters, fishers and other recreational users, to join us in realising the vision for the Marine Park. One of the first efforts of the FMP was the co-creation of best practices so that all users can enjoy SIMP while protecting and conserving its biodiversity. This was achieved through open and honest dialogue among stakeholders, where concerns and aspirations were shared, and compromises made to ensure the sustainable use of the Marine Park. Over the years since its formation, FMP has become the backbone of the Marine Park outreach and education efforts, working closely with NParks to promote responsible behaviour among visitors and raise awareness about the importance of marine conservation. Today, the FMP continues to grow in strength and champion various marine conservation causes across Singapore's seascape.

With the support of the FMP community, NParks implemented conservation measures including long-term monitoring with yearly BioBlitz surveys which complement other scientific surveys undertaken in collaboration with academic partners. To realise its full potential as a key source reef and "gene bank" that will continue to supply larvae to other reef areas in Singapore, we initiated habitat restoration and species recovery programmes to provide suitable habitats and create the right environment so that nature can "do its thing", naturally.

Leveraging on decadal local knowledge on coral reef biology and restoration ecology, we initiated targeted coral relocation campaigns to increase the number and diversity of hard corals, and the foundation of coral reefs, within the Marine Park. Where needed, we enhanced existing degraded areas by either consolidating loose substrate or using reef enhancement units. This helped to improve the suitability of the existing substrate for corals to grow on. Adding to that, in collaboration with engineering partners from our sister agency, JTC, we installed eight mega purpose-built artificial reef structures, ranging from six to 12 metres in height, on otherwise bare seafloor area. These not only created substrate for corals and other sessile organisms to grow on, but also habitats and niches for a wide range of fish species to colonise, and in the process, increase the biomass and productivity of the area. In addition, since their deployment in late 2018, we have seen an increase in natural coral recruitment within the shallow surfaces of the structures, demonstrating that the Sisters' Islands also serve as sink reefs, which have equally important ecological functions.

The marine turtle management programme was initiated in 2016 to monitor and conserve Singapore's turtle populations. Through the yearly citizen science-led Biodiversity Beach Patrols, nests that are found along Singapore's mainland beaches or around the Southern Islands are documented. Those that are laid at locations with high human traffic, in danger of predation by other animals such as monitor lizards, too close to the shoreline where high tide can drown the porous eggs, or at areas that are too shallow, are relocated to the turtle hatchery located on Small Sister's Island. The hatchery provides a conducive environment for the incubation of rescued turtle eggs by keeping them safe from predators, light pollution and human disturbance within specially built incubation cages. This has been observed to maximise the number of turtle eggs that successfully hatch. The location of the hatchery within the lagoon at Small Sister's Island also provides relatively calm conditions for hatchlings to make it out to the open sea. After the hatchlings emerge from their nests, they will imprint on the beach at Small Sister's Island before being safely introduced into the sea.

Today, NParks continues to conduct and support research and development, which helps to shape evidence-based conservation policies. Such research is facilitated in SIMP and other coastal Nature Parks and Reserves, covering areas such as marine genetic connectivity and the remote monitoring of marine megafauna.

My Personal Reflections

The marine environment has a special claim to my heart, and I am privileged to have been given the opportunities to work on it throughout my 30-year career. The last decade at NParks has been extra special because I had the opportunity and privilege to put passion to action and witness the birth and growth of the Marine Park. Although small in area, SIMP is a unique and valuable conservation area that provides important habitats to a diverse range of marine life. Its planning, designation, management, community involvement, and conservation efforts are a testament to Singapore's commitment to sustainable development and environmental stewardship. My hope is that SIMP will go on to serve as a model for other conservation areas and demonstrate the importance of protecting our natural heritage for future generations.

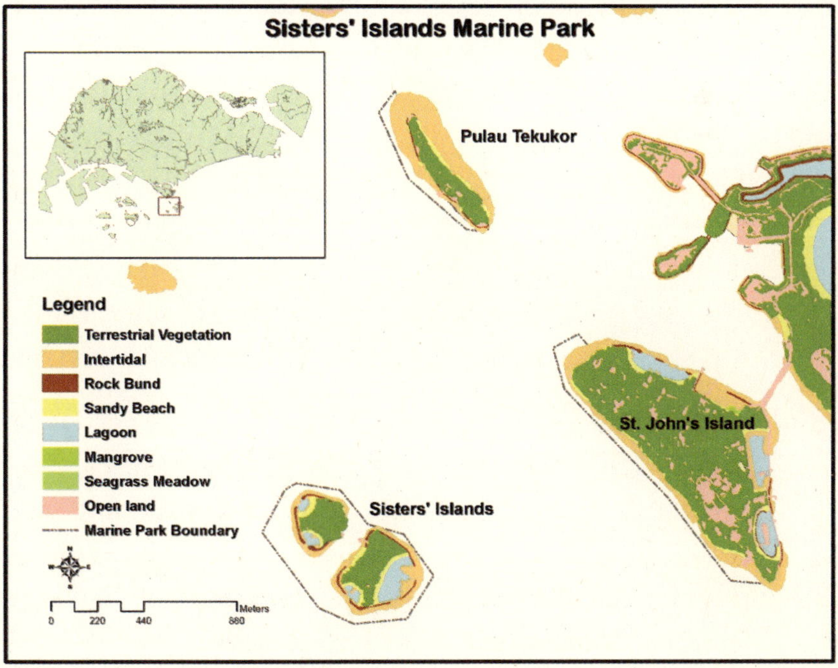

Dr Karenne Tun is Director of the Terrestrial, Coastal, and Marine Branches at the National Biodiversity Centre, National Parks Board (NParks), and her work focusses on the management and conservation of Singapore's natural areas across the terrestrial, coastal and marine environments. Her team is also responsible for managing Singapore's first Marine Park — the Sisters' Islands Marine Park. In 2021, Karenne was nominated to represent Singapore as one of 25 members of the Group of Experts for the United Nations Regular Process for the 3rd Cycle tasked to prepare the 3rd World Ocean Assessment (WOA3) by 2025.

Chapter 47

The Battle to Save the Lower Peirce Forest

Wee Yeow Chin

The Singapore Branch of the Malayan Nature Society or MNS (Singapore) came into being in 1954. Members were mainly British expatriates working in the then-Singapore Botanic Gardens, Raffles Museum and University of Malaya (then based in Singapore). Postgraduate students of zoology and botany were exposed to the activities of the society when academics like Roland Sharma and P.N. Avadhani took over the leadership of the society. It was only in 1978 when I joined the staff of the then-Department of Botany that I became seriously involved in the activities of the society. Being a new recruit to the department, I was easily persuaded to take over the post of Honorary Secretary.

The main activity of the society then was educational — encouraging locals to appreciate nature by way of talks and guided walks. In due course bird watching was introduced and proved popular among members. Things took a major change in 1986 when Richard Hale, an independent birdwatcher, stumbled upon an area of degraded mangroves and prawn ponds at Sungei Buloh. The area was teeming with thousands of migratory birds arriving to refuel in the area before continuing their journey back to their breeding grounds in the north. He approached Dr Christopher Hails who was then with the Parks and Recreation Department, now known as the National Parks Board (NParks). Christopher was then working to attract birds back to Singapore's urban environment. The pair approached the Nature Society (Singapore) (NSS) as none of the birdwatchers were privy to the area. Together, they prepared an illustrated document detailing a proposal to turn the Sungei Buloh area, now known as the Sungei Buloh Wetland Reserve, into a bird sanctuary. Richard, who was then the CEO of the local Hong Kong and Shanghai Banking Corporation, had the necessary government contacts to allow him to work behind the scenes. He managed to persuade the then-President, Mr Wee Kim Wee, the then-First Deputy Prime Minister Mr Goh Chok Tong as well as Mr S. Dhanabalan, the then-Minister of National Development, to visit the area. His "behind the scenes" lobbying succeeded. The Government subsequently abandoned plans to develop Sungei Buloh into a high-tech agricultural area and agreed, instead, to turn it into a bird sanctuary.

The Lower Peirce Reservoir forest controversy erupted at a time when the NSS had just cut off its decades-old ties with the Malayan Nature Society. It became a truly Singaporean society, instead of a branch of the Malayan society. This was in October 1991, at the suggestion of its recently appointed Patron, Prof. Tommy Koh.

In early 1992 the government proposed building an 18-hole golf course on a piece of forest around Lower Peirce Reservoir. This forest was at least 80 years old and legally protected under the National Parks Act 1990. The forest also served as a catchment to the reservoir.

This was how I became directly involved in the battle to save the Lower Peirce Reservoir forest. The first thing I did was consult our Patron Prof. Tommy Koh. He suggested that we prepare a detailed report and send it to key decision makers. I rallied members around and we undertook a survey of the forest's flora and fauna. With these data we produced an 80-page "Environment Impact Assessment" (EIA) with Tommy providing the Foreword.

The Foreword highlighted that Singapore already had 14 golf courses. And under the recently published Concept Plan, Singapore will have another 15 by the year "X" when our population reaches four million. The Urban Redevelopment Authority (URA) had already designated sites for the 15 additional golf courses, the forest at the Lower Peirce Reservoir not being one of them. The question was therefore not whether Singapore should build another golf course but whether it should be built on this particular site. Our EIA further revealed that building a golf course at this site would see to the destruction of about 40,000 mature trees belonging to 82 different species. This forest of about 80 years old, if left alone, would eventually become a primary forest. Destruction of the forest would also result in the loss of more than 485 species of fauna, of which 44 were considered endangered.

Tommy signed off the Foreword as the Chairman, Preparatory and Main Committees, at the United Nations Conference on Environment and Development. It was a lucky break that Tommy was appointed such a role at the Earth Summit that was convened in Rio de Janeiro, Brazil, later that year. And of course, this provided added value to Singapore's EIA.

Singapore's EIA Report was distributed to key government leaders. The local press was supportive and provided plenty of publicity.

This in turn got the support of the Singapore Institute of Landscape Architects, which the government responded to.

As members were impatient for a quick response from the government, a spontaneous signature campaign was organised by the Hon. Secretary, Evelyn Lim. In the midst of the media confrontations, two officers from the Internal Security Department (ISD) made an appointment via the Personnel Department of the National University of Singapore to visit me at my office (I was the NSS President then) in the then-Department of Botany. This, in turn, triggered a rumour that the NSS office was raided and the signatures seized. This of course was not true as the 25,000 signatures had already been sent to a vault in a bank for safekeeping. In actuality, the ISD officers simply wanted to know the Society's agenda and future plans — we had a friendly chat.

The first hint that the government was rethinking proceeding with the golf course came from *The Straits Times*' report on 7 June 1992. In the article titled "Don't worry about reservoir, Dhana tells nature buffs", the then-Minister of National Development Mr S. Dhanabalan was reported to say: "If it shows that great ecological damage will be done, then we will not approve it." At the same time, he urged nature lovers to be realistic in what they fought for. As an example, he cited the earlier call to preserve two ponds at Marina South, adding: "This land was reclaimed for the extension of the city. And while the city was being planned, it rained, water gathered in some places and birds came to roost and they say that we must conserve this area. I think it is ridiculous." In due course, however, the government decided not to build the golf course at Lower Peirce Reservoir.

The NSS can be proud of its success in persuading the government not to clear a piece of protected forest for a golf course. This was a second major conservation success for the society. The first was when the government agreed to set aside Sungei Buloh for a bird sanctuary.

Dr Wee Yeow Chin played a significant role as a green advocate in Singapore. He was Secretary of the Malayan Nature Society (Singapore Branch) (1978–1990) and Founding President of the Nature Society (Singapore) (1990–1995). He has also served in the Nature Reserves Board, Nature Reserves Committee, Singapore Environment Council and Work-Group on Nature Conservation. He was appointed Honorary Museum Associate of the Lee Kong Chian Natural History Museum in 2012. In 2005, he started the Bird Ecology Study Group. With more than 6,000 entries, the website has become a valuable resource consulted by students, birdwatchers and researchers locally and internationally.

Chapter 48

My Fascination with Mangroves

Yang Shufen

Mangroves in Singapore

Despite being land-scarce, Singapore, an island city-state, continues to harbour rich mangrove ecosystems. Although they cover roughly 1% of its land area, Singapore's mangroves are found in mature stands with half of the world's true mangrove flora species, along with a plethora of associated fauna, many of which are still unknown to science. On the main island, they fringe the northern coastline, continuing down to the western catchment. Mangroves stretch offshore, lacing many of Singapore's satellite islands in the south and northeast.

The conservation of mangroves is key to the realisation of the National Parks Board (NParks)'s *City in Nature* vision. Mangroves offer a multitude of ecosystem services, intricately linked to Singapore's objectives for building ecological, social and climate resilience.

Mangrove Environment and Adaptations

An enigmatic habitat, one cannot hike through mangrove forests like in terrestrial forests without the risk of being stuck in the soft mud, suffering a strong "rotten eggs" smell at times. However, with patience and time, a world of Instagram-worthy beauty is unveiled when the tide withdraws. Then the seemingly similar mangrove trees put away their modesty and reveal their secrets to surviving in an environment where no other trees can. A parade of different breathing roots appear — pencil, conical, knee-shaped, and flying buttresses, all adapted to the low oxygen and unstable environment. And taking this chance to feed and avoid being fed on, a myriad of marine lifeforms abruptly emerge, as if undecided about being fully aquatic. This cycle repeats itself, bringing life.

Working in the Mangroves

I joined NParks in 2006, as a temporary project officer to survey natural areas of Singapore, focussing on coastal and marine areas. In two years, a team of six known as the "Natural Areas Survey Team", planned, organised, surveyed and analysed the reports that set the foundation for many sites in Singapore. The team, which included me, worked with a pool of experts who volunteered generously with it and fellow National Biodiversity Centre colleagues, who helped the team with methodologies, past literature, old maps and Identity guides. At the end of the project, we had compiled over 20 reports on mangrove sites, in addition to other habitats. And as the reports piled up, these volunteers, colleagues and stakeholders became friends.

My work in NParks introduced me to a variety of mangrove types found in Singapore. Besides updating the local flora and fauna records, the team was able to collect seeds and cuttings to propagate and grow in other natural areas. It was also through these trips that I was able to record mangroves in different substrates, such as *Rhizophora stylosa* growing at a rocky cliff. These observations proved invaluable when we embarked on the coastal restoration of Pulau Tekong mangroves in 2012, carefully selecting species suited for the rock revetments. It was the first innovative hybrid engineering mangrove protection projection piloted.

NParks' Efforts in Bringing Mangroves to the People

It is rewarding and gratifying that quite a few of the mangrove areas have been successfully integrated and made accessible to public today. Working with other agencies, NParks integrated Belayar Creek mangrove into adjacent developments to the area, extending a boardwalk for visitors from Singapore's only "mangrove MRT" station (Labrador Park). While small in size, Berlayar Creek mangrove is one of the few locations where we can see *Rhizphora stylosa* trees easily, the rarest of the three species of Bakau in Singapore. It is also where I saw my first Ashy Tailorbird, who sang impatiently while I counted mangroves saplings in my quadrat. Similarly, the Sungei Cina mangrove at Woodlands, which was incorporated into the larger Admiralty Park, holds fond memories for me of mudskippers and graceful clusters of the rare Mangrove Rattan (*Calamus erinaceus*).

Mandai Mangroves and Mudflats

One of the largest mangroves and mudflats in Singapore, Mandai Mangroves and Mudflats, was announced as a nature park in 2018. NParks led a comprehensive study to ascertain its conservation value. Firstly, an extensive literature review of all past studies done on the site was conducted. Secondly, a study was designed and implemented to establish the ecological interdependency of Sungei Buloh Wetland Reserve and Mandai Mangroves and Mudflats, based on shorebirds tracking studies and benthic food availability in the mudflats. Lastly, considerations of the ecosystem services, including the local quantifications of carbon storage in the mangroves were integrated into the report holistically. These could only be accomplished due to the accumulative and invaluable contributions of over three decades, from academics such as Sigurdsson and Murphy, nature advocates like the Nature Society (Singapore), government agencies and volunteers who cared for the place.

Mangroves Restoration and Enhancement

NParks has also been leveraging on mangroves as nature-based solutions to protect and enhance our coasts. A coastal restoration project in Kranji Coastal Nature Park was recently completed. This project refined the eco-engineering solution implemented at Pulau Tekong in several ways. In addition to retaining the original mangroves and planting new coastal areas, a 400-metre-long low rock revetment was implemented in-between these habitats, with a more effective design that slows down wave energy and promotes sediment accretion and natural mangrove regeneration. A vegetation belt that follows the natural zonation from terrestrial forests to coastal and mangrove forests was also designed to provide additional habitats for biodiversity and a buffer area against rising sea levels and storm surges. A specially curated palette of coastal plant species was planted with the community as part of NParks' OneMillionTrees programme.

This science-based approach is also being taken in the restoration of mangroves in abandoned aquaculture ponds of Sungei Durian in Pulau Ubin. It applies the Ecological Mangrove Restoration method to promote self-regeneration of mangroves for long-term sustainability.

Reflections

My time in the mangroves allowed me to see a different side of Singapore. I grew up in the 80s, immersed in television, playgrounds, hawker centres and later, arcades and karaoke singing. But these forests showed me what Singapore's island was like before all of these happened — before buildings were taller than trees, before roads were paved, and even before the lazy fishing villages came to be. I did not expect to stumble upon the completely different world of mangroves. This would not have been possible if not for the opportunities presented to me in NParks. In 2017, I was tasked to report on Singapore's mangroves at the 2nd Association of Southeast Asian Nations (ASEAN) Mangrove Congress in the Philippines. It was with great pride that I shared, as a Singaporean, how even though Singapore possesses just a minuscule fraction of the total mangrove hectarage in the world, it harbours a disproportionate amount of biodiversity that continue to amaze the scholars that visit. And that many of such rich mangroves exist just a short journey away from the city centre.

Today, mangroves are riding on a wave of high interest, awareness and support spurred by collective challenges in climate change and biodiversity losses. NParks garners multi-lateral collaborations with scientists, architects, engineers, designers, and planners, to come up with solutions. Most notably, it is heartening that NParks'

Affectionately known as "flooded forests", mangrove forests are dominated by trees adapted to a life between the tides. Taken at Lumnitzera Walk, Kranji Coastal Nature Park/Sungei Buloh extension. (Photo credit: Kenneth Er)

community of volunteers continues to grow. They clear marine debris, restore mangroves, conduct guided walks, document through photographs, survey and monitor the environment — putting their hearts, minds and hands into action together so that mangroves will thrive for generations to come.

Yang Shufen joined NParks in 2006 as a project officer to survey natural areas in Singapore. In 2009, she managed the Coastal Protection and Restoration of Mangrove Biodiversity at Pulau Tekong with a multi-disciplinary team. She did a three-year stint in park planning and corporate development where she was part of the team that established Friends of Ubin Network (FUN). As Deputy Director (Sungei Buloh), she did wetlands management, Kranji Coastal Nature Park nature-based solutions and migratory shorebird conservation since 2016. Currently she is the Director (Sungei Buloh) managing the wetland Reserve, Mandai Mangrove and Mudflat, Kranji Marshes, Lim Chu Kang mangroves and Khatib Bongsu.

Chapter 49

Singapore's Freshwater Habitats: More Than Meets the Eye

Darren Yeo Chong Jinn

Freshwater Habitats in Singapore?

"*Singapore got freshwater habitats meh?*" was the response in 2010 when I suggested to a prospective undergraduate research student to survey freshwater habitats for a particular fish species. The student expressed even more surprise when we talked further about the diversity of species within these habitats. The answer to his question of course is yes; there is a tendency to overlook man-made canals, drains, and reservoirs as freshwater habitats. Additionally, forested areas in Singapore conceal many more small but natural freshwater habitats — out of sight and out of mind. Together, these artificial/urban and natural freshwater habitats drain as much as two-thirds of Singapore's land area, though it might not look it. At the start of the 1990s, I was equally as unaware of Singapore's wealth of freshwater habitats and biodiversity. My experience up till then was limited to childhood forays into *longkangs* (i.e., canals and drains) in peri-urban areas and familiarity with only a handful of *longkang* fishes, thinking there might be little else to conserve. How wrong

I was! This is where my journey to a deeper appreciation of Singapore's freshwater habitats began. Here I share a selection of what I have learned of freshwater ecology, biodiversity and aquatic invasive species in three take-home parts on (1) urban freshwater habitats, (2) natural freshwater habitats, and (3) reaching out on freshwater conservation.

(1) Urban Melting Pots: From Bare Concrete to "Natural" Environments

Artificial or urban freshwater habitats in Singapore comprise its 17 reservoirs and many smaller landscape ponds, and the approximately 8,000-kilometre network of drains, canals, and urban rivers. The waters of these habitats are mostly exposed, warm, and neutral to alkaline in pH. The reservoirs can be large and deep (for Singapore) with sluggish to still or standing waters, while the drains and canals can alternate between slow, shallow water flow in dry weather (even drying out, depending on size and location) to fast, deep water flow during heavy rains. Their waters may appear superficially to have little biodiversity, especially for canals populated mostly by non-native guppies and tilapias.

Since the mid-2000s, however, collaborative surveys between the National University of Singapore's Lee Kong Chian Natural History Museum and Department of Biological Sciences, and the Public Utilities Board (PUB), Singapore's national water agency, of hitherto unstudied reservoir biodiversity and communities in Singapore revealed diverse and unique assemblages of species in our reservoirs. These consist of mostly non-natives originating from tropical Africa (e.g., Nile, Mozambique and zebra tilapias, African sharptooth catfish), Central/South America (e.g., eartheater cichlids, armoured sucker catfish, peacock bass), and other parts of Asia (e.g., giant gourami, giant snakehead, green chromide) that are suited commonly for the reservoir water conditions, which forest-dwelling native species avoid. The survey data corroborate anecdotal observations that non-native species dominate urban freshwater habitats in Singapore. Importantly, however, a small number of adaptable native species (e.g., marbled gudgeon, common snakehead, medaka or rice fish) also persist and co-exist in the reservoirs. **Reservoirs represent therefore a melting pot of species** of multiple origins that have assembled spontaneously into functioning communities that support various reservoir ecosystem processes.

Drains and canals too now have more diversity. Bare concrete monsoon canals still hold primarily guppies and tilapias because these are the few species tough enough to thrive in the harsh conditions. But under PUB's Active, Beautiful and Clean (ABC) Waters programme, **waterways have undergone various degrees of planting and rehabilitation or "naturalisation" to less harsh and more varied environments that now support more diverse species assemblages** — albeit still non-native-dominated. This has to be an acceptable compromise because we can never completely restore our urban habitats to the very different conditions of Singapore's original tree-dominated natural freshwater habitats, which were more suitable for native species (see below).

The non-native species established in urban habitats present a conundrum at times: should we remove or control them based solely on their exotic status? My take: if they do no harm/present no threat to native biodiversity and human health — or even do a service or benefit (e.g., as food for native predators, support for the ecosystem functioning of the reservoirs, or recreational or aesthetic enjoyment for humans) then we can leave what is already in our urban habitats alone, but with a caveat. We must avoid introducing new species/

players (i.e., new unknowns) and regularly monitor the existing diversity and ecology of these habitats.

(2) Natural Strongholds: Home-ground Advantage

Natural fresh waters such as forest streams and freshwater swamps are the habitats of primeval forest-covered Singapore. We find them now only within Singapore's remaining forest fragments (most but not all situated within nature reserves and nature parks). The waters are cool from the heavy shade of the forest canopy cover, and acidic (low pH) from organic acids leached from fallen leaves (leaf litter). Forest streams are generally small, shallow and slow flowing, while freshwater swamps are more acidic, with the added elements of stained (but clear) waters and spongy substratum from accumulated, slowly-decomposing leaf litter and other organic debris. These relatively undisturbed habitats are disproportionately important because of their scarcity and their crucial role as refugia for the majority of Singapore's native freshwater fauna.

In the mid-1990s, as an undergraduate member of an aquatic survey team in the National Parks Board's Nature Reserves Survey, I encountered for the first time the natural freshwater habitats that serve as strongholds for Singapore's native freshwater fauna, including species of natural and national heritage significance such as the harlequin rasbora and Temasek shrimp, which were discovered and described in Singapore some 90 years apart. Most of these species are acid-water tolerant and unsuited to water conditions outside the forest. More special are stenotopic species, highly sensitive to changes in the environment and hence restricted to narrower ranges of water conditions found only in even rarer habitats, e.g., the Singapore freshwater crab and the muff river prawn in hill streams; and the bladefin catfish, buff-backed spiny eel, and swamp forest crab in freshwater swamp. I refer here to Nee Soon Swamp Forest, Singapore's last substantial freshwater swamp forest — and our most important and irreplaceable freshwater habitat — which holds almost half of the diversity of Singapore's native freshwater fishes in about one square kilometre.

As natural streams reach forest edges and transition into more urban habitats, native species are replaced largely by non-native species, which dominate the connected urban water bodies and waterways surrounding the nature reserves. Despite this "siege", Singapore's natural freshwater habitats remain largely uninvaded. This is due partly to environmental filtering; non-native species being generally less suited for the natural freshwater habitat conditions (but vice versa too). But what happens when non-native species tolerant of forest conditions appear (e.g., Australian redclaw crayfish, Oriental river prawn)? Biotic resistance — which involves native communities resisting non-native species invasions, e.g., through predation or competition — could possibly play a role, with native species "holding their own" in natural forest streams and freshwater swamp habitats. This, however, is **contingent on the forest habitat remaining intact and maintaining the "home-ground advantage" that native species might have.** Moral of *this* story? We must protect the overall habitat (i.e., the forest habitat) to help the native (aquatic) community protect itself.

(3) Conserving Freshwater Biodiversity and Habitats: Protecting What We Cannot See or Touch

One of the challenges of freshwater conservation in Singapore is in reaching out and exposing students and the public to natural habitats and their native biodiversity, particularly the difficulty in helping people relate to the animals and habitats without the hands-on element. In marine habitats with care and comparatively less impact, dives or intertidal walks that allow people to observe first-hand even normally hidden marine biodiversity can inform, fascinate, and enthuse. This is not as feasible in Singapore's freshwater habitats, especially for sensitive native biodiversity in natural forest streams and swamp forests. Furthermore, many of the significant natural freshwater habitat sites are located in inaccessible or restricted areas, and much of the mostly small and cryptic native biodiversity are viewable up close only when disturbed and caught. As such, we should not casually enter streams/swamps to search for biodiversity, even in accessible locations, because these habitats are generally smaller and less tolerant of repeated disturbance. The casual visitor to a nature reserve/area can therefore only catch fleeting glimpses of a small subset of native freshwater biodiversity from banks, boardwalks and bridges.

How then do we convince the public of the need to protect what we cannot see or touch in the wild? I can think of three possible approaches to consider. First, displaying live and/or preserved examples of native freshwater biodiversity at appropriate occasions and venues (e.g., public aquaria, reserves or park visitor/interpretive centres, museums). Second, allowing regulated access (but limited and less frequent) to selected sites holding less sensitive natives and non-native species. Third, producing more visual media featuring native freshwater biodiversity (e.g., brochures, books, apps, videos, documentaries). Each of these suggestions will have trade-offs and challenges to implementation, but I hope this helps at least to stimulate thought and more and better solutions for freshwater conservation outreach and education.

Freshwater swamp, the rarest and most important freshwater habitat-type in Singapore, is home to a majority of our native freshwater species.
(Photo credit: Freshwater and Invasion Biology Lab, Department of Biological Sciences, National University of Singapore)

Darren Yeo Chong Jinn is Head of the Lee Kong Chian Natural History Museum, Faculty of Science, National University of Singapore (NUS). He is also an Associate Professor at the Department of Biological Sciences, Faculty of Science, NUS, where he leads the Freshwater and Invasion Biology Laboratory. His main research interests are freshwater ecology and biodiversity, aquatic invasions, and freshwater crustaceans, which the lab investigates through studies of freshwater ecosystems in Singapore and other parts of tropical Asia.

Chapter 50

Protecting Migratory Birds in Singapore and the Flyway

Yong Ding Li

My introduction to migratory birds, as far as I can remember, seemed like a serendipitous convergence of several events in primary school. Back in 1994, I had incidentally browsed *The Straits Times* one afternoon and stumbled on an article on a little-known part of Singapore called "Sungei Buloh". I was surprised that there were still wetlands with large congregations of migratory birds in Singapore. Subsequently, I picked up birdwatching. There were few reference books available — many found at the local library were focussed on European, African or American species. As an inquisitive 11-year-old confronted with a novel hobby, I was keen to see for myself this wetland nestled within rural north-western Singapore. It must have taken me another year before I found the opportunity and courage to visit Sungei Buloh with a newly procured 10 × 25 pair of binoculars generously financed by my dad. Although hazy, I remember that visit to be extremely productive — I managed to spot nearly 30 species based on what little notes I scribbled in my notebooks 28 years ago. There was the Common Redshank, a distinctive shorebird with its scarlet red legs, and large flocks of the intricately patterned Pacific Golden Plover, a Common Kingfisher and even an Oriental Magpie Robin. With a bit of guidance from several old-timers, I fondly recall having observed the rare Asian Dowitcher from Buloh's main birdwatching hide, which I was told, to be a species that can be identified based on its "feeding pattern resembling the motion of a sewing machine". This species has declined steeply since then and is no longer found at Buloh today.

One thing naturally led to another, and soon, I joined the Nature Society (Singapore) (NSS) through the encouragement of several birdwatchers I met along the way, some of whom I still keep in touch with. Lim Kim Chuah, an old friend and a veteran birdwatcher was a constant mentor, and remains so to this day. It was comforting to know that there were people around that take a deep interest in birdwatching in particular, and nature in general. Yet another important personal milestone for me was being able to participate in the "Asian Waterbird Census" in 1998, a regional initiative to monitor migratory birds that brings thousands of citizen scientists to count birds. I wrote to the NSS indicating my interest to volunteer for the Census and was later "deployed" to Lower Seletar. If not for the telescope that a friend brought along, it would have been extremely difficult to identify what I was seeing among the flocks of shorebirds on the Seletar coast. Through the Census, I learnt that counting migratory birds was important in helping their conservation. Collecting data on how different species are faring over time can provide insight for actions needed to guide their conservation. I left Yishun Dam that day with over 20 species of waterbirds, and a lot of inspiration.

Where does Singapore fit into the bigger scheme of things for migratory birds? I wondered. How many migratory birds would pass Singapore on their journeys, and where would they be headed for after spending a few days at wetlands like Sungei Buloh and

Seletar? These were among the many questions I had. Over the 10 or so years that followed, I grew increasingly cognisant of the spectacular phenomena of bird migration. I learnt eventually that the birds that showed up here in Singapore had journeyed across Asia through what ornithologists term the "East Asian–Australasian Flyway", a series of migratory routes used by hundreds of species. Depending on species, these routes connect the very ecosystems the birds live in over thousands of kilometres — for instance, the temperate parts of Asia with the tropics, boreal forests and salt marshes with rainforests, mangroves and mudflats. Singapore and adjacent parts of Malaysia and Indonesia are clearly important stopover locations and a winter destination for many species in this wonderful Flyway.

Unfortunately, migratory birds are not a particularly well-known group of wildlife, and have not always received the attention they deserve, except among a select circle of biologists and conservationists. This should not be surprising — migratory species like plovers spend only several months each year here in the tropics — half the time, people do not even see them. Many species are not particularly colourful and do not get as noticed as the gaudy species of tropical rainforests, such as hornbills and parrots. That said, paradigms are changing, and we are beginning to learn that migratory birds have not just tremendous cultural value, but also important and diverse ecological roles. As species with large distributions, migratory birds use different habitats across the places they breed and spend their winter at the continental scale. In doing so, migratory birds effectively underpin the connectivity of ecosystems, and facilitate the movement and dispersal of nutrients. The dependance of many migratory birds on wetlands means that species like shorebirds are tremendously sensitive to deteriorating environmental conditions in such landscapes. Migratory birds therefore also play roles as indicators of environment health, and in essence, are proxies of the conditions of these ecosystems. Perhaps more so in East Asia than here in the tropics, many migratory species like cranes and storks are extremely iconic and are well entrenched in the cultures of China, Japan and Korea.

My first professional foray into migratory bird conservation started in 2016 when I was offered a role at the Iceland-based Conservation of Arctic Flora and Fauna (CAFF), an organisation embedded within the Arctic Council. When this happened, I was in the midst of my doctoral studies in Australia. I had worked extensively on the conservation of forest ecosystems and tropical birds, but less so on migratory species. The work at CAFF was a massive eye-opener and exposed me to a world of regional and global initiatives to protect migratory species. I was extremely lucky during this period to have worked alongside the late Evgeny Syroechkovskiy, a highly respected international expert on the complex policies of migratory species conservation, and a giant in shorebird ecology. Working closely with Evgeny and other colleagues in the migratory species space, we were able to update the action plan for the work of the Arctic Migratory Bird Initiative, a multi-country initiative led by CAFF to galvanise action for migratory species linked to Arctic ecosystems. Being based at Sungei Buloh (a place that I traditionally visited for leisure) also provided excellent opportunities for me to learn from my National Parks Board colleagues who manage this nature reserve, and exchange ideas on how to better protect migratory species.

My work at CAFF provided important grounding and paved my way into joining the team at BirdLife International, a conservation non-profit organisation headquartered in Cambridge in the United Kingdom, with an established global programme of work on the protection of migratory species. Taking up this new role, one of my immediate priorities was to set up as many as possible in-country projects focussed on the conservation of threatened migratory species for the Flyway here in Southeast Asia and East Asia, alongside wider activities to promote public awareness of migratory species. There are massive gaps in the conservation of coastal wetlands in Asia, and many more challenges in implementing work to protect these critical ecosystems, but the window of opportunity to take action is fast narrowing as species and wetlands are in steep decline. Three species that my colleagues and I have worked to prioritise for our conservation programmes are the Spoon-billed Sandpiper, Nordmann's Greenshank and Masked Finfoot. While these species are but a selection of the more than 600 migratory species in Asia, they are sensible choices for many reasons. They are unique, charismatic to birdwatchers, wetland dependent, and in danger of extinction — which also means that they serve well as flagships for our work to protect migratory species more widely.

Five of the most important areas for my work are the coastal wetlands of Myanmar, Thailand, Cambodia, Malaysia and Vietnam. Here in perhaps the mostly densely populated parts of Southeast Asia are also some of the most important wetlands for migratory shorebirds like the Spoon-billed Sandpiper. Many of these wetlands, however, either remain little protected or are part of production landscapes where salt or shellfish are being intensively farmed and harvested. The grey areas in the management mandates for these wetlands has made conservation work tricky to navigate through, as it is often unclear where the remit of one agency ends and that of another begins. Working with like-minded colleagues, we quickly moved in to set up conservation interventions to better understand the needs of rural communities, create livelihood incentives, while actively securing the participation of local people.

Reflecting on these last few years of work to conserve migratory birds, I am glad to say that we have made steady progress. But much more needs to be done. We need more science and monitoring, more capacity building, many more awareness campaigns and not forgetting the livelihood incentives that must benefit species, ecosystems and local people. To this end, I am enormously grateful to the people I have had an opportunity to learn from, and very much look forward to the continued work with the conservation community here in Singapore and the region, to secure wetlands for migratory birds and biodiversity over the next decade.

Yong Ding Li (right) in the field with Vietnamese ornithologist, Nguyen Hoai Bao, during a shorebird survey in the Mekong Delta.
(Photo credit: Cao Quoc Tri)

Yong Ding Li coordinates BirdLife International's work to protect migratory birds and wetlands in Asia, and is currently closely involved in the development of the Regional Flyway Initiative with the Asian Development Bank. He taught for several years at National Junior College before pursuing a Ph.D. on conservation biology at the Australian National University. Ding Li has written several books and papers on the birds and biodiversity of Asia and Australia, including the recent *Field Guide to the Birds of Malaysia and Singapore*. He paints and volunteers for the Nature Society (Singapore) during his free time.

Index

C

D

T

U

V

W

Y

Z